WOMAN IN A MAN'S WORLD

Woman in a Man's World is the first in a series of books based on interviews conducted for the National Life Story Collection at the British Library's National Sound Archive, and published by Methuen. The general editor for the series is Professor Paul Thompson, Director of the NLSC. These collections of vivid testimonies will be valuable to both students and researchers in history and the social sciences, and equally of appeal to all general readers of biography.

The first title in this series, Woman in a Man's World by Rebecca Abrams, draws on the unique ability of oral history to capture the authentic voice of the interviewee. Collected here, and related in their own words, are the private and public experiences of ten remarkable British women whose full life stories have never previously been recorded. They give voice to a generation of women whose experiences are particularly relevant to the young women of today and who, without this project, might never have been heard.

WOMAN
IN A
MAN'S WORLD

Pioneering Career Women
of the Twentieth Century

Rebecca Abrams

Methuen

First published in Great Britain in 1993
by Methuen London
an imprint of Reed Consumer Books Ltd
Michelin House, 81 Fulham Road, London SW3 6RB
and Auckland, Melbourne, Singapore and Toronto

We are grateful to the National Life Story Collection
and the National Sound Archive for their permission
to use the interviews cited in this book, which are
all deposited in the oral history collection of the
National Sound Archive.

A CIP catalogue record for this book
is available at the British Library

ISBN 0 413 66350 7

Typeset by Deltatype Ltd, Ellesmere Port, Cheshire
Printed in Great Britain
by Clays Ltd, St. Ives Plc

To my grandmother,
Tilli Edelman

CONTENTS

ILLUSTRATIONS

ACKNOWLEDGEMENTS

While relatively light on technology, oral history is nothing if not collaborative, and the process of gathering together these life stories and preparing them for publication has involved the skills, time and commitment of many people besides myself. I would like to start by thanking Robert Perks, Jean Rigby and Carol Freeland at the National Life Story Collection. Their help in co-ordinating this project and providing all the necessary administrative support was invaluable, and greatly appreciated. The financial backing of the National Life Story Collection and a timely grant from the Nuffield Foundation were also crucial, and together made possible the costly process of recording and transcribing these interviews.

I would also like to acknowledge the important role played by the Friends of the Fawcett Library and the Fawcett Society. In particular I would like to thank Alex Bennion, Linda Mowry and Betty Scarf for supporting this project in a number of ways, not least by providing enthusiastic volunteers to collect and transcribe the life stories of their members. The collaboration between the Fawcett Society and the NLSC over the creation of an oral history archive entitled The Fawcett Collection (housed at the NLSC and the Fawcett Library), has proved very successful and has provided a rich store of interviews, several of which are included in this volume. Especial thanks to Linda Mowry for permitting me to include her interviews with Hilda Brown, Mary Smith and Livia Gollancz.

I am also grateful to Dr Max Blythe at Oxford Polytechnic,

to Giles, Lisa and Cathy at Daily Information, and to Sonia Jackson, John Slim, Ewan Green, Lucia Whittle-Martin, Karen Jochelson and David Bodanis for fact-finding, fact-checking and comments on early drafts. Paul Thompson, Director of the National Life Story Collection, got this entire project off the ground in the first place, and his advice and guidance have been indispensable. I have also been very lucky in my editor, Mary O'Donovan, who has been a model of efficiency, competence and patience throughout. As ever, I am deeply indebted to my husband, Hugo Slim, who has provided support and advice well beyond the call of duty.

Above all my thanks go to the women whose lives fill these pages. The opportunity to share their memories was not only a privilege, but a very great pleasure. Remarkable women every one, their determination, courage, resilience, humour and wisdom set a daunting and admirable example. For their support, for their time and for their memories, I am immeasurably grateful to Helen Brook, Lucy Faithfull, Josephine Barnes, Sheila Parkinson, Hilda Brown, Jean Graham Hall, Mary Smith, Livia Gollancz, Una Kroll and Betty Boothroyd.

PREFACE

Woman in a Man's World is the first title in an important new series to be published by Methuen in conjunction with the National Life Story Collection at the National Sound Archive. Both the series and the archive collection on which it draws are ultimately a response to profound social and cultural changes which have taken place during our century. Victorian Britain, like most societies in recent centuries throughout the world, was sharply divided between a minority who were used to expressing themselves in writing, and a majority who could perhaps read, or sign their name, but had neither the confidence nor the practice to write about themselves. The literately expressive minority has given us a British auto-biographical tradition of exceptional richness, and also a wealth of personal documents – above all letters and diaries – for historians to quarry. We have a more convincing account of the personal and emotional life of Queen Victoria from her family letters than is ever likely for her successors; and even a man as busy as Gladstone, when Prime Minister, might produce thirty handwritten letters to colleagues in a day through which his shifts in political opinion and strategy can be pinned down in detail. Today we produce much more paper than the Victorians, but it is often less revealing. On the one hand, those in public life are more cautious of what goes into the written record, so it is more systematically filtered and cleaned. On the other hand, communication in writing has lost its exclusive pre-eminence. Television and radio have larger audiences than newspapers and we conduct our confidential discussions by telephone rather than through letters. Paradoxically, the easier it has become to communicate directly and intimately across distance, the fewer traces have been left for the historians and biographers of the future.

It is fortunate that these same transformations have also provided an alternative new source in the tape-recorded retrospective interview. In recent years there has been a rapid growth of 'oral history' and 'life story' work, both in books and broadcasting, in historical and social science research, in health and social service work with older people, in theatre, and in schools. Oral history is now recommended as one of the first steps for exploring the past in the National Curriculum; and equally to Oxford's history students. I have written fully about its development and its potential in my own book *The Voice of the Past*.

It has taken much longer for the archival world to recognise the importance of this change, and the preservation of audio and audio-visual records is still much less systematic than that of written or printed material. It remains national policy, for example, to preserve a copy of every newspaper issued, but only a fraction of radio and television broadcasting. And many other countries – among them the United States, France, Israel, Sweden and Australia, were earlier in recognising the importance of building national sound collections of autobiographical recordings.

In this context the setting up of the National Life Story Collection and the establishment of an oral history section with its own curator at the British Library National Sound Archive has been an important step forward. During the last five years the National Sound Archive, through providing a safe place of deposit for nationally significant collections, has become Britain's leading archive for oral history. At the same time the National Life Story Collection, as an independent charity based in the archive, has secured funding support for a series of new projects designed to meet some of the obvious gaps in the existing record. They range from projects recording leading sculptors and painters (with the Tate Gallery) or the City of London's financial élite, to survivors of the Nazi holocaust, ordinary schoolteachers, GPs, immigrant families from Barbados, and the steel industry from top to bottom. All these interviews, like those used in this book, are housed in the National Sound Archive's oral history archive, and almost all of them are available to the general public through the archive's library and listening service.

Each book in this series brings together a set of edited testimonies recorded for one of these National Life Story Collection projects. *Woman in a Man's World* draws partly on a set of interviews with leading women of the generation between the suffragettes and contemporary feminism which were specially commissioned from Rebecca Abrams by the National Life Story Collection, and partly from a further twenty interviews recorded by a volunteer team, with funding assistance from the Nuffield Foundation, in a joint project on 'Forgotten Feminism' with the Friends of the Fawcett Library. A second set of these latter interviews is deposited in this historic feminist library, originally of the suffragist Fawcett Association, now housed in the City of London Polytechnic.

Rebecca Abrams describes very vividly in her note, 'Using Oral History', some of the difficulties which are inherent in editing spoken life stories into written form. It is worth adding two other general points here on the nature of retrospective oral testimony. The first (which it shares with written autobiography) is the nature of the memory process. Both memory and recall are inherently selective: an attempt to make sense of the past. It is certainly possible with most people to reconstruct through memory reliable outlines of a career or key events in family life and also, especially for earlier life, the patterns of everyday work and living. But there is a tendency –although usually less so when about the more distant past – for matters felt shameful to be withheld. The passing of time also brings new evaluations: for example a parent, once bitterly criticised, may become better understood, even forgiven. And in making sense of the past memory can play tricks, fusing separate events or transposing them from one context to another. Gradually historians have come to realise that these subjective re-evaluations and even distortions can be as valuable as more reliable factual memories, for they provide vital clues to understanding the consciousness of individuals and the social groups to which they belong. *Woman in a Man's World* needs to be read in this spirit. Like all autobiography, it presents perspectives.

The second characteristic of tape-recorded memory is new and marks a crucial advance in our ability to understand the recent past: for it allows us to bring into history not only the life experiences of the powerful and the literate, but of those innumerable men and women in all walks of life who would never have had the skills to write their story, nor even thought it worthwhile to do so. Through this oral history can help to rectify many imbalances in the historical record. We can hear the voice of the fisherman or the foundryman as well as the politician or professor; of the criminal as well as the judge; of the black migrant as well as the white colonial civil servant. One of the most fundamental biases in most past history has been the neglect of the life experiences of women: a neglect which operates both at the level of ordinary working women, and of those who have achieved eminence in their sphere. It therefore seems especially appropriate that the first in our series should be these fascinating testimonies of eminent women, which thus prove so revealing, not only of their own lives, but of their whole generation.

Paul Thompson
Oxford, 1993

USING ORAL HISTORY

This book is the fruit of a three-year oral history project for the National Life Story Collection. It consists of ten life stories drawn from a larger pool of in-depth interviews conducted by myself and trained volunteers from the Fawcett Society between 1989 and 1992. All the interviewees were women aged sixty and over, and each interview lasted between three and eight hours, giving interviewees the opportunity to describe in detail their entire life story, including their childhood memories and any background information they could supply on their parents and grandparents. The interviews were semi-structured and particular emphasis was given throughout to the interviewees' experience *as women*.

The ten life stories in this book are edited versions of transcripts of the original taped interviews. The questions have been removed and the answers edited to run, as far as possible, continuously. Inevitably in editing these interviews for publication they have undergone change. When Samuel Coleridge said of literature, 'the infallible test of a blameless style is its untranslateableness without injury to meaning,' he could have been describing the dilemma facing the oral historian. One of the problems of translating an oral history interview into book form is that meaning is injured in the process. Meaning is held not simply in the words, but between the words, in the pauses and hesitations, in the emphasis, inflection, intonation. These things are hard to translate from the spoken voice to the written word, as are irony and a certain kind of wry humour beloved of this generation of the English middle class for whom understatement, self-control and modesty were an integral part of behaviour extending into language. In the process of reducing 130 pages of transcript to a twenty-page chapter, words have been lost and with them, inevitably, nuance, stress and certain subtleties of meaning. Shortage of space made it necessary in places to condense sentences and elide phrases. Nevertheless, my intention throughout has been to try and capture in the printed word the idiom and inflection of each woman's speech, conveyed so well in the taped interviews.

Several of the women interviewed here were aware that they were in some sense offering their lives up for 'translation'. One woman had reservations about the whole process of being interviewed, particularly since she had had prior experience of her words being distorted and misused by journalists. Another contributor decided to withdraw her interview, not only from this book, but from the NLSC archive, for fear of misrepresentation. The evidence of oral history is no less prone to misrepresentation than that of written evidence once it has undergone a process of editing. The integrity of the interviewee depends on the integrity of the editor, and a relationship of mutual trust becomes important. The two-way dynamic which exists between interviewee and interviewer in the giving and taking of a life story is both the strength and the limitation of oral history. As Paul Thompson says in *Voice of the Past*: 'This is material which you have not just discovered, but in one sense helped to create.' In editing these ten interviews I have tried to preserve as far as possible the character of each woman and the essence of her story as I think she intended it.

Some interviewees were anxious about the possible 'inaccuracies' contained in their interviews, and this is a criticism frequently levelled at oral history by its detractors. The unreliability of memory, particularly in older interviewees, can present difficulties, but in the quest for 'accuracy', people often miss the true function and value of oral evidence (which can, in any case, be substantiated with factual accounts of the period or events concerned). What is important and valuable is the individual's *perception* of events, the emphasis that a particular memory places on aspects of an experience, the darkened corner that is illuminated by that person's specific perspective on an event. The so-called inaccuracies in themselves are of interest.

It has been suggested that oral history interviewing is exploitative: that the interviewer plunders the memory of the interviewee and then hoards the riches found there for his or her own ends. But in my experience, this kind of interviewing is inherently reciprocal. Certainly, I feel immensely privileged to have had the opportunity to share these women's memories, experiences and insights, but often they too expressed satisfaction and even gratitude at the end of an interview for the chance to talk uninterruptedly for several hours about their lives, to recall their achievements and to reflect on their struggles and their successes.

Whatever its limitations may be, oral history undoubtedly also has many strengths. Theodore Zeldin once wrote that 'the history book that has the most to offer is written from the basis of rich personal experience.' In this respect oral history is at an advantage: through personal testimony it can uncover entirely new information; convey colour, tone and atmosphere missed in written documentation; provide a unique perspective on events, and yield significant insights into a subject's personality and psychology. For oppressed, socially disadvantaged or minority groups it has a special purpose in giving them a voice. Oral history can go beyond the official version and provide an alternative vision of recent and contemporary history. For feminist historians oral history therefore offers an important way of correcting the male bias in historical interpretation and challenging a past seen predominantly from a male perspective.

INTRODUCTION

'You have to be a woman of your time.
Twenty years before I wouldn't have
begun. Twenty years later there are all these
excellent women going. You had to be just
there at the right time, almost without
knowing it.'

Jean Graham Hall

'Occupation is essential,' wrote Virginia Wolf in her diary on 8 March 1941. She used the word 'occupation' to mean, simply, busyness, a state of being occupied, but in the fifty years since she wrote this the question of a woman's occupation, in the sense of paid work, has indeed become essential. This century has seen for the first time the large-scale emergence of women into the traditionally male sphere of paid work. More women now work than ever before. They still encounter discrimination in the workplace in a number of ways, but a woman's occupation is no longer defined exclusively in terms of housework and child-rearing. Women are still responsible for and very occupied by these concerns, but fewer and fewer women now give up work when they marry, and children increasingly tend to interrupt rather than terminate a woman's working life outside the home. For middle-class women in particular there has been nothing short of a transformation in both attitude and policy. Before this century, with the exception of the teaching profession – the traditional preserve of single genteel women – paid employment was rare and eccentric for middle-class women: motherhood and marriage were thought occupation enough. The combined impact of suffragism and the First World War profoundly challenged such preconceptions, and this century has witnessed the continuing struggle between these two notions of what a woman's occupation should be. Undoubtedly, those who make it to the top of their profession are still too few and the obstacles in their way too great, but their achievements serve as an example and an inspiration to the many other women coming up after them.

The ten women whose life stories are collected here have played an important part in the ongoing transformation of female work this century. They provide both example and inspiration. Born between 1907 and 1929, they represent a small but determined number of pioneering professional women. Each of them pursued a career with enthusiasm and resolve, often in the face of considerable obstacles. All ten worked outside the home for a large part of their adult lives, and it is this that makes them particularly unusual: they pursued careers at a time when most women did not. Furthermore they all achieved a degree of distinction in their chosen field: eight of the ten were made CBE, OBE or DBE in recognition of their achievements. To the extent that it was still the norm for women of their generation to stay at home after having children, each can be said to have been, for at least part of her life, a woman in a man's world. By this I mean that they were active in the sphere of paid work in the public domain at a time when the professions were still male-dominated. The professions chosen by these ten women include law, medicine, politics, publishing, family planning, social work, the army, the Church and the civil service. Seven of the women came from middle-class families, and are therefore unusual in having worked at all. The three who came from working-class backgrounds, in which women have always done paid work, stand out for having determinedly pursued careers which propelled them into high-powered positions and into the heart of middle-class professionalism. Only one of the ten remained in the traditional female mould of the voluntary do-gooder – Helen Brook, founder of the Brook Advisory Centres – but she easily earns her place in this dectet of women with more than thirty years of intense activity in family planning, during which time her unpaid work helped professionalise the field and revolutionise attitudes to birth control. Furthermore, as the wife of an eminent man, she was unusual in having such a marked realm of activity beyond the conventional demands of married life.

A word about the notion of 'success'. This is a particularly ambiguous term when applied to women's lives, since fulfilment is rarely linked purely to professional achievement. Many of the women interviewed here are aware that they succeeded in their working lives because of sacrifices, shortfalls or disappointments in their private lives. For these ten women (and I will argue later that their experience is representative), success was often bought at a high price.

These ten women are linked not only by having pursued careers, but also by the social and political backdrop to their achievements. All grew up between the Wars. The eldest was eleven when the First World War ended, the youngest eleven when the Second World War began. They come from a generation of women who were post-suffragette and pre-feminist, a generation often neglected by historians. Unlike their mothers and daughters, they were motivated not by political ideologies so much as by social and economic circumstances: the two World Wars that framed their formative years, the prevalence of single and widowed women in the 1920s, the economic austerity of the 1930s, the sudden availability of jobs for women in the 1940s. To appreciate the contemporary relevance of these ten stories, it is therefore necessary first to understand the historical context in which these women were living and working.

The Historical Context

The inter-War generation of women has often been portrayed as inward-looking and reactionary, easily overshadowed by the more dramatic activities of its suffragette predecessors and feminist successors. It is a period depicted as recovering from one World War and preparing for a second, characterised by qualities of cautiousness, self-control and conservatism, too often assessed in relation to what came before and what came after, its self-defining autonomy denied. Yet for women in particular this was in some ways a time of increased freedom and opportunity. Women over thirty had won the vote in 1918 and full suffrage for women over twenty-one was granted in 1928. New feminist groups were created in the 1920s, a feminist journal, *Time and Tide*, was established, and significant legislation was enacted which improved the status of wives and mothers. Between 1918 and 1927, twenty laws were passed which improved women's status. The 1923 Matrimonial Causes Act, for example, enabled women to sue for divorce on the basis of adultery, as men could.

However, as pointed out by Harold L. Smith in his article 'British Feminism in the 1920s', 'most of the legislation enhanced the status of mothers, thus encouraging women to view motherhood as a woman's primary function, rather than facilitating new roles.' The 1925 Guardianship of Infants Act, for example, which established equal parental rights once a dispute went to court, was not as far-reaching as it appeared. Full equality for mothers was not in fact won until the 1973 Guardianship Act, almost fifty years later. Married women during the 1920s were still unable to obtain birth control information through a public clinic, a situation that remained unchanged until 1930. The Sex Disqualification (Removal) Act of 1919 also appears less progressive in retrospect than at the time. It did nothing to ameliorate the iniquities of the marriage bar, which prevented women from working after marriage, and which was in extensive use right up until the Second World War. During the 1920s the marriage bar was used for the first time to dismiss married women teachers, and it also became common practice in the civil service and local government during that time. Many other discriminatory measures were also in operation still: for example, Cambridge in the 1920s did not allow women to be full members of the university. The first woman barrister was accepted in 1922, but by the end of the decade the number of women at the Bar had increased only to twelve. As late as 1970 medical schools were still covertly operating a quota system to keep women medical students below twenty per cent.

Despite the many remaining social, political and economic inequalities, support for feminism waned dramatically between the Wars. Brian Harrison, in his book, *Prudent Revolutionaries*, has charted the increasing popularity at this time of the Women's Institutes and the Townswomen's Guilds, both of which 'catered for women who acquiesced in their conventional domestic role but wanted to broaden out their relevant interests and skills.' The strident tone of something like Lady Rhondda's Six Point Group, founded in 1921 to campaign for feminist causes, 'jarred with an inter-War generation of women who wanted organisations of a more recreational and utilitarian kind.' Social questions emerged as the new religion for the mid-Victorians, the mothers of the ten women whose lives we are concerned with here. Self-discipline and public spirit were the cornerstones of individual endeavour. Humanitarianism was a more pressing call than feminism between the wars, a woman's duty more important than her rights. At this time, as Jane Lewis suggests in *Women and Social Action in Victorian and Edwardian England*: 'the only unifying force was the powerful commitment to social action, which each woman had to reconcile with an equally strong commitment to domestic duties and to late Victorian ideas about female propriety.'

The well-documented decline of collective feminist activity after 1918 is often seen as an indication that feminism itself was in decline: the vote had been won, the fight was over. But as the women interviewed here show, the matter was not so simple. While they were reluctant to adopt the feminist language of the suffragists and recoiled from the noisy exhibition of collective action, nevertheless at an individual level they *assumed* what their mother's generation had fought for and *acted on* the changes in attitude towards women's education and employment. In many ways it is true that they withdrew into traditional female roles once more, and certainly they eschewed the strident words and deeds of the previous generation of women, but they conducted themselves with a new sense of self-worth and a new commitment to self-determination. If the inter-War period was one of social and economic retrenchment after the massive expenditure of financial, emotional and human resources during the First World War, it was also for women a necessary and significant period of assimilation and individual progress.

Alison Light in *Forever England* makes an important contribution to our understanding of this period and its subsequent impact on women's lives by challenging the usual view of the middle class in the inter-War period as politically and socially conservative. 'As the nomenclature suggests,' she says, 'the "inter-War" years are easily seen, from the masculine point of view, as a kind of hiatus in history, an interval sandwiched between more dramatic, and more historically significant acts. Ironically, feminist studies of the period, with their perspective shaped by the battles for suffrage, have also tended to confirm that view.' Light identifies 'a contradictory and determining tension in English social life' which she terms 'conservative modernity', and describes 'a conservatism itself in revolt against the past, trying to make room for the present.' Women during this period who would not dream of calling themselves feminists were nevertheless, Light suggests, 'linked by a resistance to "the feminine" as it had been thought of in late-Victorian or Edwardian times.'

Embedded in this period were the seeds of future radicalism. The generation of women growing up between the Wars were influenced by the mid-Victorian and Edwardian values of their parents' generation, but their lives have also spanned the period that saw the ending of the marriage bar, the creation of the National Health Service, the disappearance of the servant class, the decimation of the male population, a reduction in family size, and greatly increased class mobility.

A historical overview that places too much emphasis on the shift to collectivism and the growth of the welfare state can easily miss the persistent and powerful strain of individualism that survived in the very generation who oversaw the arrival of the welfare state, and which has flourished in Conservative Britain of the eighties and nineties. Conversely, a historical overview that stresses conservativism can overlook the modernity that characterises the attitudes of this generation of women. The First World War had ushered women into the workplace in unprecedented numbers and if the post-War years saw them ushered out again, the experience had nevertheless altered perceptions of both men and women's social and sexual roles. The strenuous young heroines of D. H. Lawrence's later works (notably, *Women in Love*, written in 1920, and *Lady Chatterley's Lover*, in 1928) reflect both the burgeoning sense of possibility and the anxiety roused by these altered perceptions. This was not only a period of retrenchment and conservatism, it was also a time of careful exploration of enlarged boundaries, a time of quiet advances and individual progress.

The Life Stories

i Work

When were these ten women working? What did work mean to them? Why was work so important to them? What was it that made them pursue careers when so many of their middle-class contemporaries seemed content with marriage and motherhood?

The working lives of these ten women span from 1937 to the present day. Work has meant many things to them. For some it meant fulfilling a social and moral obligation, for others it was a financial necessity. Some relished work for the independence it gave them, or for the intellectual satisfaction, some for the influence and power it provided. Others worked because they were bored at home. Few achieved what they did professionally without first overcoming certain obstacles and opposition, whether from parents, friends, children or colleagues. Jean Graham Hall, who became a Crown Court judge in 1970, discovered when she was doing her pupillage in the early fifties that many chambers would not take women and even those that did, might not put work their way.

> *It wasn't until . . . I actually started to try and practise that I realised it was a man's world where it was a disadvantage to be a woman . . . We were very dependent upon the goodwill of a few men to begin with. When I came to the Bar . . . my clerk would really rather have given the work to somebody else . . . I remember going in there one day, and I must have been in a real temper, and banging my hand on the table and saying, 'Look Edgar, you're doing this to me because I am a woman, because you're afraid. It simply isn't fair. I'm going elsewhere with my five solicitors.' Goodness knows where I was going to go to. He didn't want to lose them, so he said, 'All right, Miss Hall.'**

There are similar tales of overt discrimination against women in nearly every interview. Considering the range of obstacles that faced these women, it is not surprising to find that they had to have a great deal of determination and commitment to their professional lives. Josephine Barnes was married with three small children at the same time as she was a consultant at Charing Cross Hospital and running a private practice in Wimpole Street. Combining home life with an extremely demanding professional life was not easy. She describes washing nappies by hand at six o'clock in the morning before going to work. As well as employing a nanny, she depended heavily on her mother and friends to provide child-care during school holidays. But asked if she had ever considered giving up work, she replied with an emphatic 'No!' She even made it a condition of getting married, that she should be allowed to continue working. The fact that she needed her husband's permission in itself says much about prevailing attitudes towards women in the medical profession at that time. Asked why she was so determined to work, she answered:

* *All quotations in this section are taken from the main text of the interviews.*

I'd passed all these exams, I'd had all this training, all these skills – why should I throw them away? . . . Once you're committed, as I was, totally committed, there's no question. I couldn't go back.

The pressure on a woman to give up work once she married was intense, and particularly so immediately after the Second World War, when for many women the demands of small children were also in direct conflict with professional aspirations. Mary Smith, who worked all her life in housing management and became President of the Institute of Housing Management, describes how once the men came back after the War, the assumption was that women would leave to get married. Of her six female contemporaries at work, all except one gave up their jobs in housing management after marrying. Three later became teachers, which was seen as acceptable employment for women since it could be fitted around their traditional primary role as carers. As Mary Smith was well aware:

Not very many of them were so career-orientated as I was. I married, and didn't *leave housing. That was the difference.*

If the end of the War was a contributing factor in women being squeezed out of the workplace, it is important not to overlook the critical role that the War had previously played in opening doors for them. In 1939 Josephine Barnes went to work as a gynaecologist at the Samaritan Hospital in London. As she herself puts it:

Women doctors were at a premium once the War started, because the men were all being called up and having to go away. In fact, when I arrived, the hospital secretary looked at me and he said, 'You're the first woman we've had here since the last War.'

Livia Gollancz had a similar experience. For many years the Director of the publishing firm, Victor Gollancz, she had first pursued a successful career as a professional musician. It was during the Second World War as a horn player in her early twenties that she benefited from increased demand for women players, although positive discrimination had its limits as she explains:

> *In the Hallé they depended very much on women because there were so few men around. Women were treated very well there, very much on merit . . . but if there was a choice between you and a man as a player they would probably take the man. You accepted it. You just considered yourself jolly lucky for what you got. I suppose fair enough – if the men had families to support they needed more money really.*

Determination to succeed is frequently offset by this kind of shoulder-shrugging acceptance, and it is noticeable throughout these interviews that these independently-minded and undeterrable women often seemed surprisingly prepared to accept the status quo. When they challenged so much, it is striking what they seemed not to think of challenging. This suggests that while they were prepared to pursue change on an individual level, there was a distinct reluctance from many of these women to take on the male establishment by standing up for broader notions of 'women's rights'. Self-interest and women's interests were clearly not perceived at this time to be at all the same thing.

Several of these ten women worked in, or were involved with, the traditionally female world of social work. From the late nineteenth century right up until the Second World War an army of middle-class women had undertaken social work on a voluntary basis. What is significantly different for these women is that their involvement coincided with the professionalisation of social work; they witnessed and partook in its metamorphosis from the customary form of voluntary work for well-to-do women with time on their hands, into a paid job with a career structure, stratified pay, pensions, competition and discrimination. Helen Brook, who went on to found the Brook Advisory Centre, worked in family planning from the 1950s and saw these changes taking place:

The doctors [in the clinics] were women who couldn't have a full-time practice because of being married. The male doctors really despised the family planners. They thought it was just pin money for lady doctors. It wasn't until the sixties that they saw there was money and a career and some prestige in it and they started jumping on the bandwagon. And then of course bossing us all around.

Mary Smith witnessed similar changes in housing management, another area of work traditionally left to women:

When it was a fairly low-paid job, then the women were there; once it became a big job and the salaries went up accordingly, the men took the directors' jobs.

Professional lives do not take place in a vacuum and in nearly every case these women seemed to feel that the involvement they gave to their work inevitably caused a shortfall elsewhere in their lives. Una Kroll combined being a GP and a deaconess, and as such had experience of two very male-dominated professions. She was also married with four children. For much of her married life her husband was unemployed and as a result there was considerable financial pressure on her to work. While she experienced great fulfilment through her career, she emphasised that it would not have been possible without her husband's full co-operation, and she felt that to some extent both he and her children suffered.

Supportive husbands were mentioned by several women, as were resentful children, yet however grateful they were to the former, however resistant to the latter, the external validation provided by professional success seems seldom to have entirely eradicated the internal guilt that these women felt. A note of defensiveness or apology creeps in when they describe themselves as hopelessly undomesticated: 'He made bread much better than I did' (Una Kroll); 'I was no cook. I didn't really live up to his expectations' (Hilda Brown), while their children's pleas for them to stay at home and 'be like other mothers' clearly roused complicated emotions. Hilda Brown, now in her seventies, described how her daughter had criticised her for working, yet has in turn become a working mother. 'So opinions change,' she says, fitting many shades of emotion into those three words.

What is clear is that if the juggling act is difficult now for working women, it was considerably more so then. It is noticeable that the higher a woman got in her profession the smaller the degree of her domestic responsibilities: of these ten women, five were not attempting to combine the two worlds of home and work, and to some extent felt them to be incompatible. Betty Boothroyd, who has been an MP for twenty years and in 1992 became the first woman Speaker in the 700-year history of the House of Commons, is quite explicit about the irreconcilable demands of her private and public lives:

> *I think sometimes, when I look back on it, maybe I have missed out in not marrying and creating a family of my own . . . but I had a job to do, I had a full life which I enjoyed enormously . . . To have a husband, to have a home, to have children, and still have a very big professional life . . . I'm not sure that I would have been able to do it . . . You've got to make choices in life, and maybe unconsciously I made my choice.*

The further up the scale these woman climbed and the more traditional the profession they sought to progress in, the less compatible it appears to have been with the more conventional expressions of female fulfilment, marriage and motherhood. These women were ahead of their time: they were challenging notions of how a woman could live her life. But what they could not always do was find the men who would also accept their revised versions of female identity: men remained largely unchallenged and unchallengeable in both the domestic and the professional sphere. To succeed professionally, it was often necessary to align oneself with male codes of behaviour which left little or no room for either conventional or radical expessions of the female self. Those women who did succeed in combining marriage and career had the full support of their husbands. Like the generation of feminists before them, partnership proved vital if the two aspects of a woman's life were to be realised. Millicent Fawcett, Emmeline Pankhurst and Emmeline Pethick-Lawrence, for example, had all enjoyed their husbands' full support.

For those women who were not able to combine marriage and career, there have been compensations: intense pride and involvement in work is one, the respect of colleagues and peers is another. Power and influence are mentioned, as are growing self-confidence and the sense of having done something worthwhile with one's life. Jean Graham Hall says of being a judge: 'It is absolutely engulfing. The day passes. You don't even know it's begun.' For Betty Boothroyd work is a source of great personal pride: 'I feel very honoured by it. To have had the confidence of my peers is something that I cherish very much. That makes up for a great deal of what I miss in other things.' It is the note of these 'other things' that persistently creeps in, a reminder that compromises can easily shade into sacrifices, that success in one area of one's life may well be qualified by perceived failure in another. The 'unconscious choice' that Betty Boothroyd describes remains the indictment of a society that continues to resist genuine flexibility in domestic and professional life for women and men, and ensures that there is still a price to pay for women who resist the traditional roles allotted them. Una Kroll summed up the situation very well when she said:

> The best of feminism and the best of societies would somehow enable both mothers and fathers to have enough time for their children . . . But we haven't reached that stage. Meantime women have a double burden to bear. I don't think women should [not fulfil themselves because they] sacrifice themselves for their children. But at the same time, part of the fulfilment of yourself is to be a mother. You have to make a whole series of compromises.

ii Family Background

What, if anything, did these women draw from their own family backgrounds? Were their families the springboard for their future success or the lions' den from which they fled? What role, if any, did their grandparents play? How much support did parents provide, and how much opposition? What impact did their upbringing have on their adult lives?

Childhood experiences seem to have played an important role in shaping attitudes towards work. Lucy Faithfull, who became Director of Social Services for Oxford and is now a Conservative peer, remembers deciding at the age of six, shortly after the death of her father, to commit her life to providing the stability in other children's lives that her own so drastically lacked. Betty Boothroyd was deeply impressed by the relentless harshness of life for her working-class parents in industrial Yorkshire in the 1930s. Josephine Barnes, the eldest of four children, was competitive with her clever brothers. Her determination to do as well as if not better than the boys stood her in good stead throughout her medical career: 'I reckoned that if I was competing,' she says, 'I had to be better qualified.' Jean Graham Hall echoes her words almost exactly: 'If a woman wants to get anywhere, she's got to be better qualified than anyone just to get started.' In their gritty determination sounds the echo of the suffragettes, the difference once again being the individual rather than the collective focus of their endeavours.

Another way in which family background was influential can be seen in the strong sense of social duty that these women inherited from their parents' generation. Charitable work was by no means restricted to those who would later go into social work as a career. As Helen Brook put it: 'In my day it was natural to work for the poor. People like me always did something.' A keen desire to be of service to society was a legacy of Victorian paternalism and Christian duty, but for these women, the religious energies of their parents' generation were gradually being replaced by a humanitarian impulse and a political commitment to social action. Wanting to be of service to society was a reason for working cited by eight of the ten women. It was wanting to do so in the context of a career which differentiates them from the generation before and links them to the feminists of the sixties and seventies, a period in which many of them were at their most professionally influential.

Grandmothers in several cases played an important part in these women's lives. Livia Gollancz has clear memories of her feisty suffragette grandmother; Sheila Parkinson also speaks with admiration of the resilience and independence of her maternal grandmother. Lucy Faithfull's grandmother provided key financial support after her father's death. Grandfathers do not seem to have been such an overtly positive influence. They are referred to occasionally as eccentric or lovable characters, whose presence coloured weekends or holidays, but otherwise had limited bearing on the future direction their lives were to take.

Fathers, on the other hand, are mostly notable for their absence or their opposition. This applies to seven of the ten women. Lucy Faithfull's father died when she was six; Una Kroll's walked out before she was two; Sheila Parkinson's father left the country when she was ten, returning only to legalise the divorce when she was fourteen; Hilda Brown's father seemed 'very far away, very remote' and was taken up with his work in China throughout her childhood. For Jean Graham Hall and Livia Gollancz, fierce arguments with their fathers were an uncomfortable feature of their adolescence, although Livia later established a working relationship with hers when she joined the family publishing firm. Three out of the ten had very positive relationships with their fathers: Mary Smith's engine-driver father was the prime mover in her education; Helen Brook adored her father and had a blissful year living with him in London while her mother and siblings remained in the country; and Betty Boothroyd found in her father a friend and companion as well as a role model in manner and temperament.

In striking contrast to the descriptions of their fathers is how these ten women describe their mothers. 'She did the most extraordinary things' (Helen Brook); 'a most outstanding person' (Lucy Faithful); 'You name it, she could do it' (Josephine Barnes); 'an unusual individual' (Hilda Brown); 'a very remarkable woman' (Betty Boothroyd); 'I was like a pale dull shadow compared with her' (Una Kroll). Is it that they are idealising their mothers in retrospect? Or might remarkable women themselves be the daughters of remarkable women? Perhaps the process of identifying some special quality in their mothers bolstered their own sense of self-worth and provided an extra spur to their determination. Closer examination, however, shows that hyperbole at times thinly veils a more complex dynamic in the mother–daughter relationship that involves guilt, regret, pity and fear as well as admiration, respect and gratitude. Una Kroll is the most direct, saying simply: 'I was passionately adoring of my mother, fiercely loyal to her, but also frightened of her.' Betty Boothroyd admired her mother's personal qualities of kindness, warmth and loyalty, but never forgot the sheer hard grind of daily life for working-class women in the North of England between the Wars. When Boothroyd herself escaped that life to make her way in the world of Westminster, she had to reconcile herself to the contradictions inherent in her success: she was both rejecting her mother's way of life and at the same time fulfilling her hopes. Lucy Faithfull also expresses great admiration for her mother, who was a young War widow left to bring up two children single-handed, describing her as: 'a person who was prepared to sacrifice everything for the children. She was always enchanting, and she was always deeply loving and considerate, but she had that incredibly sad look.' Lucy Faithfull in turn has dedicated her life to children, perhaps as much in an attempt to repay a heavy debt of gratitude as to provide other children with what she felt her own childhood lacked.

The description of the typically Victorian mother that Josephine Barnes offers is not unusual: 'My mother was generous and open, but rather reserved, not a person with whom you would discuss emotional problems at all.' Sheila Parkinson describes a world of nanny and nursery maid: 'We saw very little of my mother. We weren't expected to be about.' And a note of perplexity creeps into Livia Gollancz's voice when she says of her mother: 'She was a wonderful person, a lovely person, very sensible about everything. She was a good mother, but she had a curious air of detachment.' Yet it is these perplexing, often unreachable mothers who so often provided the key impetus for their daughters' careers, as well as vital back-up later on. Josephine Barnes's mother supported her financially through medical school and later looked after her children while she went to work. Una Kroll's mother at one point had to beg for her school fees. Jean Graham Hall's mother backed her decision to go to the London School of Economics to study social work against the wishes of her father, who initially regarded it a waste of time and money. Livia Gollancz stayed every weekend with her mother when she became Director of Victor Gollancz: 'She would look after me and I would just work.'

The experience that these women's mothers had of work also seems to have been significant. Lucy Faithfull's mother was a trained nurse and worked as a matron in a preparatory school; Betty Boothroyd's mother always worked, so did Una Kroll's. These women supported their families without the help of a husband's income and their daughters learnt from them that economic survival could and did come from women's work. The example set by their mother's lives implicitly challenged the assumption that men were the breadwinners. All three in their turn became the sole or main breadwinners in their own households and have always worked. Even when mothers had only briefly worked, their small taste of employment was clearly influential. Hilda Brown's mother got a science degree at Manchester University and then worked as a missionary teacher in China before the First World War; Livia Gollancz's mother had trained to be an architect at the Architectural Association.

Both women had stopped work on marrying and as a result neither had utilised her education or training. Both were very ambitious for their daughters, instilling in them the value of education and of work, attempting perhaps to achieve more through them than they had been able to in their own lives. Hilda Brown, who went on to work in the Factory Inspectorate and ran some of the first courses in personnel management, remembers how her mother's ambitiousness made her a difficult person to get close to, but is nevertheless grateful that 'she did assume that the daughters would get a degree as well as the sons.'

In all but three cases, it can be said that a mother was a most significant presence for these women, and played a critical role in their future success, whether through explicit example, indirect influence, practical help, emotional encouragement or financial support. Where mothers were lacking, other older women often filled the breach: Sheila Parkinson's mentor, Olwyn Easton; Helen Brook's redoubtable Mrs Shadwell; Mary Smith's Auntie Grace. Often these women were unmarried or had been widowed young. As strong, practical, independent women, they proved admirable role models for striking out into the world; what they could not do was provide clues as to how to combine the professional and moral satisfaction of a career with the social and emotional obligations of a family. That was the dilemma facing this generation of women, a dilemma for which there were neither role models nor easy solutions.

iii Marriage, Divorce and Widowhood

Born between 1907 and 1929, these women, as a group, married relatively late for their generation, at an average age of twenty-eight. Their married lives span sixty-five years. Helen Brook was the first to marry in 1928, and is still married, to her second husband whom she met in 1936. She is also the only one of the ten to marry more than once. Una Kroll, the last to marry in 1957, was widowed in 1987. Of the seven marriages, five took place after the start of the Second World War, and in three cases were prompted by the outbreak of war. Two of the seven marriages ended in divorce. Four of the ten women did not marry at all. In this respect, these women as a group presage a shift towards marrying later and delaying childbirth that by the 1990s has become the norm (see also Conclusion).

Most of these women came from significantly larger families than they in turn produced. Between them they had just thirteen children, whereas their mothers had had a total of thirty-one offspring. Four of them came from families of four children or more, whereas only one had more than three children herself (see Fig. 1). They are unusual for their generation in having either smaller or larger than average families, bifocating into having one or no children, or else having three to four children.

Fig. 1

	Total siblings in family (including self)	Total number of children
Josephine Barnes	5	3
Hilda Brown	5	2
Livia Gollancz	5	0
Helen Brook	4	3
Sheila Parkinson	3	0
Jean Graham Hall	3	0
Lucy Faithfull	2	0
Mary Smith	2	1
Una Kroll	1	4
Betty Boothroyd	1	0

The smaller family size clearly reflects the changes that had taken place since their mothers' time: wider availability of contraception, for example, had a demographic impact.

Economic austerity after the Second World War and the fact that the government was encouraging smaller families (in contrast to its attitude after the First World War) also had some bearing on family size. Non-marriage is a significant factor in explaining the reduced fertility rate in this group, although it is hard to know what relation this has to the pursuit of full-time professional work: did they not marry because they were working, or were they working because they were not married? The shortage of men during the Second World War, at the time these women would have been marrying, is certainly a factor to be taken into consideration. But any direct connection between career and reduced family size is contradicted by Una Kroll and Josephine Barnes who between them had more than half of the children in this group and yet were both married and in full-time employment.

Statistically, the married women in this group were also widowed relatively young: Sheila Parkinson, married for just four months, was still in her twenties; Hilda Brown and Mary Smith were in their forties; Una Kroll was sixty-two. The impact of widowhood, emotional, social and professional, is described vividly by these four women. It ushered in a period of despair, loneliness and anxiety, increased the burden of domestic and financial responsibilities, and brought social isolation and sexual frustration. But widowhood (and also divorce, which affected two of the ten) played a crucial role in facilitating their professional activities. Hilda Brown recognised that her husband's death at the early age of fifty-two brought her a new degree of freedom:

> *When you're married, you're so busy contributing to the home and the family, it's very difficult to find time for outside things. Your focus is much more on the present circumstances. But after I was widowed and began to wonder what the rest of the world was doing, I became more politically active . . . I could do things which I wouldn't have wanted to take the time to do [before I was widowed].*

Widowhood in some cases provided a socially acceptable

reason for full-time work, and one which to a certain extent let the individual woman off the hook, providing a convenient veil for her 'unwomanly' behaviour. Widowhood enabled them to lead professional working lives that might not otherwise have been possible. It also seems to have alleviated somewhat the perceived professional and social stigma of being a single woman, a source of some dread to a generation who had grown up surrounded by spinster aunts, and for whom divorced women were still considered morally questionable. When Helen Brook divorced her first husband in 1931 she experienced a degree of social approbation and sexual harassment, which were still painful for her to recall sixty years on. Even in the 1960s, there was stigma attached to the divorcee, as Hilda Brown explains:

> *At work I felt fortunate that I was single not because of a divorce, but because I was a widow. It did make it easier to hold up my head. I knew I hadn't been neglected or walked out on.*

Widowhood has been found to have similarly positive effects for women in a very different cultural context. Helen Watson's book, *Women in the City of the Dead*, is based on oral histories of Muslim women in a small, impoverished community in Cairo. It describes how the women are often compelled to work in order to feed their families, but go to great lengths to conceal their paid activities from the outside world in general and from their husbands in particular, who consider it shameful and emasculating. In this traditional Muslim culture widows stand alone in having a legitimate entry into the work place. The cross-cultural similarities are sobering: as late as the 1960s in Britain to be single was still to invite censure. Widowhood, as Hilda Brown found, was a respectable front for an independence that many still found threatening in women.

In exploring why it was that these women prospered in their professional lives, it is impossible to ignore the striking fact that only one of the ten, Una Kroll, remained married to one man throughout her working life. Of the others, two were divorced, three were widowed (all before the age of forty-six) and four did not marry. And in Kroll's case, it is worth noting, there were highly unusual circumstances which precluded the possibility of her stopping work or getting divorced. This is not to say that she would have done either, but rather to emphasise that even she is in certain ways far from typical. All ten of these women were therefore unusual for their generation in terms of marriage and motherhood.

iv Attitudes to Femininism, Femininity and Womanhood
What did these women feel about feminism? How did they define what it was to be a woman? How did they feel about motherhood? How was their sense of identity affected by having a career? To what extent did they consider themselves fulfilled as women?

Clearly for these ten women fulfilment through motherhood is central to their concept of self (their attitude towards marriage is less straightforward), and those whose lives did not afford opportunities to explore this aspect of their identity experienced a degree of disappointment. Of the women who did not have children, all expressed regret that that was so, none more poignantly than Jean Graham Hall:

> *In my heart of hearts I always wished I had married and had children. I've felt deprived in not having them . . . When I realised I wasn't going to have any children of my own, I thought it was the end of the world, but I've come to terms now with any regrets. When you're old enough to know how to play Juliet, you're only able to play the nurse.*

For this generation of women, motherhood was closely connected with sexuality: contraception was only available on proof of marriage and virginity was a highly-prized as well as burdensome asset. The sexual double standard (i.e. that sexual activity outside marriage is condoned for men, forbidden for women) was still largely unchallenged for their generation and locates them historically perhaps more than any other factor. Helen Brook was offended by this double standard from a very young age:

I had to guard my virginity like mad until I was married, because I wouldn't have been acceptable had I not been a virgin. Well, what a terrible thing to do to a human being! . . . I could never understand why it was all right for men to sow wild oats with some people's daughters and keep other people's daughters as virgins.

Having received no sex education, the twenty-one-year-old Helen was not to know that the Whirling Spray her husband brought home had no contraceptive value whatsoever. (Since he claimed not to want children, it is only to be guessed that he did not know this either.) Her first child was born the following year. Later, as a family planner, she witnessed for herself the toll that repeated pregnancy and labour took on women and was incensed by the hypocritical attitudes towards female sexuality still prevalent in the 1950s. She remembers the jubilation that accompanied the arrival of the contraceptive pill:

It was wonderful, it was absolutely wonderful. I can't tell you, it was like all the public holidays that you've ever enjoyed all together, it was really Hallelujah!

Undoubtedly, the arrival of the pill fundamentally changed attitudes to female sexuality, but for these women it happened too late. For their generation, sex was only acceptable within the confines of marriage, with procreation considered as its primary function rather than female pleasure or self-expression.

While Helen Brook dedicated much of her later life to making contraception available to women of all ages and helping them to take charge of their sexuality, Sheila Parkinson's job had been to keep it in check. Responsible for one hundred FANY drivers during the Second World War, one of her key duties was to 'guard the English womanhood'. Her life story vividly conveys the sense of burgeoning female sexuality during the forties and fifties barely restrained by traditional prohibitions. This in turn points to an irreversible shift in female identity that insisted, however conservatively, upon recognition, a shift which society would eventually have to attempt, or at least appear, to accommodate.

The attitude towards feminism that emerges from these interviews is more complex, and given the insistent movement towards change that is discernible in these life stories, it is perhaps surprising how fundamentally anti-feminist many of these women appear to be. Several had seen their mothers working and had in early childhood years absorbed the atmosphere of the suffragists, yet few happily called themselves feminists or were interested in a collective cause or identity. Some were overtly hostile and critical, others simply dis-associated themselves from the collective on the grounds of age: 'I probably would have been a suffragette if I had been born in those days, but I wasn't, and if a woman can't get her equal rights, I think it's a very funny do' (Lucy Faithfull); 'You asked me about feminism: it came after me' (Jean Graham Hall).

A number of factors may have encouraged them to internalise rather than politicise the obstacles and disadvant-ages they faced. The First and Second World Wars, for instance, led to widespread economic hardship and to the prevalence of single-parent families, but these were hardly issues which women could band together and protest about. Similarly, the War-time spirit, although bringing greater work opportunities for women, fostered a stoical attitude in which the shared goal was the ability to endure opposition rather than counter-attack. They were also swimming against the tide of post-War anti-feminism, which was attempting to push women back into the home. This generation of working women needed to be individuals to achieve what they did. Had they identified more closely with the collective group of women, they would never have pushed as far as they did into the pervasively male world of paid employment. It was by *not* identifying themselves too closely with other women, by seeing themselves as different, that they found the impetus quietly and determinedly to challenge the status quo.

Some of the women in this group became dislocated not only from the traditional domestic realm of women's lives, but also from the 'community of women'. In this respect age appears to make a difference. The women born after 1920 were more politicised: Una Kroll, for example, describes herself as being 'highly aware of discrimination against women, and very loving of my own sex.' The older women, however, those born in and before 1920, tended not to identify thmselves with a 'women's cause' and were not predisposed to helping other women, despite the determination and resolve it had taken them to suceed professionally. Lucy Faithfull distinguishes between 'a child's issue and a woman's choice', while Josephine Barnes insists: 'I haven't worked for women's rights. I've worked for women – not for their rights.' Helen Brook is the exception, being the oldest of these women and yet in some ways the most ardently feminist in action and outlook. This difference in attitude and perception may well be explained by the fact that she was old enough to have been influenced more directly by the pre-1918 suffragist movement, as well as coming from a distinctly unconventional, not to say Bohemian, background in which women would have enjoyed a greater degree of sexual and social freedom than was usual for that time. Of all these women, Livia Gollancz was the one in the best position to help other professional women: as director of her own company she could have instituted whatever changes she wished. But asked what provision was made for women who wanted to have children and continue working, she insisted:

It just didn't arise. There were only three or four of us high enough up in the company for it to apply to. A publishing firm is like an hour-glass: if you don't get through the little gap into the top bit, you leave at the gap . . . Once you've got through the gap and you've got into the upper echelons then you've probably got past the age when you want to be having a family anyway. Most people by the time they'd been promoted didn't have children. They either didn't marry or they didn't have children.

The motivating force for these women was inherently contrary to a notion of feminism with its emphasis on collective consciousness and collective action. The group identity was simply not there, in part because for this group of women no community existed with which they could have identified. Since there were no professional female role models ahead of them, they had to fit into a man's world on male terms. They had to be individualists to get on professionally. Feminism was a luxury they could not afford.

Professional success seems to have been bought at a high price, and on a profoundly private level the cost may have been to their female identity. Many of them became isolated from other women in the process of rising professionally and became divorced from the shared needs and common goals of women. How much this was a result of their career and how much a reflection of personal ideology is not entirely clear, but it would seem that professional success for this generation at least could often only be achieved on very male terms. The experience of working in a predominantly male world isolated women from other women (socially, economically, intellectually and emotionally) and in turn made them more identified with a male culture than a female one. In terms of how they spent their time, what they talked about, who they saw etc, the emphasis in their lives would have been predominantly male-defined. This may well have brought about a split in their self-identity: unable to realise both the male and the female aspects of their personality within either of the roles available to them, career women of this generation may well have been forced to neglect the latter in order to liberate the former. It may, therefore, be more appropriate to define this apparent anti-feminism instead as a necessary process of de-feminisation.

In an oral history interview you have access not to one generation but to three or four. These ten women tell us also about their grandmothers, their mothers and their daughters. As Brian Harrison points out: 'Each generation finds its bearings by re-evaluating its predecessors.' But each generation also finds its bearings by re-evaluating itself in relation to the generation that comes after it. In the course of the interview, several women referred frequently to their daughters, whose experiences and opinions not only interested them greatly, but seemed to provide a context in which to understand their own. Changing attitudes towards sexuality, marriage, motherhood and domestic responsibilities were often mentioned. Not surprisingly, the childless women were far less likely to cross-refer to the younger generation of women. This is a further reason why they were also less likely to set their own lives in a continuum of female experience.

The emphasis on individualism, and the resistance to a collective female identity, can be seen through these inter-views to have had a number of causes: economic and political factors; the identification through work with a male rather than a female world; diminished opportunities, as a result, to cross-reference one's own experience with those of other women; cultural emphasis at the time on obligations rather than rights; lack of role models among women who combined career and family, and the need to de-identify with the majority of women in order to achieve.

It must also be remembered that the tendency of oral history itself is to resist generalisation and to emphasise the individual and the particular. In the life stories of these women diversity of experience is immediately striking. Their political allegian-cies range from Tory to Communist, and their religions from Methodism to Judaism. Some were university educated, some were not, one did a degree by correspondence course in her thirties. Only six married, of whom five had children, two divorced, and four were widowed. One had servants, most had domestic help of some kind, one had a house-husband. Their role models range from parents, friends and teachers, to characters from the Bible; some had strong fathers, others had strong mothers; three would call themselves feminists, three would object vehemently to the label.

The challenge to the oral historian is always how to respect the diversity of individual experience, while at the same time searching out the similarities from which conclusions may be drawn. In a sample of this size conclusions are more elusive than usual; nevertheless, it is possible to set the experiences of these ten women into a wider social and political context and to identify the themes that unite them, both as women of their time and as women whose experiences can reach across the generations and acquire a contemporary relevance. Each woman tells her story in her own words. While the individual interviews respect the uniqueness of each woman's experience, seen as a whole the similarities and the differences in their accounts are fascinating and throw interesting new light on how the perception of self has changed for women during the twentieth century. The cumulative voice that emerges from these interviews describes vividly a female identity torn always between the collective and the individual.

Rebecca Abrams
Oxford, 1993

HELEN BROOK

Helen Brook, founder of the Brook Advisory Centre, was born on 12 October 1907 into the very heart of artistic London. Her father ran the Chenil Galleries in Chelsea and her childhood was populated by such characters as Augustus John, William Walton, Osbert Sitwell and Jacob Epstein. It was an idyllic time which ended abruptly with the Depression when the Galleries had to close. After a brief spell working as a waitress, Helen Brook married in 1928 and the following year gave birth to her first child. When the marriage ended in divorce, she went to Paris where she studied at the Sorbonne. She returned to England and in 1937 she married Robin Brook, a businessman who later became a director of the Bank of England, with whom she had two more children, Sarah and Diana.

When war was declared she was living in London and immediately joined up as an air-raid warden. She was then absorbed by her domestic duties until 1952, when she took a part-time voluntary job at the Islington Family Planning Clinic in Spencer Street. This modest step was to change her life. After the death of Dr Marie Stopes in 1958 she became director of the Clinic, then in Whitfield Street, and in 1959 took the highly controversial decision to open the doors for the first time to unmarried women. In response to sustained demand, the Young People's Advisory Centre (for advice and counselling) was officially formed the following year. In 1963 the first Brook Advisory Centre was opened in Dawes Street, Walworth, and in 1966 Helen Brook again caused uproar when she made contraception available to the under-sixteens. There are now twenty-four Brook Advisory Clinics and nine branches across the country.

No stranger to controversy, Helen Brook, as chairman of Family

Planning Sales, the commercial subsidiary of the FPA, was responsible for authorising the slogan 'If you want to have it off, put it on.' She was also at the forefront of the drive to introduce a proper system for sex education into schools. In 1978 Brook set up the Education and Publications Unit, which published its own literature and supplied sex education material and training to schoolteachers. This in turn led to the creation in 1981 of the Schools Publication Group. She is still involved with family planning as president of the Brook Advisory Centre, trustee of Family Planning Sales and a member (and vice-president) of the Family Planning Association. She lives in London with her husband Robin and has three daughters, seven grandchildren and six great-grandchildren.

This interview took place in three sessions in 1990 at Helen Brook's home near Regent's Park. The walls are hung with paintings collected over a lifetime, which to her frustration she is no longer able to see. A woman of tremendous passion and commitment, keen to suffering and intolerant of injustice, Helen Brook answered each question with careful consideration. At times indignation would break through (when talking about women's suffering and sexual indignity), at other times enthusiasm (when recalling her blissful childhood). She expressed great sadness that her role in the family planning movement has so often been misunderstood, and was at all times modest about her achievements, emphasising that it was down to teamwork rather than individual success. Her final words were, 'I'm sure I haven't talked nearly enough about all the other people who were involved.'

I was born in the Chenil Galleries in the King's Road, Chelsea, during the first one-man exhibition of Henry Nevinson. My mother was very young and didn't realise that the pains she had was actually me, and I shot out into the world among all the prints and the smell of turpentine. My mother was totally uneducated and she wasn't the least bit interested in education. She imagined that girls just grew up to get married and boys grew up and went off and ruled the world. She was that kind of old-fashioned girl. She was a very handsome woman, full

2

of life, and she adored babies. She had four children by the time she was twenty-one and I am the eldest. My father was twenty-two years older than she. He was running the Chenil Galleries and my mother was one of the young lovelies of that time and they met and were married. She must have been sixteen. My father was not an artist, but he was involved always with artists. He was a very charming man, an idealistic man, very imaginative.

Walter Knewstub, Helen's father, was the son of the painter J. W. Knewstub, pupil of, and then assistant to, Rossetti. Walter's sisters also married artists – William Orpen and William Rotherstein, known respectively by Helen as Uncle Orpen and Uncle Rotherstein.

We lived in Chelsea until I was five years old and then we moved, first to Rye in Sussex, and then to Pett Level which is on the edge of the Romney Marshes. We were right on the sea, within 250 yards of the sea, and behind us this amazing Romney Marshes. It was completely wild, there was nobody there but the fishermen. We were a very small community, fifty or sixty people at the very most, probably even fewer. There was a shepherd who lived out on the Marshes, and he looked like the pictures of shepherds from the Bible with a great beard and his flocks all over the Marshes. And Reg Cook, his son, just knew every single bird, everything that moved. We used to go with him collecting birds' eggs and mushrooms and he used to take us out fishing and shrimping. It was blissful. That's the worst of it really, because nothing has ever tasted or smelt or been so beautiful. My mother always had her hair down her back, looking like a gypsy, and we used to be barefoot, no shoes or stockings or anything. We bathed without clothes. That caused a tremendous chatter. It was so idyllic. We had such enormous adventures all the time.

I remember well the day the War started because we had all been bathing and it was a very, very hot day and we came in and found the weekend guests in the house in a fuss. Everything was buzzing. The War on the marshes was absolutely marvellous, because things were happening all the time. We were bombed by Zeppelins, and a bomb dropped just behind Jacob Epstein's house. It was very exciting. I was seven that October and started at the village school up in Pett village, about a mile and a quarter away. I continued there until I was about nine and a half. On the way we used to go birds'-nesting and pinch apples and all sorts of lovely things. These children going to school in buses, they don't know anything about life.

We weren't poor, but we weren't rich, we were just an ordinary family. My father was in London at the Galleries and he'd come down on Fridays. Mother was there all the time. She was like one of us. She was really just a girl herself. She did the most extraordinary things. She and two of her friends got into a tub that was washed up and went off to sea and they had to be rescued. Although she was always there, my memories are much more of my father, whom I really loved. It's very bad luck on mothers really: they look after their children, but the fathers are heroes to their little girls. My father was to me. He and my mother were useless as parents for growing children – they simply didn't know how to help us grow up. They weren't interested in our education at all. We weren't prepared for life at all. I think nowadays they all grow up too soon, they're shoved out into the world before they know where they are, but you can also be too protected, you can stay young too long. I must have been about twenty-five before I was really grown-up.

A Mrs Shadwell came to live at Pett and she was a Roman Catholic convert and was out to convert the world. She immediately got hold of my young mother and before Mother knew where she was, she was converted to the Church, which meant that we all had to be redone. And then of course I had to go through my first confession and Holy Communion. I was dressed like a little bride and I was told that everything was going to change and I took the host and I waited – and nothing happened. I can't tell you what a disappointment it was! When I made my first confession I couldn't think what a sin was. I'd

4

never heard of sin. I couldn't think of anything. I've always found that difficult. How can a child have sins? You can only have sins later on.

Mrs Shadwell really took control over us and she arranged all our educations. I went to school at the Burlington High School, which is now no longer, and I stayed with my father up in London. That was a most blissful year and I found I was really very bright and awfully good at gym too. By the end of that year, when I was eleven, Mrs Shadwell had decided I should go to a convent school, the Holy Child Jesus at Mark Cross. It was absolutely awful. I've never been able to learn since really. All the things that I was good at weren't the sort of things that were much good in a convent school. I was never a Child of Mary or any of those things. I wasn't ever good at sewing. And although I have nothing against praying, it took up such a terrible lot of time.

All during the War Father was keeping the Chenil Galleries open, but all the time dreaming and planning of rebuilding the Galleries as an artistic centre with a school, a restaurant, music. By some means or other he got enough people together and slowly this dream of his became a reality and the New Chenil Galleries was built. It attracted everybody you can think of: Augustus John, William Orpen, the Sitwells, William Walton . . . John Barbirolli got his chance to become a conductor from the Chenil Galleries. It was rather marvellous. Everybody would be sitting in lovely chairs, listening to heavenly music, pictures all round – Father's idea of heaven. I remember William Walton chasing me round the Galleries! And Osbert Sitwell taught me how to bet on horses. Eric Kennington was around, doing portraits and things. Everybody was there. It was that sort of world. It was a tremendous time.

Things began to go wrong in 1926. There was a great depression and suddenly there was no money, no nothing, and the Galleries had to be sold. My poor father had not only put every bit of himself into it all, but everything that he owned.

Suddenly within a few months we were without a penny. We hadn't got a home, we hadn't got anything. It was unbelievable. My father was so humiliated by all of this, instead of coming out and fighting and getting himself a job, he just disappeared. My mother had left him. My dear Aunt Grace had to come to the rescue. Uncle Orpen had helped my brother Casper to go to Australia, my sister Wendy was still at school. I got taken on as a nippy for Joe Lyons Corner House people. I was at the tea house on the corner of Gloucester Road and High Street Kensington. That was really quite an eye-opener. You got twenty-one shillings a week and tips. If you were pretty you got sixpence, and if you weren't so pretty you only got threepence. I was very lucky and people gave me lots of tips. My shop-mates were terribly nice, but I think they saw that I was totally stupid and they never told their stories in front of me, or swore. I was so innocent. We'd had no sex education. I was a virgin. I was really still about twelve years old in experience. I gathered, because you know you can't help hearing, that they were having male friends pay for them. Even in those days it was pretty rotten for women. They always had to pay sexually. And even then I thought it's really revolting and it's not going to happen to me. I've never thought of it morally at all. I just can't bear women being used. From a very young age and so ignorant, I felt fierce about this. I've never been a women's libber, but I've always thought of women as equal.

During this time, Helen Brook struck up a friendship with George Whitaker, a distinguished violinist of the day, and a member of the Chenil Chamber Orchestra. After a six-month courtship, they were married on 10 March 1928. Helen was nineteen.

He was a marvellous musician and a very intelligent man. It was very nice for me to be back talking to my own civilised world again. He was the leader at Covent Garden, so I went to rehearsals at Covent Garden and it was all great fun. Then my daughter was born about eighteen months after. George was playing *Tristan and Isolde* the night she was born, so she was called Christine Isolde. The problem was that George was never there, because if you're a musician you're always somewhere else. It meant that I really didn't have any kind of social life. We lived in a flat on Haverstock Hill and it was a very nice area, stuffed with painters and musicians, and everybody knew everybody and it was terrific fun, but it was very difficult for a young woman to have a life mostly without a husband. We had a single-parent relationship really. Eventually I got a divorce, I think it was 1931, and then I went off to France, leaving my little girl with my father. The moment you were a divorced woman you were fair prey, or fair play – one of those things. It was horrible. My family would have nothing to do with me. I first of all stayed in a girls' finishing school by the Lac D'Annecy for the summer and then went to stay in Paris with the two sisters who ran the school, and I entered the Sorbonne for two terms to study French literature. That was wonderful. I had lots of friends by then, and things were happening in the Thirties, and everybody was talking in the cafés. I was very fond of Germany, but I was absolutely totally anti-Hitler.

Anyway I came back to London and I went to a dinner and in came Robin Brook. Robin was then working with a firm in the City. This must have been towards the end of 1935. And the awful thing is I fell in love with him. I mean *real* love. I'd never been in love with a human being. It was the first time and it was terrible! I knew I really would die if I didn't marry Robin. That was the most agonising year of my life. Eventually he asked me and we were married in June 1937. It was a completely different world. His family were very upper-middle-class and were quite surprised by me. There I was, a woman who had a child, had no money and had divorced her husband. Their way of life was so safe, so well-fed, so predictable. I liked all that. And I adored my mother-in-law, who was a very intelligent, highly educated woman for her time. It was another world altogether. I had to change. But I'm good at changing and I soon learnt. When I married my husband I made up my mind that I would stick it out, whatever happened, through thick and thin. Nothing would ever make me change my mind.

We had hardly been married before the War started. Robin had a house in Devonshire Place and we occupied the top part and let consulting rooms to Jewish [refugee] doctors. I then decided I'd better have a child, because I thought, if he's going I'll be left without anything of his. And then of course I was unable to conceive. I understood then how terrible it was for women not to have a family when they thought they could do so easily. It went on month after month with this desperate disappointment and at last I went to a consultant and had an operation, and it worked and we got our beloved Sarah. She was born in 1941. By then the Battle of Britain was on and I'd gone to stay in Ludlow to be away from it all. Christine was at boarding school then, she must have been twelve when Sarah was born. Then I went up to Yorkshire to stay with Robin's mother and aunt for a while, and I then joined a friend of mine in Didcot and we both became VADs [members of the Voluntary Aid Detachment] and worked in Didcot Hospital. Mary had a plan that should we be attacked by the Germans, she would stay and entertain the troops with masses and masses of condoms which she'd got stored away, and I would have to crawl to Didcot for help. Thank goodness it never had to be put into action!

I came back to London and had my second child, Diana, there in 1943. After she was born, we went to Dorset and then we went to Wales – we spent all our time trying to get away from London. I had such a caravan by this time: three children and a nanny and six hens in a laundry basket and a Pekingnese dog. Robin stayed in London. He was recruited to SOE [Special Operations Exercise] and then posted to the Ministry of Economic Warfare with Hugh Dalton in charge and Hugh Gaitskell as his private secretary. So all that was going on in the background.

Anyway we got through the War. I had the opportunity to

move up to a beautiful house in Hampstead owned by some friends of ours, so I was back where I felt I belonged. There were all the political people and artists and musicians and painters. It was like going back to heaven. Robin was in Germany, by then he was a real soldier, and then he came home and of course he hated it all. He loathed having to go to London on the tube. He liked to be near the office. And eventually I had to go back to Devonshire Place. I got very depressed and couldn't paint or anything. I was in real despair. I didn't know how I was going to get on with my life at all.

It was at this time that a chance meeting one morning in 1952 with a friend, Mrs Nancy Raphael, in Cullen's Store on Marylebone High Street set off a chain of events that was to change her life dramatically.

Nancy said to me, 'Helen, I suppose you wouldn't like a job?' And I said, 'Yes!' I would have said yes to anything. 'What is it?' And she said, 'They need an interviewer at the Islington Family Planning Clinic.' I said, 'I don't know how to interview.' 'Oh,' she said, 'Don't worry. Come on Wednesday and I'll show you how.' So I went.

The next Wednesday I went up to Spenser Street and did some interviewing by myself and that was fine. We used to work in pairs, so you'd go up once a fortnight and you covered for each other. I loved it, I absolutely adored it. After about a year they invited me onto the committee and I remember walking home as though I'd won the football pools. I was on air, it was so exciting. I'd never thought of myself as being a committee woman. And eventually they made me chairman.

We were teaching the woman how to use the cap – we only had the cap in those days – you know, lifting your leg on the side of the bath and all that, and you do it about six o'clock so you're ready for the evening and it's all romantic. It began to cross my mind that maybe it wasn't like that for everybody, so I visited the homes of the women down by King's Cross and Euston, and it was terrible. And the stories were awful, really pathetic – husbands would burn the woman's cap if they could find it, things like this. The lavatory was out in a backyard, a stinking, awful thing, and they went down to the public baths once a week to have a bath. People had to live like this. It was terrible. And there we were saying . . . I don't know how they ever did it.

Then in 1955 the West Indians arrived. They were another problem: many of the women became pregnant and they couldn't be seen in family planning clinics because it wasn't their habit to marry and we didn't see unmarried women. That seemed to me very foolish. It all seemed so ill thought through. I went to see Philip Rogers who was the official at the Colonial Office concerned with these West Indians and I put to him the problem about family planning. He said, 'I think you'd better talk to the High Commissioner.' The High Commissioner was quite receptive, and things did start to happen: after about a month or two, the chairman of the Family Planning Association, Margaret Pyke, was able to announce that we would see West Indian women so long as it was a stable relationship. Which of course none of us knew. We had no idea. How were we to know? What we really wanted to do was to help them, so it was allowed.

In my day it was natural to work for the poor. People like me always did something. I had [previously] been involved with a group that used to take people in the King's Cross area and give them an outing, a treat. There was always a church element in it, and I was part of that, making sandwiches and cups of tea. I never thought about it, one did that automatically. Family planning clinics very much started out being for the poor. Our clinic had been started way back in the thirties by a number of Bloomsbury women and doctors. By my time it had become much more formal and people were paying to see the doctor, though only three shillings or something, very little. We were committed to the idea of family planning, of actually making it possible for women to decide when to have children and how many children to have. We'd seen women dying young and having too many babies and being unable to bring them up properly. It was quite horrifying to think that human beings were treated like this. Women's lib and women's anything didn't really come into it. We were really just worked up about what was happening to our country, our children.

In 1958 Marie Stopes died and during that year I was invited to take on the clinic at Whitfield Street as the new director and we started to modernise it. The place was buzzing. It was always open, there was always a session, evening, morning, afternoon. I was still part of the FPA and I was still working at Islington, but I was doing Marie Stopes as well. I was there a great deal, but it all worked and fitted in. I had a studio on the top floor, and I would be there in the morning with my little Pekingese, Humphrey, and get into my overalls and be painting up there and still be on the spot. As soon as anybody wanted an interview or there was business or whatever, I was available. Occasionally I would come covered in paint and they must have thought, odd body, but it worked marvellously.

I was by then on the national executive of the FPA and I travelled with my husband to India and Iran and Russia and Japan and all over the place, where I could see what family planning was going on. It was all very interesting and it occupied my thoughts. The work was all voluntary; except for the doctors, nurses and clerical staff, nobody got paid. I've never been paid a penny the whole of my family planning life. Only the people we employed got paid. The doctors were women who couldn't have a full-time practice because of being married. The male doctors really despised the family planners. They thought it was just pin money for lady doctors. It wasn't until the sixties that they saw there was money and a career and some prestige in it and they started jumping on the bandwagon. And then of course bossing us all around!

When I'd been [at the Marie Stopes Clinic] about eight months, I became deeply aware that here was the opportunity to start a session for all unmarried women. We had FPA doctors, but we were not under the rules of the FPA. Marie

Stopes had always made it clear that it was quite separate. It took a bit of persuasion, but I found a doctor and a nurse who would see unmarried women, and in November 1959 we saw our first. We didn't say a word to anybody, it was deadly secret. We didn't *need* to tell anyone: the news got round like wildfire! [Women were coming] from everywhere – from Cornwall, from Scotland. It was extraordinary. The telephone never stopped. It was almost too much for us. When the thing got almost out of hand, we divided into the mature patients and the younger ones. We were then still in Whitfield Street, and we were called the Young People's Advisory Centre. They were all around eighteen, twenty. They would come and see the doctor and the doctor would talk to them and unless there was some major reason why not, they would be given a contraceptive. The young people were pouring in. It really was extraordinary. Terrifying!

Then John Trusted of the Ionian Bank said he'd like to help, and he gave me £15,000 on condition that I called it the Brook Advisory Centre. I was rather reluctant to do this, because in family planning we were all anonymous and nobody took credit for anything. But then, you know, £15,000 – it meant we could really get our own centres. So that was it. We had to get ourselves organised and have a committee and a board and then I had to become chairman. It all became very official. I really detest being a chairman, it's the one thing I can't bear, but anywhere there I was, a chairman, and these important people on the board. I really was very nervous about it, because I am not that kind of woman. However, there it was, and we eventually opened our clinic at Dawes Street, Walworth [in 1963]. Lord Braine, the president of the FPA, opened it and made a wonderful speech. We had a terrific amount of publicity and it was received very well by most of the papers. We always had a lot of battles with the *Telegraph*, but you know, you need enemies if you want to get on – it's free publicity. They do the whole work for you!

Brook started off by being a substitute mother. I furnished [it] like a nice little sitting-room, so that the girls would feel at home. I wanted these girls to talk to first-class doctors who would be able to be in the place of parents and help them to understand their problems and what it was that they were needing. What we were trying to do was make them responsible. We were trying to tell them the facts of life, the plain facts, and what it is to be a responsible human being and not lumber the world with unwanted babies; that you have a responsibility not only to your own body and your own future, but also to your parents and your family. That was very important to me, and still is. People have never understood this; they thought we were encouraging girls to be promiscuous, encouraging abortion. They only had to read what we stood for, but nobody ever does. We were *against* abortion. Of course abortion must be available, but I believe that it should be used most rarely, when it's totally necessary and not as a contraceptive. Brook stands for the *prevention* of abortion, the prevention of the unwanted child. I'm rather emotional about this, and I don't speak very clearly about it. To use abortion as a contraceptive is totally unfair to women. It has absolutely nothing to do with religion at all, it's just I'm very much a woman and I cannot bear that women should have to suffer such unnecessary trauma. I always thought it quite horrifying that women should have to go through that, for what? I think males don't really know how unpleasant it is.

I have never been able to endure the thoughts of women being treated as second-class human beings. I've always found even these sorts of jokes totally offensive. I just had that tightly in me always. I also wanted to make it possible for women to be as free as men, and to be able to choose, and not to depend on sexual intercourse as a way of life. I, for instance, had to guard my virginity like mad until I was married, because I wouldn't have been acceptable had I not been a virgin. Well, what a terrible thing to do to a human being! At the time I just took it for granted and never really thought about it, only that it protected me from men's advances. But I could never understand why it was all right for men to sow wild oats with some people's daughters and keep other people's daughters as virgins. All these things were churning around inside me.

I'd never used birth control at all. My first husband didn't want children and he'd come home with a thing called a whirling spray. It [had] a rubber ball on the end which you filled up with water and then put inside you and squirted. Of course it didn't work and I became pregnant very soon. You never talked about these things, you see. Nobody ever talked about them at all. You know: your sex life is your private life and you don't talk about it. My mother, for instance, said to me when I was thirteen, 'Some time during the coming year you will find something in your knickers,' but they didn't tell you anything. My friend Kitty was the same age and we read the Bible, because you find out a lot of things there, but nobody talked about these things. One girl was expelled for looking inside her knickers. There wasn't any contraception, so there was no talk about it.

When my first child was born the waters broke and I was in full labour straight off, just like my mother, without any preliminaries. I was dashed off to the nursing home and was standing on the steps, almost holding the baby in. You stayed in the nursing home for a fortnight then. The matron had worked down in the docks when she was a young woman and I remember vividly her saying how when the husbands came back from work, even though the wives had just given birth, they quickly wanted to have sex again. She said, 'We used to sew them up with very coarse gut, so that if he did want intercourse it jolly well hurt him!' That was their way of protecting the women. That stuck in my mind. It seemed to me so horrifying. Many years later, in the 1950s, I was in Iran and exactly [the same thing] was happening there: the women were having babies and by nightfall they were back cooking their husbands' dinners and having to have sexual intercourse again. The women simply never had a moment off. These memories all strung along and I suppose turned me into the kind of woman I am, which is protective of women. I think women are marvellous, and should be treasured instead of wasted the way they've been since the world began.

During those hectic months when Brook was first going, I was behind the desk, answering the telephone, taking the money, making the dates, organising this, that and the other. It really was very, very hard work. But when you're starting something new you manage to do amazing things. I used to sleep very little. I would be awake by half past four or five and any writing or thinking I would do very early in the morning. In fact, I was a terrible nuisance because I would forget that people weren't up and I'd be telephoning, you see. My desk was at home. I had an enormous king-size double bed, and my bed was mainly where I did my work. I used to get it all out and spread it all over this great bed. I still use my bed for putting all my things on. My husband was very busy in his world and I was always dressing up and going out with him. There was also cooking and housekeeping and all that. And I used to go to the clinic every day. I was always in the clinics, always around. But I had fantastic energy. And I was not alone, I had these amazing colleagues and friends who were just as involved as I was. None of us had any training, we were learning as we went, making out of nothing a great cause. It was a cause, a wonderful cause. We were a movement, all working together to make family planning acceptable. You always had another hill to climb, another battle to win. It was really something.

It was 1967 that I took in the under-sixteens. That really blew the lid off. It was really a very funny occasion, if it hadn't been so horrific. We were in the middle of the FPA AGM and goodness knows what did it but I stood up and said, 'Brook will see the under-sixteens from now on.' I hadn't spoken to my committee or to my doctors or to my anything. But you couldn't go back on something like that. The *Evening Standard* and all these papers were making a tremendous to-do! The *Evening Standard*, of course, was one of my greatest champions, it was a most wonderful paper. The *Daily Mirror* was another. I can't tell you how good those two papers were;

they always saw what we were doing and why we were doing it, they never got it wrong. Unlike everybody else!

What I had in mind was that Brook would hold the fort and as soon as the climate of opinion had changed, then Brook would be absorbed by the FPA. It was holding the fort, you might say, for the Family Planning Association, until we could get it to change its mind and accept the unmarried. Year after year we had our AGMs and year after year this subject was debated. Well, now the Family Planning Association's clinics have been absorbed into the NHS and we're still here. But Brook was really done as a holding operation. It was not done from ambition, there was nothing in it of that sort. I am not an ambitious woman, nor have I ever played a great role making history in a way I suppose I could have done. I've always tried to keep in the background and have other people running it.

There were many things that were unforeseen about how young people and their contraceptive needs were going to develop. In the fifties home life was still central: people had meals together, mothers and fathers still counted much more. But suddenly it all broke down when the pill came in. The change from the young people of the fifties to the young people of the seventies was quite extraordinary. When I went into family planning a great many young people in their twenties and thirties, schoolteachers and nurses and people like that, were seeking back-street abortions and unable to get contraceptives at all. Even when they'd got the right to a contraceptive, they often wouldn't use it, because then it looked as though they wanted it! There was this extraordinary hypocrisy about the whole thing: women weren't allowed to look as though they wanted a sexual relationship. The pill changed this in a flash. It was wonderful, it was absolutely wonderful. I can't tell you, it was like all the public holidays that you've ever enjoyed all together, it was really Hallelujah! To think that at last women could be in charge of themselves, decide for themselves. Women were really going to be free.

Of course, the males were always finding ways of undermining people's confidence. We'd hardly got it and they all pretended that you were going to get cancer or heart attacks or goodness knows what. The other thing was that it cheapened women in men's eyes in many ways; they thought, oh, well, she's ready. That was rather horrible. I think they've got over that, I don't think there's quite so much stupidity about as there was then. But for quite a time in the sixties, I felt sometimes as if I'd been helping to take the lid off Pandora's Box. It was quite frightening. It was as though people had suddenly lost their reason for a little while. It changed everything. It really changed *everything*. A lot of this was blamed on Brook, of course, in that we allowed people to become more sexually aware, made it easy for them. Quite untrue, but we *had* made it less hazardous.

Quite a number of people were quite cruel towards me and I had some very unpleasant experiences. I became really rather shy, quite nervous. I had sleepless nights! I would never let on, or talk about what I [was] doing, but there was always somebody who would notice my name or something, and then before you know where you are, it's out. And because I was in something that was to do with sexual intercourse, men would come up and start telling me the most awful jokes. I found this one of the most trying things that I had to suffer from family planning. It was rather like when I divorced my first husband – the moment you were divorced, men thought you were something you were not. Being in family planning, and notorious in a way, was the same thing. There is a certain kind of man who really takes advantage of women in one way or another and these men, I must say, I totally despise. Of course, there were very marvellous men, too, men whom I respect, Lord Braine, for instance, and Sir Theodore Fox. Without such men I don't think we would have achieved so much. [My husband] started off by rather ignoring [us], and then being rather hostile, and then by seeing that what we were doing was something to be respected. He became a member of the board, and eventually he became treasurer of Brook and treasurer of the Family Planning Association, and he followed me as chairman of Family Planning Sales. He is really totally committed to family planning. And, well, I don't know what I'd do without him.

Since my sight has gone, which is such a burden, I've had to make a new little life for myself. The life I led before included painting and gardening and cooking, but now I study music as much as I can.

I'm still the president of Brook and the trustee of Family Planning Sales and a member of the FPA. I just belong in an elderly way. I go to their meetings and all that sort of thing. I resigned from Marie Stopes in the seventies. The clinic had been taken over and had been set up to do more general contraception, which included many more referrals for abortion. It was a very good way of making money then, because an abortion referral centre took quite large fees. I have nothing against medical abortion for women and girls who get raped for instance, but this was quite against my family planning training, and my whole feeling about abortion as a contraceptive.

If I was starting again from scratch, I'd be working for the two-parent family. That would be my banner, and I would be setting up clinics everywhere! I would be really working towards a two-parent family. I'm not talking about marriage, but I mean two people committed to bringing up their family. I think that a main human right is that a child should be able to expect its mother and father to see it through its education to the moment when it can start to earn its own living. I think that is *the* human right. All the others I don't care about. But while there are young people on the streets, knocking around the way they do, I find this very unhappy. It shouldn't be, not at the end of this century. We've done a lot of good, and we have helped a great many people, but people still don't understand about their responsibilities, and I regret very much the fashion for the single parent. That seems to me to be going backwards. So that's what I would like to do, start again, fighting for the two-parent family.

What we were doing, we were doing together. I don't understand half the time why my name came up on top. I had energy, and I am always bursting out with ideas and am on the whole a bit of a nuisance, you see, but when I look back, we were *all* doing it. We were all of us working for each other, to provide something that we really believed in.

LUCY FAITHFULL

Lucy Faithfull was born on 26 December 1910 in Boxburg, South Africa. Upheavals in her early family life as a result of her father's death in France in 1916 during the First World War made a deep impression and contributed to her lifelong commitment to providing other children with stability and security in their lives. She spent five years on the Birmingham University Settlement, both as a student and later as a member of staff. She then worked in the East End of London for four years as a care committee organiser. The outbreak of the Second World War interrupted her plans to become a psychiatric social worker and she became involved instead with the evacuation of children as a regional welfare officer for the Ministry of Health. After the war she moved to the Home Office as an inspector and in 1958 was appointed children's officer in Oxford. After twelve years in that position, she was made director of social services in Oxford.

On retiring from the social services she was awarded a life peerage by Margaret Thatcher and has since played an active and important role as the only social worker in the House of Lords. She is chairman of the council of the Caldicott Community, a school for disturbed children, and a governor of Bessels Leigh School near Oxford. She has sat on the council and executive committee of Barnardos and is a patron of the NSPCC. Since 1975 she has been president of the National Children's Bureau. She is co-president of the London Boroughs Training Consortium which trains social workers, chairman of the Family Courts Consortium, and a patron of the Conciliation and Mediation Service. She is also chairman of the All-Party Parliamentary Group for Children at Westminster, which she set up during the Year of the Child in 1978. She gave evidence to the

Piggott Report, which dealt with the methods and procedures by which children should give evidence in court in cases of child sexual abuse. Currently, she and five other trustees are involved in the setting up of the Faithfull Foundation, providing centres for the treatment of men convicted of child sexual abuse, and also a child and family centre which will provide social workers, probation officers and teachers with the skills to deal with abused children and their families. She is an honorary member of the British Paediatric Association, and of the Royal College of Psychiatrists, and has recently been elected an honorary fellow of St Hilda's College, Oxford.

The interview took place at Lucy Faithfull's cool and orderly home in North Oxford in two sessions in May 1989 and July 1990. An interval of fourteen months separated our meetings due in part to Lucy Faithfull's heavy burden of commitments, and in part to the death of her brother, to whom she was extremely close. On both occasions she was helpful, courteous and patient.

I was born in Boxburg, just outside Johannesburg in South Africa, and we lived in a long, low bungalow looking onto a lake. One of the things that I remember was playing on the balcony and looking across and seeing a lot of men practising at a shooting range, and saying to my mother, 'Why are those men shooting?' And she said, 'Oh, they have to practise, because you know there are wars.' That always lived in my memory. My life seems to have been dominated first by the Boer War, then by the Great War, and then by the Second World War.

My father was the chief inspector of mines and had a wide circle of friends, and my uncle had been town clerk of Mafeking and he used to come with his friends, and I remember the house with an enormous number of people coming and going. Of course, entertaining was easy because you had the staff, as everybody did in those days out in South Africa. We had two or three staff and we had the most marvellous 'boy', as they were called, Twopence, and he was the gardener and general handyman and lived in a hut in the garden. I absolutely loved Twopence, I used to follow him around.

Then came the Great War. My father fought in German Africa, but then decided that he should join up with the Royal Engineers, so in 1915 he came to England. I remember clearly seeing him off on the troop-ship. I remember standing on the quay when he sailed: he was just one among hundreds of men on the ship. I remember that very clearly. My mother sold up the house in South Africa and followed him. But very sadly, in 1916, my father was killed in France, he was only a young lieutenant when he died, so we never saw him again.

My mother had to bring the two of us up on a pension of £207 a year. She was a most outstanding person. I mean, you're a widow, you've only been married five years, you're left with a pension of £207 a year, and you bring up two children and send them to good schools, and me to university and my brother to be a solicitor – I think it speaks for itself: she was a person who was prepared to sacrifice everything for her children. And quite apart from that she was a delightful person. She had trained as a nurse in Cape Town which is where she met my father. She was small and very delicate and very attractive. She was always enchanting, and she was always deeply loving and considerate, but she had that incredibly sad look. I used to look at her, and wish that she wasn't quite so sad. She never let it impinge on us if she could help it, but it was inevitable.

We lived first of all with an aunt and uncle in Newport, and then we moved to Boscombe in Hampshire and she became very friendly with a family called the Peaks who ran a boys' prep school. They were short of staff, as everybody was, and when they heard that she was a trained nurse they did a deal with her: she came as matron to the school and in return they [gave] my brother free education. I was sent to boarding school, to what was then the Bournemouth High School. The night before I went I remember having the most terrible nightmare, and when Mother actually left me there, I looked over the banisters to see her go, and I froze. It was such a terrible experience that I've never forgotten it. Given my life again, I wouldn't want to go to boarding school so young – I was seven and a half. From the point of view of one's early childhood affecting one, when I had to remove a child from home it always hurt most terribly because I remembered that night and first day at boarding school. You mustn't let your own feelings affect what you're doing in your professional life, but in fact they're almost bound to, and I really felt strongly that one should never move a child from home unless it was absolutely necessary. During the war, I worked with evacuees and separating those children from their homes was a very sad thing.

This experience influenced Lucy Faithfull in her work as a children's officer, and later as a director of social services as well as in her part in passing the Children's Bill through the House of Lords. She believes that, wherever possible and practicable, children should not be removed from their families unless absolutely necessary.

I wasn't really happy between seven and twelve. I found the mass of people trying; children need to be by themselves sometimes, and at boarding school you never are. We weren't allowed in the dormitories during the day, and I used to creep up and creep under the bed, and it was an absolute relief to be by oneself just for a bit. But having said that we were wonderfully well looked after. The school was beautifully run, the staff were so devoted. It seemed to run on affection between staff and children, and children and children. You couldn't have called it a highly disciplined school, and yet everything ran like clockwork, simply because the headmistress, Miss Broad, was so beloved. I was appalled, when I first took up social work, to see that some children were not treated as I had been treated.

I loved school, absolutely loved it, and it was a constant factor in my life, but my childhood was never settled because we had no home. We would sleep in six different places during the year. We would go for Christmas to the aunt and uncle in

Newport; at Easter we would go to Boscombe to be near my
father's parents – we used to go and stay in what were called
'rooms' [where] Mother would do the shopping, and the
landlady would do the cooking – and then in the summer, we
would go to friends in Kent. For ten years we did that. I look
back on those years as being very happy, but always recognising that there was something missing. Then my grandmother
died at the age of ninety and left us money and we bought a
house in Bournemouth. For the first time, at the age of fifteen,
I had a home. And it was lovely, it really was, to have
one's own bedroom and not to have to move and to be able to
stabilise. It was lovely to have the peace and security of home.

*Between school and university, Lucy Faithfull went to live in
Paris where she worked in the nursery of La Residence Sociale,
a settlement in the Levalois Perret district of the city run by a
remarkable Frenchwoman named Mademoiselle Bassot. In 1930
she returned to England to take her place on the social studies
diploma course at Birmingham University, studying under
Professor Sargent Florence. During this time she lived and
worked at the Birmingham Settlement. After two years as a
student volunteer, she became a member of staff, first as club
leader and then as sub-warden. Birmingham at that time was an
outstanding local authority, with a strong Quaker ethos and a
deep commitment to serving the community. It was an exciting
place to be and an exciting time to be there.*

When I first went to the settlement, an extraordinary woman
came to lecture, and she said, 'If you're going to be a good
social worker, you work yourself out of existence. While you
must be compassionate to those who are in need of money,
and in need of a house, and in need of goods, your ultimate aim
must be to help them to be completely independent, so that
they can develop themselves and not be beholden to anyone.
We [still] haven't really worked this out properly: how, on the
one hand, you do not allow the vulnerable to sink below the
poverty line; on the other hand you do your very best to help
people to be independent.' This seemed an extraordinary

thing to say to a group of people just starting out on their social work training, but I always remembered that.

It's impossible to really analyse why one went into social work. What [inspired] me to do it or why I should have wanted to do it, I don't know. I just knew from the age of about fourteen exactly what I wanted to do. My grandparents and a favourite uncle were missionaries, so it was, so to speak, in the blood. And I remember reading Dickens, Mrs Gaskell and Disraeli, and being quite appalled at some of the things I read – Dickens was my favourite from about twelve to fourteen. And although I was never angry or upset about it, I think I was conscious of the fact that we'd had no home for ten years, and that we had no father, and that my mother had a very difficult, hard life working to keep us. I was conscious of all those things without being resentful about them. We had had a very stable, happy life out in South Africa and then our family life had been completely disrupted. I remember very well when I was about six standing in the nursery of some friends and thinking [about this], not unhappily, but at the same time realising that things weren't quite right. I said to myself, all my life, when I'm grown-up, I'm going to work for children who are not happy. It really does seem the most extraordinary thing for a very young child to say, but I can remember the moment, I can remember the place. And really, I have never deviated from then, and here I am, still doing it at the age of nearly eighty!

The university settlement was in quite the worst part of Birmingham. It was back-to-back houses and very poor, and the unemployment in those days was appalling. Anyone who was in trouble would come and ask for help. We ran clubs and took them to theatres, took them to plays, arranged games for them, arranged country holidays for them. We used to take the children away for weekends in the country and in the summer we used to take them for a fortnight to a little village called Powick where we had the village hall.

We ran clubs for every age – for little ones, for the school-children, for the young men and women, and we ran a dance

every other Saturday night for the adolescents. Then there was
the mothers' club and the fathers' club. We had sixty
volunteers and some of them would come and teach art, and
some of them would come and teach dressmaking, and some
of them would come to the boys and teach metalwork. In any
one week, there were about four or five hundred [people]
coming to clubs. It was morning, noon and night. Every now
and then one felt that one really must get away. You could get
on the tram and go out to a farmhouse in the Lickey Hills
where the farmer's wife used to serve one with the most
marvellous teas. But it was an exciting time. There were really
exciting people, they were stimulating, there were ideas. My
mother came to stay and she thought it was the most terrible
place and she never came again, but I simply loved it.

We used to go and work on the new estates they were
building. The one we worked on was called the Kingstanding
Estate. The planning of it was terribly bad and I disagreed with
the housing policy. I thought that the back-to-back houses
should have been pulled down and new houses built in their
places, instead of moving people right onto the perimeter of
the town. It would have been far better if they had rebuilt the
old area, and kept the people as a community. Although their
conditions there [were terrible] – they had one wash-house to
eight houses, and two loos to about sixteen houses – there was
a real sense of community. I used to be quite distressed at them
being moved out to their lovely little houses, miles away from
their friends, from their relatives, from their work. They were
very lonely. In those days there were no social facilities. There
wasn't a library, there wasn't a swimming centre, there
weren't churches, there weren't many shops; there were just
houses and houses and houses. We were so upset about it that
we used to run clubs in the evenings in a school for them, in
order that they would have a feeling of being connected with
the place from which they had moved.

On a Monday morning, all the students had to collect
money for the Birmingham Provident Fund. You had a bag
and you visited every house in your district and you tried to

persuade people to pay into the Provident Bank. They would pay in twopence, threepence, fivepence, and you would mark it up on their card, and mark it in your book. I always visited Brearley Street, which was one of the worst streets. We always went alone, and we always carried these bags of money. Everyone knew that we'd got a bag of money and never at any time was any one of us attacked. Yet it was such a bad district that the police used to go about in threes! But no harm ever came to any of us. When I look back on it, it was extraordinary.

In 1935, after five years at the Birmingham settlement, Lucy Faithfull decided she needed more training and was given a grant by the British Officers' Fund for six months training with the Charity Organisation Society, now known as the Family Welfare Association. For the next three years she worked for the London County Council, as it then was, as the care committee organiser in Bermondsey and Rotherhithe.

Rotherhithe was a most exciting place: the East End people were so full of life and vitality and humour that one enjoyed visiting the dockers. The care committee organiser was responsible for about twenty-six London schools; if the school felt that a child needed clothes (and some of them did), or needed food (and many of them did), or that there was something uphappy about the child, or something unhappy about the home, one of your volunteers [would] go and visit the home – or if there wasn't a volunteer you did it. You provided a link between the school and the home. I ran a team of voluntary workers. They were practically all women from the West End. Married women didn't do jobs in those days and it was a great interest to them to come down to the East End. I don't expect it would work now, but it did then: the social structure of England was different then, the East Enders were not resentful of the West Enders and the West Enders had a tremendous sense of service.

In 1938 she went to work in Islington, where poverty and crime were both acute problems. It was here, due to her work at the Canonbury Child Guidance Clinic, that Lucy Faithfull became interested in the psychological and emotional needs of children. As a result of this, in 1939, she decided to train to be a psychiatric social worker. The arrival of the Second World War, however, took her in an unexpected direction.

When the Second World War broke out I was delegated to take parties of children, and also mothers, out into the country. The children were all wildly excited, because in those days people didn't travel as they travel now, and it was a tremendous excitement for these children going out, with their little gas masks bumping on their back, and their little suitcases. Then, as the time came for the train to go off, a kind of silence fell, and the women would weep, and the children began to be apprehensive, so that when the train pulled out there was this tremendous silence among the children, a terrible apprehensiveness at what was going to happen.

Late in 1940, a remarkable woman called Miss Geraldine Aves, who worked at County Hall and who was the chief welfare officer, asked me if I would act as a regional welfare officer, advising local authorities on the welfare and well-being of evacuees in the area of Derbyshire and Leicestershire. Now, Derbyshire is a most delightful county, but it was a very 'County' county, if I can put it that way, and the Dowager Duchess of Devonshire rang up the minister and said how absolutely awful these children were, and that they were being billeted in very nice houses and that they couldn't even carry out their natural functions properly, they would do them on the drawing-room floor. She and all the ladies of Derbyshire said that they thought these children ought to be put in camps instead of billeted. And I was delegated to address all the women of Derbyshire in the town hall, and they all stood up and said that they were prepared to do their bit for the War, but this was really going too far. So I said, well, if they are all put in a camp, and a bomb drops on them and they're all killed, what would you then feel? There was dead silence in the hall, and one woman got up and said, 'That settles it, we must have these children.'

I learned two things [as a regional welfare officer] which in a way influenced all the work I did subsequently: it made me realise what families meant to children, and how much damage we did to children, taking them away from their homes even if they weren't good homes. A lot of the evacuees were very well looked after physically, but emotionally, while some of them came to terms with their separation from their families, a lot of them didn't. When the War was over, I went back to London and we carried out an inquiry. We took several streets in Islington and visited all the families in those streets. We divided them into those where the children had been evacuated, and those that had stayed at home with their families, not going to school, sleeping in the underground with their parents, not having school milk, The outcome of that inquiry was that the children who had stayed with their parents were taller, were heavier, were emotionally better balanced, were psychologically at ease with themselves, and the only thing that they lacked was education. Whereas the children who had been evacuated, many of them to very good homes, were not as tall, were not as heavy, and were, in a number of ways, disturbed in their emotional behaviour; sometimes deeply disturbed, sometimes only minimally disturbed, but disturbed.

This taught me that, wherever possible, and wherever practicable, a child should be left with its family. And in my later life, as an inspector in the Home Office, as a children's officer in Oxford, and as a director of social services, I always worked towards keeping children with their families where possible and practicable. Both Bowlby and Winnicot influenced me enormously. Their research accorded to what I thought and what had been my experience. I recognise that there are some children who are so deeply disturbed – because they have been unloved, because they've been cruelly treated, because they've been sexually abused – that they need therapeutic treatment away from home. It would be wrong to say that every child must stay at home, but it would be equally wrong to say, we must get as many children away from home. One's got to strike a balance, and do the best for each child in each case. In the Cleveland affair, for instance, I think children were doubly abused by being removed from home without consideration, at the drop of a hat. When I was dealing with abuse cases, wherever possible I used to try and leave the children with the mother, unless she was involved. The man should be the one to be asked to leave the home. In my own experience, I regretted very much not being at home, and not having a home; I regretted that I went to boarding school so young, and my brother went to boarding school even younger than me. I recognise that people who run children's homes and boarding schools have got much to offer, but in the final analysis it really is home and family which counts.

The responsibility of being a regional welfare officer during the War was so great, and I really felt at that stage that I needed a breathing space; I didn't feel that I was ready to be a children's officer, it would be a 100 per cent commitment. Being an inspector, one wouldn't carry the ultimate responsibility and one would have more time to read and go to lectures, so I applied to be an inspector in the children's branch of the Home Office. You had to inspect local authorities' children's departments. You had to inspect the way the department ran administratively. You had to inspect their foster parent system, and visit foster parents. You had to visit children's homes, nurseries, approved schools, and submit reports following your visits – to establish and maintain a standard of child-care, and to disseminate good ideas that you had picked up from different people.

In 1958, when I was already forty-eight, I felt I was now ready to take ultimate responsibility, and I applied to be a children's officer in Oxford. I had to run the office and be responsible for the administration. We had six children's homes, one family centre and two hostels, and then we had foster parents and two day nurseries. All that's been cut down now. It was my responsibility to see that the homes were staffed and well run; to see that the child-care officers carried out their duties with regard to the foster parents. Adoption was quite a big part of our work: we were responsible for about 300 children. Being a children's officer was very stressful. In the Home Office you were never ultimately responsible for anything, because if anything was wrong you handed it on to your seniors. One of the funniest things was, sitting in the office, my first week in Oxford, I had a phone call from Bristol Juvenile Court, saying, 'There's an Oxford child up in court, and the magistrates would like to make a Fit Person Order, will you accept the Fit Person Order?' Being a civil servant I said, 'I will certainly consider it and let you know.' There was a howl from the other end of the phone, and the clerk to the Magistrates Court said, 'The magistrate's sitting there waiting for an answer.' I wasn't used to giving an answer straight away like that, and I thought well, I'll be wrong positively rather than negatively, so I said, 'Yes, we'll accept it'. But I realised that when you are actually doing the work, it is quite different from working in the civil service: you had to ultimately decide yourself, then and there very often, what you had to do.

In 1970, after twelve years as children's officer, Lucy Faithfull became the director of social services for Oxford, a post she held for four years until she retired at the age of sixty-three.

It was a very big change. As children's officer in a small authority, you had a lot of responsibility and power. I knew, or knew of, every single child that we dealt with. I knew every member of staff, I knew every cleaner, I knew all the caretakers. I knew them all absolutely personally – and I enjoyed that; you had personal responsibility for them. Being a director of social services you weren't only doing children, you were doing the mentally ill and the mentally handicapped; you were doing the chronically sick and disabled; you were dealing with the elderly . . . You couldn't possibly know everybody individually or every case or even every member of staff. You were a manager. It was a management job. In a way, I missed not knowing the children; I missed not knowing the staff and being responsible for them. I enjoyed being director of social services, but I did miss the personal contact with the cases.

[When I left the social services in 1974] I had no ambitions whatsoever, other than to retire gracefully. I'd got my retirement all mapped out. I'm very keen on bird-watching and I wanted to go back and live in France and perfect my French. I wanted to see friends and travel – my brother and I were going to travel far and wide. And then there was this extraordinary phone call from Mrs Thatcher at nine o'clock in the morning. 'Lucy, I'd like you to go to the House of Lords,' she said! And I said, 'Oh, how simply awful, I don't want to go into the House of Lords!' There was a frightful silence at the other end of the telephone. She simply couldn't believe her ears! She said, 'But don't you realise that there are queues waiting to go into the House of Lords?' and I said, 'But Mrs Thatcher, I'm not in the queue.' And she said, 'You mean to tell me that you're turning down a peerage?' So I said, 'Well quite frankly it would terrify me out of my wits, and I don't think I'm really bright enough to go into the House of Lords.' So she said, 'Well, isn't that for me to say?' I said, 'But you don't know me, how can you know?' So we had quite a little ding-dong. And then she said, 'Well, think about it and I'll ring you back at one o'clock.' So I went to the public library and I looked through all the peers and found that there was no director of social services in the House of Lords. Then I rang up my brother, who was a most remarkable man, and he said in that sort of drawly solicitor's voice, 'Well, if you go into the House of Lords you will regret it; if you don't go into the House of Lords you'll regret it, so you'd better regret positively rather then negatively!' When she rang back I thought she's going to say she doesn't want me, because after all, if anyone goes and refuses a peerage . . . She rang back, and I said, 'If you continue to offer it to me I'll accept.'

I voted against the Government on several occasions on their social policies. I'll give you three examples: I agreed with the abolition of the Greater London Council, but I supported an amendment that there should be an inner London co-ordinating committee. Mrs Thatcher was so worried in case Livingstone would want to run it that she wouldn't have it, but if you didn't have a co-ordinating committee of the inner London boroughs, who was going to decide about traffic, and about sewers, and about roads? I disagreed with her over that. I disagreed with her over the poll tax. It's quite wrong that the Duke of Westminster only has to pay 480 [pounds] a year instead of whatever he used to have to pay on his rates. So I opposed her over that. I moved an amendment saying that the poll tax ought to be based on the ability to pay. I opposed her on child benefit. I feel very strongly about child benefit; for a woman to be able to draw seven pounds twenty-five a week for her child, which doesn't go to the husband, is very important.

When the Criminal Justice Bill of 1985 passed through the Lords, Lucy Faithfull pressed for children and young persons to be helped in their homes and communities rather than committed to care and institutions. Here again this was linked to her own experience as a child and her work with the evacuation scheme in the Second World War. She recognises that there are, of course, cases when children do need specialised help away from home.

Asked if the concept of women's rights has been of any interest to her, Lucy Faithfull replied:

Absolutely none. I get bored with women's rights, quite frankly. I know that the Equal Opportunities Commission would be absolutely horrified if they heard me. But I believe if a woman really wants to get somewhere, she'll get somewhere. Somebody from the Equal Opportunities Commission said to me the other day, 'I can't understand it, we fight for women and they don't fight for themselves,' and I remember saying to them, 'Well, perhaps you're wanting for them what they don't want for themselves.' This business of fighting, I can understand in the days of the suffragettes, and I think I probably would have been a suffragette if I had been born in those days, but I wasn't born in those days. If a woman can't get her equal rights, I think it's a very funny do. I've hitched my star to what I wanted to do with children. The question of women's rights really hasn't come into it. If a woman feels that she's going to go mad looking after her baby, then I can quite see that she wants somebody else to look after [it]. I don't think that she ought to be pressurised by circumstances to either looking after it or not looking after it. I am worried about our present policy with regard to working women. I question whether the present system whereby women are encouraged to go out to work and place their children in workplace nurseries from six months upwards, is wise, [but] I don't believe it is a women's issue, I think it's a *child's* issue. It's a child's issue and a woman's choice. I think women have got to make up their minds for themselves – and then we've got to provide the facilities.

Ideally I would like to see a division in the Ministry of Health called the 'Family and Child Division', to deal with all children and young persons up to twenty-one. [As director of social services,] I found it difficult working with two ministries, Home Office and Ministry of Health; it would have been much easier to have worked with one. Children and young persons are [currently] divided between *three* ministries: Education, Health and the Home Office. In the last ten years there's been a great cut-down of the duties of local authorities, and a lot of work is now done by voluntary organisations. A new concept has entered now into the field: the private sector. I think it has to be very carefully watched. In the House of Lords – and don't forget I am the only social worker in the House of Lords – you get letters coming to you from all over the country, and there's no doubt about it, you need to have a focal point for families and children. Until we get one department responsible we shall never get a coherent policy in the country.

I'll be eighty next birthday [and] I think I'd like to subside . . . spend time in the garden . . . but I shall always be interested in [these issues]. Getting children out of prison: I don't think that women and children ought to go into Holloway, and to put young people in prison is absolutely wrong, we ought to deal with them in different ways, in the community. I really feel very strongly about this, because if you don't give a service to those children, those are the ones that are going to commit murders, and those are the ones that are going to be very costly, both in emotional and financial terms, to the community. I'm also deeply interested in the training of social workers. I'm the president of the London Boroughs Training Consortium, which runs training courses for social workers, and whenever I'm in the House of Lords and training comes up, I speak about the training of social workers because I think that much more money ought to be given to the training of social workers. It's very important that they understand human growth and development, the development of a child, emotionally, physically and educationally. It's absolutely vital. Housing is very important too: all the social work in the world isn't going to help people if they haven't got a home. You could say that I never had a home, and therefore why should I press for other people to have a home, but I know that I lost not having a home.

It was pointed out that she had nevertheless overcome the difficulties of her early life and done very well. Lucy Faithfull did not agree:

When you say 'do so well', what do you mean? I'm not married, and I haven't got children. Admittedly that was due in part to the Second World War, but I think at the back of my mind, when I was young I thought that I wouldn't make a good wife and mother because I hadn't had the background. From a career point of view one may have done well, but one may not have done well perhaps in all spheres of life.

All the children that we had in care in Oxford, the only thing I cared about was that when they left care they were independent and able to run their own lives, and I think by and large they were, because I still see them: they all come and see me.

I had a very interesting letter a little while ago, from a young, well, he's not a young man now, he's, I suppose sixty, called Bernard who was a club member at the Birmingham settlement, and he wrote, saying, 'You taught us how to run our lives, how to make personal relationships, how to make good marriages, and now I'm married happily and I'm a father and a grandfather,' and he said how he remembered that we never gave anything material, but that we gave people a sense of confidence in themselves, sense of belief in themselves, and we opened the horizons so that they were all able to stand on their own feet and have their own families and children. I think in a way that's been my philosophy. I don't think that you ought to give welfare rights to everybody; I think welfare rights ought to be a net to catch those who can't manage for themselves. One of the reasons why I am a Conservative is that I really do believe that one wants to organise society so that people are independent, so that they make their own choices and run their own lives.

JOSEPHINE BARNES

Josephine Barnes was born on 18 August 1912. Her great-grandfather, John Francis Taylor, was one of the founders of the Midland Bank. Her father was a Methodist minister and her mother an accomplished musician. As a girl, Josephine Barnes combined music and religion by spending Sunday evenings turning pages for Sir William Harris, then organist at Christ Church. Music was to remain an important element throughout her life.

A first from Oxford (where she was one of only five women out of forty-three medical students), and a scholarship to University College Hospital, marked the beginning of a distinguished medical career which was by no means concluded in 1989 when she became president of the British Medical Association, the first woman to hold the post. Along the way she has been a member of three influential maternity surveys (1946, 1958, 1970), written three books and sat on two of the most significant Government committees since the war, the Lane Committee (1971–4) into the workings of the Abortion Act and the Warnock Committee (1981–4) on Embryo Research.

From 1946 to 1976 Josephine Barnes had a private practice in Wimpole Street and in 1954 she became the first woman consultant in the Department of Obstetrics and Gynaecology at Charing Cross Hospital. In 1960 she was a member of the Medical Research Council Committee on Analgesia in Midwives, and from 1961 to 1977 she sat on the council of the Medical Defence Union. She was president of the Medical Women's Federation from 1966 to 1967, and from 1965 to 1968 sat on the Royal Commission on Medical Education (Todd). She led the campaign in 1977 to keep the Elizabeth Garret Anderson Hospital open. She has been a governor of Benenden School for the last twenty-five years and is also president of the Friends of the Girls' Public Day School Trust. She is a fellow of King's College, London, and an honorary fellow of Lady Margaret Hall, Oxford, and of the Royal Holloway and Bedford New College. She is the only woman to hold the fellowship of all three Royal colleges, the FRCS, the FRCP and the FRCOG. In 1974 she was made a Dame.

This interview took place over two days in October 1990 at Josephine Barnes's home in West London. Tea was offered at four o'clock but it was clearly a concession to the interviewer and considered by Dame Josephine herself as somewhat frivolous. The room in which we sat was dominated by a grand piano and photographs of her three children and eight grandchildren, which she showed to me with great pride, enunciating the achievements of each in turn – after which she insisted, 'But we're not a very special family, not at all.'

I was born in Sheringham, in Norfolk. Not because we come from that part of the world, but because my mother happened to be there at the time. My father was a Methodist minister. I don't think I tasted alcohol till I was twenty. When I was a child, we were expected to go to church on Sundays, both at eleven in the morning, and at six-thirty in the evening. For some curious reason, we never went to Sunday school. I don't know why; I never could find out. He was at the Battle of the Somme in the First World War as a chaplain [and he] had a very bad time there, 60,000 casualties the first day, and he had to deal with the wounded and the dead, conduct the funerals, write the letters of condolence. I think that really shook him.

My mother's name was Alice Mary Ibbetson. We were all very close to her, not just me and my brothers and sister, but my grandchildren too. She was a very splendid musician. She went to the Royal College of Music at the age of sixteen, which was quite a thing for a Victorian girl to do in 1900, and she stayed there till she married. She was the second woman fellow of the Royal College of Organists when she was twenty-three. She was a super musician, a marvellous pianist, accompanist, organist, choir trainer; you name it she could do

it. My dear great-aunt, Anne Jane Taylor, who was unmarried, took a flat in Kensington to look after my mother.
My aunt went to the chapel where my father was officiating,
and that's how they met. They were married on 5 September
1911. In 1921 my mother inherited some money and we went
to Oxford [in 1925]. (We had two houses in Oxford, 1 Hernes
Road – it's still there, I saw it last week – and 30 Norham
Road.) My oldest brother was then at Balliol, my sister was at
the Oxford High School, and my youngest brother was at the
Dragon School, so Mother bought the second house [in 1934]
to save on boarding fees.

I've got three brothers and a sister. My sister, sadly, died in
1979. She was a civil servant in the Admiralty. I was the eldest,
unfortunately! With five children, the eldest is always left to
do a certain amount of the discipline and I think my brothers
have always resented my being older. I was always the one
who was blamed. 'Why did you let Teddy do this?', sort of
thing. I always got the blame; because I was the eldest, I was
supposed to be responsible. When I was fifteen I remember
my parents went away on holiday and I was left in charge of
them. When you're a child, you're terribly uncritical, you tend
to accept things as they come to you. It was a very happy
childhood indeed. I never remember resenting anything,
until, oh no, not until my twenties.

My oldest brother was at Balliol, my next brother was at
Hertford and my youngest brother was at Oriel. So I think my
parents did jolly well to get four of their five children to
Oxford. My father started from nothing. I don't remember
discussing ideas at home at all. My brothers were younger
than me, remember. We'd spend most of our time playing
cricket, or rowing or punting on the river. And my father was
a lovely person, everybody who met him liked him, but he
had very, very rigid views and you didn't argue with his
views; you just listened, you didn't say anything. I can tell
you one small story: when we were married, we did have a
reception and we had some white wine. The Methodist
Church then was strictly teetotal and no drink was allowed in

our house or anywhere. My father afterwards said, 'You know, I don't think it was right, we had that wine in the church hall.' So I said, 'Well, you know, there's quite a good precedent for wine at a wedding.' He had to give in on that one! I think that was about the only time I ever disagreed with him. My mother was generous and open, but rather reserved, not a person with whom you would discuss emotional problems at all, never. Never ever. They were typical of Yorkshire Victorians, which is what they were.

I went up to Oxford, to Lady Margaret Hall, when I was eighteen, to read science. That was 1930, when there was a quota for women students in Oxford. Five hundred, I think, something like that, between the five colleges. Lady Margaret Hall was only allowed to take, I think, fifty-six students a year. In addition to that, there was a quota for women medical students, so that out of forty-three medical students there were five women. It just came to me when I was about thirteen, that this is what I wanted to do. I never thought of doing anything else from then. There were all sorts of reasons: the idea of service, if you like, if one is being highfalutin; intense interest in the workings of the human body – those were the main ones. I mean, I never wanted to do anything else, ever. Didn't occur to me.

I loved everything about Oxford. It was lovely, just heaven. One worked jolly hard, of course. The trouble with medicine is that you're always taking examinations. One had to work. But it was just wonderful. I had lots of friends and a lot of freedom. I sang a lot in the Bach Choir, and various other groups; I played hockey for the university and for the county; one had friends. Those friends, the friends I made at Oxford, are probably the ones that have endured longest. The person I was closest to at school, I used to see, but she died last year, which was very sad. When you get to my age group, they begin to die, you know.

There were some very, very famous people at the Oxford Medical School. Sir Charles Sherrington was the professor of physiology, his great thing was the nervous system. There was a chap called Douglas, who worked on respiratory physiology and had actually been to the Andes to see what happened to your breathing at high altitude. There was Sir Rudolf Peters, in biochemistry, and D. C. Correy in anatomy. The professor of anatomy was Arthur Thomson, author of *Anatomy for Art Students*, but the important part of the department was left to a very remarkable woman called Alice Carlton, who everybody thought was wonderful. Professor Thomson thought it was indelicate for young men and young women to dissect the body together, so the young women were relegated to his studio at the top of the building. I found myself up there alone with a corpse and a book and told to get on with it. Alice Carlton came and rescued me. I don't think anybody knew I was there!

During my vacations I used to go home to York, where my parents were then living, and I'd go out with the doctors from the York Dispensary, which was a charity for the poor of York. I used to go and hold the children's heads while they had their tonsils out. And I used to go out to the slums with the women doctors, down Whipma Whopma Gate and the poor parts of the city. One really did see appalling poverty there: children who were not sick, but were never well. Women and children had nothing except for maternity and child welfare, which didn't treat them, it only assessed their condition. I found the same thing when I came back to London, because at UCH we mostly looked after the railway workers from the King's Cross St Pancras area. There one did see poverty that was unbelievable, even by modern standards. If you asked a woman how much her husband earned, she would always say, three pounds ten a week. That was what he gave her out of his earnings. The rest he kept to spend on himself. There was a lot of wife beating, there was a great deal of back-street abortion. These poor women were desperate in their poverty. I did once go up the Rhondda Valley, which was worst of all, people were literally starving. Many of the pregnant women died. Things were pretty desperate. I didn't think it was something I was there to do anything about. I was there to look after their medical problems, to do what I could. It didn't affect me politically. I just felt desperately sorry for them. I'm fairly tough. One of the first things you have to learn in medicine, and you omit to learn this at your peril, is that you must not get emotionally involved with your patients' problems. Whether you're a doctor, a lawyer, a parson, solicitor or an accountant, you can't be a professional if you involve yourself in your client's emotional problems. It's not callousness, it's simply professional.

After securing a first from Oxford, Josephine Barnes got a scholarship in 1934 to University College Hospital Medical School in London.

UCH were given a special endownment of money to admit twelve women medical students a year. They didn't like it, but they took eight from University College London and four from outside. We were a fairly select lot, one in five [there were about sixty men]. I think it did give us a certain advantage. It made us rather conspicuous, mind you. We had to behave ourselves and we had to work. And we had to be better [than the men], because unless you were good you didn't get in at all.

At first I was living in a bedsitting room in Cartwright Gardens, and it was the most ghastly place, full of elderly women secretaries. Between 1920 and 1940 there was a surplus of about two million women because of the First World War and these poor ladies had no hope of marriage; they all had to earn their living. It was a terrible place, infested with mice. One Sunday there was a scream from one of the rooms, and one of the good ladies had found a mother mouse and a whole lot of baby mice under her mattress!

I did a lot of singing while I was a student. I sang in the London Philharmonic Choir and we had people like Sir Thomas Beecham and Fürtwengler conducting us. I went to the theatre and the opera a lot. One summer my parents gave me a season ticket to the Promenade Concerts, which meant I could go to any concert I liked. That was a marvellous musical education. Sir Henry Wood was conducting all that time. One afternoon I went to the Albert Hall and paid sixpence for the gallery and heard Fritz Kreisler play three violin concertos, one after another. It was a pretty remarkable afternoon. Music is in the genes, I think it must be. My next brother, Francis, writes music now and we go singing together in the summer, we used to sing together in the Bach Choir. My sister was a competent singer and pianist. My children and two of my grandchildren are musicians. My second granddaughter, Alice, is a terrific cellist. My son-in-law, Martin, is the organist at Westminster Abbey. Music is part of the family, it always has been. There's never been a time when one was without music, even in wartime.

[After medical training] I got a job as house physician at University College Hospital. There were very few house jobs and you had to take an examination. I qualified in July and had to wait until November to get a house job, and even then I had six months which was unpaid. It's rather hard after seven years to go to your parents and say, 'I've got a job, but I'm not going to be paid anything.' To fill in that time, I spent a month in Cambridge as a general practitioner. I was very wet round the ears. I'd only just qualified, I was full of confidence, I didn't think anything would go wrong – and it didn't, actually. The only patient who defeated me was a mother with a baby with a feeding problem: I hadn't the slightest idea what to do about it! That was the only thing that defeated me; I was a very confident person in those days. I've always been rather, perhaps over, confident. It never occurred to me I'd fail in anything.

At UCH we all had to live in what was called 'Residence', which was the height of ambition because you had your own room. Looking at it now, it's the most awful sordid place. In the morning a cup of tea would be put down beside you and then you would get up and you'd go down to breakfast, then you'd go on the wards and you'd do a round of all the patients. We were directly responsible to the consultants. One was called John Hawksley, who's still alive, and his main interest was in stomachs so we had to do gastrocopies at nine o'clock on Monday mornings. Andrew Morland, who was the most delightful man I could possibly know, taught me about chests and tuberculosis. Dinner was a formal occasion. You weren't allowed to come in to dinner in your white coat. There would be about twenty of us, presided over by the Resident Medical Officer, and if you were late, you had to apologise to him. There was no official time off at all but it was a marvellous six months. We worked twenty-four hours a day, seven days a week; we weren't working all that time, but we were expected to be there. One would get called out at night quite often. Those were the voluntary days, before the Health Service. All the chiefs were volunteers. They were only paid for teaching and relied on their private practice to live. Junior doctors were not paid at all. We were given board and lodging and laundry, so you lived free, but I think some of them probably had a pretty rough time. I had a little money fortunately. My mother had given me some capital, so I had enough.

I gave about 200 anaesthetics in that six months. At four o'clock in the afternoon the honorary anaesthetists would go off and give anaesthetics in nursing homes and earn their living, so one of us house physicians had to go and do anaesthetics. I became quite good at it. No one died that I gave an anaesthetic to. Mostly chloroform or ether in those days: the anaesthetics were not as pleasant as they are nowadays, but they were much safer. You'd have sickness and gastric irritation the next day, but they were quite safe. It was almost a cottage industry. We hadn't got the powerful drugs, we hadn't got the elaborate machinery, we hadn't got monitors.

By the time I qualified in 1937 I had pretty well decided that I would do obstetrics and gynaecology. I did two months in Mundesley Hospital and then I went as house surgeon to the King Edward VII Hospital in Windsor for six months. Windsor was awful. It was the only hospital for 3,000 people in Windsor and 30,000 people in Slough. We were desperately busy. I mean, talk about the juniors working now, we worked like they work. A lot of the work was done by the local general practitioners who had to rely on fees from patients. The dermatology was done by one; ear, nose and throat by another. We did the anaesthetics as well as the surgery. We had eight obstetric beds and in the six months I was there, I saw every obstetric emergency.

I liked obstetrics: you're dealing with normal women, doing a normal event. I enjoyed that. As a medical student we had six months of obstetrics and gynaecology – now they get eight weeks – and we had to deliver twenty babies. Something like twenty per cent of births took place in hospital in those days, so I delivered babies in their own homes and in hospital. Childbirth is much safer now. Mothers don't die having babies and many fewer babies are stillborn or die the first week of life. In 1958 it was thirty-five per thousand, and now it's down to eight per thousand or less. And there's no doubt at all that babies are safer born in hospital, where you've got the monitors, you've got the equipment, you've got the anaesthetic equipment, you've got blood transfusion, you've got everything. Eighty per cent of pregnant women will be perfectly all right, but the other twenty will get into some serious trouble of one kind or another. Even perfectly healthy women, like my daughter-in-law, who had an awful haemorrhage after my last grandchild was born. I always feel that one should make the best use of the facilities you have. No woman should suffer unnecessary pain in childbirth, for example. Epidurals have their risks, their side-effects, and you don't want to have one unless you need one, but no woman should suffer unnecessary pain.

In 1939 I passed the FRCS [Fellow of the Royal College of Surgeons]. By then the War had started; women doctors were at a premium, because the men were all being called up and having to go away. I was invited to go and work at the Samaritan Hospital in Marylebone Road. I had six months there, doing gynaecology and filling in for surgeons who had been called up. It was fantastic. I don't think I'd have got that job as a woman [under normal circumstances]. I was the first woman they'd had. In fact, when I arrived the hospital secretary looked at me and he said, 'You're the first woman we've had here since the last war.' I've never been a feminist and I'm not now. I think women should be allowed to do what they want to do, they shouldn't be prevented as they were earlier, but I haven't any particular feminist views. It never worried me [that medicine is a male-dominated profession]. I just got on with what I had to do. I knew what I wanted to do. I had to wait, I had to hang around for jobs, and I had to take more examinations. I reckoned that if I was competing, I'd have to be better qualified. That's why I got three fellowships. But I wasn't thinking, 'Here I am a woman, I must do this and this and this,' not at all.

In 1940 I went to Queen Charlotte's Hospital in Marylebone and then the Blitz began and it was horrific. One evening I came back and the fire of London was burning and I could read my newspaper in the street. The air raids were appalling; we were on the path of the German bombers and they used to fly in, turn round and aim for Paddington, Marylebone, Euston, St Pancras, King's Cross and Liverpool Street, in a straight line. We were on that line, just behind Marylebone Station, and you could hear these bombs come down. The women got terrified and insisted on going down to the basement. They didn't appreciate that over their heads were the gas pipes, the steam pipes, the hot water pipes and the electric cables. People had this curious troglodyte feeling. We had all sorts of obstetric emergencies: one lady had twins and the ambulance wouldn't come until the air raid was over. About halfway through my time at Queen Charlotte's the chairman of the hospital was almost knocked down by a bomb and so we moved to Hammersmith, the whole lot, lock, stock and barrel, from Marylebone to Hammersmith in one day. It was quite a thing. I delivered a baby that evening, sitting on the floor. There was no blackout, there were no curtains, we couldn't have any lights on, so I had a lantern and I sat and delivered this baby on the floor.

Some of the more old-fashioned gynaecologists would keep patients in ten days after a minor operation. I wouldn't do that.

I think there's everything to be said for not keeping people in hospital. All my patients had to get out of bed the day after an operation. When I was at Windsor Hospital – I didn't get into trouble for this, but I could have done – I started sending patients home a day or two after operations. That was a revolution! At Queen Charlotte's we started getting women who'd had babies out of bed because of the Blitz. And at UCH we got everybody out of bed and made them carry their babies downstairs so that we could evacuate the building if it caught fire.

My husband was in the army. I'd known him as a student at UCH, but we met again in 1942. We met, we decided we liked each other and we got married – in six weeks. People did that in the War. You felt, 'Well, let's do it now, or we may not be able to.' We were supposed to have a fortnight's honeymoon, but in fact we got four days; we went to the Old Ship in Brighton. Then he went off to the army and I went back to work. I had great difficulty after I was married because I was still living in the hospital and they wouldn't allow the wife to sleep with her husband. Although I offered to pay, they wouldn't even let my husband have breakfast in the hospital. They were very anti-marriage. It was considered not the done thing at all. When my husband came on leave, we'd go and stay sometimes at the Savoy. It was quite cheap in those days. I'd always ask for a room on the top floor. We were very unpopular with the staff, but I always thought you were safer at the top than if you were underground: there's nothing to fall on you. We had our first child within a year. I would rather have waited a bit longer, but my husband said, 'I may be in Africa tomorrow, let's see what we can do.' I think he was right; I wasn't that young, so it was just as well to get it over.

I had Penny in 1943. I wasn't very clever at having babies; I ended up with three Caesareans. I was still working at University College Hospital and the Elizabeth Garrett Anderson Hospital and also worked at the Hospital for Women in Soho Square. I went on with that until about 1945, so I was pretty busy. My mother was marvellous, and I'd got a

lady, Mrs Smith, who'd come and give Penny her lunch, take
her out in the afternoon and put her to bed. Mother could cope
up till lunchtime quite well. So that's how I managed.
Amanda, my second daughter, was born in 1948 and Antony,
my son, in December 1953.

I never had any intention of not working. Never. Never
ever. In fact, I thought I'd better make it absolutely clear
before we got married that I was intending to go on working. I
made it a condition when we got engaged. I said, 'I'm not
marrying you unless you allow me to continue working. I'm
not going to give up work.' I made him go away and think
about it. I said, 'You're marrying a working woman, and I
intend to go on working. You'd better go away and think if
you still want to marry me.' He came back in three days and
said, 'I still want to marry you.' I'd passed all these exams, I'd
had all this training, all these skills – why should I throw them
away? It's just not my thing. I'm not domestically minded.
I'm a nervous wreck if I'm left at home all day with a small
baby. I'm not a nervous wreck if I'm spending the day
working.

Work intruded all right. No question. I always reckoned
that the thing that defeats the working mother is the measles.
If your children are ill, you feel awful about having to leave
them and go to work. The other problem I found when they
went to boarding school was that they would have sixteen
weeks' holiday a year and I had six, so there were ten weeks to
fill in somehow. They went to stay with friends or with my
mother; they'd go camping; when they were smaller they'd go
away with the nanny. I was very lucky in getting the most
wonderful nanny. I always did the night feed when the
children were babies, even though we had the nanny, whether
I was breast-feeding or bottle-feeding. I never got Nanny up
in the night. I don't feel I missed all that much; I don't think
they minded too much either. I never could go along with Dr
Bowlby; he did an awful lot of harm. He made mothers feel
guilty. I do remember Penny once saying, 'I wish you were
like other mothers.' And I said, 'Well, I'm awfully sorry, I

can't be.' Because once you're committed, as I was, totally committed, there's no question. I couldn't go back. I'd had all this marvellous training, and I didn't want to waste it.

My husband came out of the army in 1946 and he had no job and no money.. There was still rationing of clothes and food after the end of the war and that period, between 1946 and 1951, was about the most difficult time in my life. We even had rationing of bread and potatoes. I used to have to drive round in the car with the ration books to pick up bread and potatoes for the household. We found a rather derelict house in Chester Square, which we bought and shared with another family. They had the top half and we had the bottom half. It really was a very, very difficult time. The rationing was the worst thing of all. You had to queue up for fish; if you were lucky, you got a bit of liver or a few sausages. It was an appalling time. We got just about enough to eat, but that was all.

I was working at University College Hospital and the Elizabeth Garrett Anderson, and I started my private practice in Wimpole Street. (I went on at the Elizabeth Garrett till 1977; UCH I left in 1953; private practice I still do.) The Elizabeth Garrett Anderson Hospital was founded in 1866 by Elizabeth Garrett Anderson, the first woman doctor to qualify in this country. The idea was that it would be a hospital for women and children staffed entirely by women doctors. I went there as locum in 1945, and stayed until I retired in 1977. It was my first consultant job at a time when it was very hard to get one. The men were coming back from the War and jobs were very hard to come by for women. We'd been doing their jobs for them. (At UCH six women had been running the entire hospital.) In about 1973, Barbara Castle said she was going to close the Elizabeth Garrett – it was terribly expensive. But we were determined that it should not close; it still had a function in providing facilities for women who wanted to see a woman doctor. You can't guarantee that in any other hospital. Some Muslim and Jewish women don't like seeing a man doctor and if you've got a National Health Service it seems fair enough that you should provide women doctors to see them. I was chairman of the committee to keep the hospital open, and thanks to Mrs Thatcher we got a grant to rehabilitate the hospital, so it never closed.

The creation of the NHS in 1948 affected my life in that I was paid for my hospital work which I hadn't been paid for before. It wasn't very much, but it was enough. One had to supplement it with private practice in order to educate children and run the house and so on, but one was paid. I was sceptical, but I didn't feel it was my business. I had children to support and a living to earn, so I was glad to be paid, quite honestly. I remember when the Health Service came in, people rushing off to their GPs and demanding shampoos and wigs and teeth and spectacles. Just because they were free – at taxpayers' expense. It just gets more and more expensive every year, and doesn't necessarily give people a better service.

In 1954 Josephine Barnes went to Charing Cross Hospital as the hospital's first woman consultant gynaecologist.

I was in charge of a unit of beds and the junior staff and I had to organise teaching. It was quite a responsibility, as the first woman, because I felt if anything went wrong, they would say, 'Ah! That's what happens when you have women on the staff.' They'd never had a woman consultant before at Charing Cross. We had six separate departments of obstetrics and gynaecology. I saw the patients in London and operated on them at Mount Vernon Hospital. We were doing about 2,000 births a year at Kingsbury Maternity Hospital. I did the outpatients on a Saturday morning, which is not very popular with the staff but very popular with the patients because the husband's home to look after the children and the wife doesn't have to give up time from work if she has a job. I was there for twenty-three years and no woman ever died that I operated on. I'm quite pleased with that!

I think the staff all liked me. I did my job and I expected them to do the same. When I retired, they gave me a dinner and one of my young men who'd worked with me as registrar came back and he said, 'I always remember one thing about you. You were always punctual.' Now, I think that was terribly important. I was always there on time, and if an operating list started at two o'clock I made a great fuss that the first operation started at two o'clock. The juniors knew this, the theatre sister knew it, the anaesthetist knew it, everybody knew it. And unless there was a very good reason, my operation list started on time. I think my staff respected the fact that I liked things done properly. My children are the same. They were expected to be there for meals on time, merely as a courtesy to the cook. If they weren't going to be there on time, they were to say. I think that's fair enough, don't you?

I was then paid a good deal more, of course, which was good. I would get up about half past seven, and the house-keeper would bring us a cup of tea. The children would then be brought down ready for school, by the nanny, one hoped they'd been washed. They were made to eat a cooked breakfast every day, I insisted on that. Then I usually took them to school, unless I had a very early start. I could get them there at half past eight. And then each day would be different. I'd have a clinic one day, an operating session another day, a session in private practice another day or a lecture. If there were emergencies at night, I'd have to go to the hospital, and if a private patient had a baby at night, I would go and deliver it. I preferred them at night, actually, it's much, much easier.

I was involved in the three maternity surveys, 1946, 1958, and 1970. In 1946 we were looking at the social costs of child-bearing, in particular relation to poverty. We were looking at how much the woman spent on things like prams, cots, baby clothes, nappies. A lot came out of that; I think it had a big influence when the Health Service was set up. The 1958 survey was called 'The Perinatal Survey' and looked at the reasons why babies died. We looked at 18,000 births. A lot came out of that survey about maternity services, paediatric services, anaesthetic services. It did stimulate people to do better. The

1970 survey, 'British Births, 1970', was looking at the care of mothers and babies. The surveys were made public and, we hope, led to improvements. But improvement to the maternity services is a gradual process. Every time there's a new discovery it's like dropping a stone in a pond, it spreads out till everybody takes advantage of it. It doesn't happen overnight. For example, up until six or nine years ago, abortion was the commonest cause of a pregnant woman dying; now there are hardly any deaths from abortion. We had forms of birth control for people; they wouldn't use them. The Brook Advisory Centres were formed through a great necessity, but the impact is terribly disappointing in that the number of abortions goes up each year and the number of teenage pregnancies doesn't diminish. I used to do an abortion counselling service and I was sometimes a bit tough with these very silly girls who'd got themselves pregnant for no apparent reason except that it was an impulse. It was difficult not to get a little bit cross!

One of my achievements in the Health Service is that I got rid of my waiting list. I know there are a million people waiting for operations but waiting lists are essentially un-necessary. When I got to Elizabeth Garrett Anderson, there were about 200 people waiting for operations. To begin with I got them out of bed so they went home sooner and would then be seen in out-patients. The other thing I did was to write to every patient on the waiting list every six months and ask them if they still wanted to come in. A lot of people are counted on waiting lists who are not really waiting at all. It's a ridiculous thing the politicians throw up. The matron said, 'There won't be anything for my nurses to do,' but I found far too much for them to do because they had a constant stream of patients coming in. This business of waiting lists is almost totally unnecessary, so we got our waiting lists down. The authorities then tried to close the hospital. The number of operations we were doing had trebled, we were doing more work than ever before, but we hadn't a waiting list and that didn't appeal to them. Really the NHS is a huge, terrifying bureaucracy. I could say a lot more about the Department of Health, but I won't.

Josephine Barnes was president of the Medical Women's Federation and has been president of the Women's Nationwide Cancer Control Campaign since 1974. In 1965 she was appointed to the Royal Commission on Medical Education and throughout the sixties travelled extensively, looking at medical education and facilities all round the world, including America, India, Russia and Nigeria. She sat on the Lane Committee from 1971 to 1974, investigating the workings of the Abortion Act, and in 1981 was appointed to the controversial Warnock Committee whose findings became the basis of the Human Embryology Bill. Both committees were chaired by distinguished professional women: Lord Justice Lane, the first female judge, and Dame Mary Warnock, Principal of Girton College, Cambridge. From 1961 to 1987 she sat on the council of the Medical Defence Union, dealing with cases of negligence and other medico–legal decision matters. She was also made an inspector in nullity and was the official inspector in the case of April Ashley, a male transsexual whose marriage was annulled on the grounds of non-consummation. A great landmark in her career was becoming the first female president of the British Medical Association.

That was something quite terrific. It was marvellous. As president, you are an absolute monarch, you're not supposed to be concerned with the day-to-day running of the association. Something like seventy to eighty per cent of doctors belong to it. Every year there is the Annual Representative Meeting and when I was there, we had our scientific meeting in Hong Kong, which was great fun. I was very lucky. Being president involved attending council meetings, lecturing all over the country, conducting the meeting in Hong Kong. It was quite hard work. I didn't want to make any errors or say anything I shouldn't.

I retired from the National Health Service in 1977. I'd reached retirement age. In some ways my working life has become easier, in some ways more difficult. I miss the junior staff, the people I had to help me, the fact that, if I'm not there, there's no one to do the work for me. I'm president of the Royal Medical Benevolent Fund, which provides financial help for doctors and their dependants who have fallen on hard times – and it's surprising how many do. I'm also president of the Family Planning Doctors, Family Planning Nurses and the Obstetric Physiotherapists, so I have a good deal to do. I do a lot of charity, some consulting, writing reports, court cases, attending committees.

I'm not a feminist. I don't like the screaming women. I can't stand them. I think women should earn their rights and deserve them. They shouldn't expect them to be handed on a plate. I don't think one should think about gender. I think one should get on with doing the best job one can do. I haven't worked for women's rights, I've worked for women, not for their rights. Except perhaps the Royal Commission on Medical Education when we did agree – but this was nothing to do with me – that women should be admitted to medical school on merit and not on a quota system. That if you like is a feminist issue.

I take life as it comes. The next thing I'm asked to do, I get on with and do. I don't suffer from stress. I just do the next job as it comes along, I get on with it. I set out when I was thirteen to study medicine, to become a doctor and to practise medicine all my life, and I'm very lucky that I've managed to do that and keep it going even until now. I never stopped. I'm proud of my achievement in the examinations, they were better than most. I'm very proud of the fact that I have three healthy children. In June 1990 I was awarded the honorary degree of Doctor of Science at the Encaenia in Oxford. I would regard this in some ways as the most important achievement in my career. At the time I was very conscious of the courage of my parents in taking us to Oxford in 1925. Had they not done that I would never have achieved any of the things I have managed to do up to now. In a lifespan there is a certain amount that you can achieve, and I've achieved as much as I reckon I can. I wish I could achieve more, obviously everybody does, but I think that within the limits that you have in any life I've achieved as much as anyone can.

SHEILA PARKINSON

Sheila Parkinson was born on 5 August 1913, the eldest of three children. Her life has been full of determined women: from her grandmother, widowed in her early thirties and left to raise four daughters; to Lady Sidney-Farrar, a legislative councillor for a gold mine district in Kenya in the thirties; to the 100 FANYs she was in charge of during the Second World War; to the Belsen survivors whom she met at the anniversary of the Liberation of Natzweiler in 1977. She has needed a degree of determination and courage too: the Second World War claimed the lives of her husband and her brother, and her only sister also died in tragic circumstances.

An ardent traveller all her life, starting when she went to Palestine and Kenya in her twenties, Sheila Parkinson has been to Lebanon, Sardinia, Cyprus, Russia, Iceland and many other countries besides. She has driven in the Belgian Congo, panned for gold in Uganda, built a house from wattle and daub, ridden across the Kenyan highlands, confronted a live cobra and drunken Masai warriors, travelled on the Red Ball Route, attended the Nuremburg Trials, been inside the harems of Kuwait and slept in a hearse.

In 1937, at the age of twenty-five, she joined the First Aid Nursing Yeomanry and she has remained a dedicated FANY ever since. During the Second World War she was with the supreme head-quarters of the Allied Expeditionary Forces and led a FANY driving company in England and France. In 1964 she was appointed head of the FANYs and in 1977 she was awarded an OBE in recognition of her services to the force.

Founded at the start of the century, the FANYs have now served in three wars. In the First World War they drove horse-drawn ambulances, bringing wounded soldiers back from the front line and transporting unexploded shells. Later in the War, they switched to mechanised ambulances and made a reputation for themselves as drivers. Throughout the Second World War the FANYs provided staff-car drivers for the army, as well as working closely with the Special Operations Executive and the Polish army. In 1991, during the Gulf War, the FANYs were again involved with army communications.

As corps commander for twenty-five years from 1964 to 1991, Sheila Parkinson played a vital role in establishing the reputation of the FANYs as a significant peacetime organisation with valuable skills to offer both the army and the police in a civilian context. She was also responsible for directing and focusing the FANYs at a time when they could easily have lost momentum. She developed the training courses available to new recruits and registered the FANYs as a charity, which has helped to secure their financial future.

A modest woman, Sheila Parkinson has approached the many varied experiences of her lifetime with a combination of curiosity, enthusiasm and good humour. Now retired from both civilian and military work, she is facing the next stage of her life with equanimity, arranging her move to a retirement home, looking forward to the chance to garden and to read, and planning a trip to Venezuela.

This interview took place at the National Sound Archive in London in 1991.

For the first eleven years of my life I lived at a house called Fishinghurst in Kent. It had been a Huguenot settlement and was reputed to have two or three ghosts. There were certainly two ghosts, both of them very benign and dressed in the clothes of Huguenot women. My grandparents on my father's side started a silk mill in Macclesfield. My grandfather on my mother's side, Louis Rivett-Carnac, was Adjutant-General in India. He died very young, killed playing polo. My grandmother was a splendid woman, Mabel Rivett-Carnac. She was a very independent, clever woman and after her husband died she brought her four daughters back to England and educated them over here. She had a large house in Bath for a number of years and my memories of the house are [of] a smell of curry. She made curry properly: it took four days to mature. And she insisted that everybody ate their curry off paper plates. She had a beautiful singing voice and was a very good pianist. She was ninety-six, I think, when she died.

Like other Anglo-Indians, she travelled backwards and forwards to India with the children all her young married life. Her great contention was that it was important that my sister and I must travel when we were young, to find out about countries from the people who lived in them. I well remember her coming to see me off for my first bit of travel, at the age of seventeen, when I was going to Palestine. She handed me a travelling rug and an enormous piece of adhesive plaster, and she told me very firmly that if I put this across my ribs, I would not be seasick, because no self-respecting passenger should be seasick. Unfortunately my skin was allergic to it and the medical doctors on board had considerable difficulty getting it off without pulling off my skin. A rather better way of not being seasick, was on my return journey. There was a group of Indian Army colonels and I landed at their table. They made the point that I had to attend every meal, and we had curry and coffee laced with brandy. They said there was no need to be seasick. I turned out a good sailor, so my early training on curry and brandy was a good idea.

I was a disappointment, being a girl. My father decided that if he hadn't got a son to take hunting, he would take us. He was a keen huntsman and we had two or three horses. So every morning at six o'clock we used to be got out of bed by Nanny and taken down to go over jumps until we could stay on. I didn't enjoy hunting. We were very small, I was eleven and my sister must have been about eight. You were blooded with your first hunt and given the paw of the fox, which I've still got mounted with the date. It was a sickening performance which sticks in your mind, but it was part of the tradition.

We saw very little of my mother. We weren't expected to be about; it was a world of nanny and nursery maid for us. Nanny was very good to us. She stayed with us until I was fourteen and she was a more important figure [in my life than my mother], because other than going out riding and for walks, life was in the nursery, entirely in the nursery. The nursery maid brought the meals up from the kitchen. We used to be dressed up and taken down to tea and that was about it. Mother was very pretty and very popular. She was a very good shot: there were a lot of shooting parties. (My grandmother, incidentally, was the best shot in India and got the Gold Cup. Back at the end of the last century, shooting was quite a usual thing for the women in India.) It was a full life in its way, a life of entertaining, until 1923 when my father nearly went bankrupt and there was no money. When I was fourteen there was a divorce and that was when we went to school for the first time. I was at a boarding school in Camberley which no longer exists. It exasperated my sister and I that my brother would always have an enormous tuck box and we were told it was quite unnecessary for us.

Despite getting good enough results to go on to university, the money available was designated to Sheila Parkinson's brother. Instead she was despatched on the 'fishing fleet' to Palestine.

It was a standing joke. It was how the young officers were supposed to find brides. Although we were all out visiting relatives ostensibly, it was a marriage market – though I honestly can't remember anyone getting engaged. My mother knew the Government Medical Officer and his wife, and I lived with them. It was a festive time. Everybody was young, everybody was enjoying life. Palestine was British Mandate then and the Jews and the Palestinians were living amicably side by side. The repercussions from the Balfour Declaration hadn't permeated. The first sign of trouble between the Palestinians and the Jews was that the Palestinians strewed all the roads with nails at night. It was the most effective way of drawing the entire place to a grinding halt. Everybody spent their entire life mending punctures. There was a Highland Regiment out there, so [there were] an enormous number of eligible young men and only nine single girls. There was one Austrian hairdresser who did the most magnificent hairdos, and you danced the night through with reels and bagpipes on the black-and-white marble floor of the King David Hotel. I had plenty of boyfriends. I mean, who couldn't? Nine girls and a Scottish regiment! And during the day I played a lot of tennis. It was great fun. I can remember the Shah of Persia visiting: I was delegated to take the Shah's wife and daughter to buy hats. Too silly, all these things, aren't they!

I was very nearly killed one night on top of a petrol storage tank in Jersualem. My boyfriend of the moment, to ring the changes a bit, said, 'The thing to do is to look at the moon from the top of the storage tank.' Which we did. But a young lieutenant and his platoon, all armed with live ammunition, who were guarding it, mistook me in my long dress for an Arab who was blowing up the petrol tank. It was very fortunate that I laughed about something just before he gave the order to shoot. He was devastated, poor man. And my boyfriend was sent home. So that was the end of that.

I was out there for five or six months, then I came home and in 1937 I went to Kenya for two years. A woman called Olwen Easton, whom we knew, wanted somebody versatile who could do the preliminaries of education for Frances, her three-year-old. I had nothing else in view and this seemed a wonderful opportunity. Olwen said the only essential was that I should acquire 200 words of Kiswahili on the journey, because I would be running the house – she hated anything to do with housework – and looking after the houseboys. It was also my job to feed the labour force. They came every evening for crushed maize and salt and meat. Their job was to till the ground and do the maize, which was known as the 'mahindi'. They came out from their reserves for six-month periods and they usually left their wives and children at home and then brought the concubine with them, attractive little things. It was also my responsibility to do the sick parade, although there was little in the way of medicines. The neighbours were all bachelors who'd 'gone native' and there were a lot of coffee-coloured children.

We were up-country, at a place called Turbo. It was a farm, a rather poor farm, four hundred miles from Nairobi and five thousand feet up. We used to go and stay with Lady Sidney-Farrar at a place called Mau Summit, eight thousand feet up in the highlands of Kenya. She was one of the Duke of Buckinghamshire's daughters and she was an admirable woman. She was used to getting what she wanted and she had a very successful life there. She and her husband grew pyrethrum in enormous acreages. You baked it and crushed it and sent it back to England and turned it into a fly-killer called 'Flit', now considered to be deadly dangerous. Everybody used it for years before they discovered this. When her husband died young, her boy went home to school and they said she should pack up and come home. She said, 'No such thing.' She became the first woman legislative councillor on the Kenya Legislative Council and she represented a Kakamaga, a gold mine section. She was a woman of considerable personality.

The FANY camp in Kenya was her camp. Olwen Easton was her senior mechanic and did all the mechanical repairs. Olwen was a FANY to her back teeth. I became a member of the FANYs in 1938 in order that I could drive myself about, because you weren't allowed to drive on your own in Kenya unless you were a FANY – you could never go anywhere without a boyfriend. You had to be able to strip down an engine and put it together again (I'd learnt changing tyres in Palestine). You also had to know a bit about wood: you cooked on an open range and you had to know which wood you needed to produce an even heat. The King's African Rifles down in Nairobi balloted as to who should teach us drill. We used to march up and down on a piece of ground full of rabbit holes. And you had to be a good shot on the FANY camp. Rifle and revolver. You had to shoot. Olwen insisted that part of my household duties was to shoot buck. I could skin a buck and hang and butcher it, but I would never shoot anything because one night I was in the car on my own and I ran over a buck which leapt out. I stopped and I heard it screaming in pain so I had to kill it. I took the base of the jack and went back and killed it, but I decided then that I would never shoot anything again. I was very unpopular because of that.

I loved Kenya. Loved it. If Olwen went away, I was perfectly happy to be in the house with nobody within three miles and a village of four hundred labourers and their families. There was never any feeling of distrust between the Africans and the British. One time we were staying with friends and they had a prize herd of cattle – good cattle were very hard to come by because of the tsetse fly. They also had a garden with rose trees in it, of which they were extremely proud, and they had a ha-ha round the garden so that no cattle could get in. That night they'd all gone off and I woke, to my horror, to hear the sound of cattle outside, and there they were, chumping around the rose bushes. The Masai who were guarding them were drunk. They knew there was only me about and they had had a good drinking party. There were a lot of leopards about that would attack the cattle, so I went out in my pyjamas and gumboots and a Burberry and a revolver to look for the drunken Masai and get these animals back again. My Swahili was sufficient to say, 'Get a move on.' There was me in my gumboots and my Burberry, and the Masai in nothing but their spears, and rather drunk! We got them all in the fold again, but I couldn't disguise what had happened: there were hoof marks all over the grass.

Another time a friend of Olwen's husband died and she'd got no money and nowhere to live, so Olwen said, 'We'll build you a house!' We went and bought books on how to do it and we built her a house of wattle and daub with two bedrooms and a bathroom. The important thing was to get the pitch of your roof right, so that it would neither blow off, nor the rain come in. The fire is important too: you've got to build it at exactly the right angle, otherwise the smoke comes back on you. The floor itself was made of the same clay material as the walls. You mixed it with ox-blood, so that it came out a deep rosy red. It was a laborious process, but it was a very successful house. And it proved that it was quite possible to build your little single-storey bungalow, with the aid of a couple of books and the material to hand.

Olwen decided we should take two cars and drive from Kenya to the Belgian Congo. We had to drive two days on a little narrow road through these enormous primeval forests, where you never saw the light. The tribe that lived there used bows and arrows for killing their animals. They wore nothing and they were absolutely black. You saw them flitting between the trunks with their bows and arrows. We stayed in amazing places. We spent a couple of days in Uganda up in the Mountains of the Moon panning for gold. It was very hot, I can remember, and you fill a large shallow pan with earth and mud and you keep putting water in and swilling it until you suddenly see these tiny little bits of gold. It's quite extraordinary what an effect it has, seeing those little bits of gold. You feel so primitive. Actually finding gold! It made the most inexplicable impact.

Every night, sitting in the middle of nowhere, we used to listen to the nine o'clock news and Big Ben, and it became more and more obvious that there was going to be a war, so in July 1939 we went home. War was declared in September. It was a glorious sunny day. I was [visiting] Olwen and her father in Cardiff. Unbelievable. This extraordinary voice [of Chamberlain], 'We are now at war.' You just couldn't believe anything had happened. Very shortly after that, I got a telegram from the FANYs saying, 'Report to Porthcawl.' I sent a thing back, saying 'Impossible!' And then, you know, the facts of life began to dawn: I realised that if I didn't do something now, I wasn't going to, because there were queues of people wanting to join the FANYs.

The FANYs had a good reputation from the First World War when they took their horses and ambulances over to France and Belgium. So in 1938, even before the official outbreak of war, the FANYs were asked to provide structured driving units for the Army Commands.

I ended up at the Headquarters of Western Command in Chester. Our job was staff-car driving. You had to be able to pick up any car that was free and then you took these pompous brigadiers and generals round visiting. We were told to be extremely respectful and we were to wrap them in a rug. I said, 'That's enough. If there's any rug going, it's for me' – I was sent to Tycroes for being difficult!

Tycroes was an enormous anti-aircraft station, very wind-blown, in Anglesey; and it was one of the most interesting intellectual experiences of my life. I had to sit for hours on the gun site, with a stretcher bearer, looking at Snowdon. My stretcher bearer was a Welsh miner and amazingly well-read, and he'd say, 'Read that tonight, and we'll talk about it tomorrow.' He was an absolute delight and we covered the most extraordinary range of books.

I met my husband at Tycroes. Lance Parkinson. He was the medical officer there. We decided almost immediately that we would get married as the doctors were being sent out overseas. So on 13 September 1941 we got married. Three months later he was sent out to Singapore with his medical unit. They went up through Burma and were beaten back by the Japanese, and they came back to the main hospital in Singapore and the Japanese came and killed everybody in the hospital – the patients, the nurses and the doctors. We were married in September and he was killed in February. It came as the second blow, because my brother, Michael, who'd gone into North Africa as soon as the campaign began, was killed in November 1941, burnt to death in a tank. And then Lance was killed in February 1942.

I never remarried. I had no lack of people who thought I'd be a great help around the place, but for a long time I had no wish to think of anybody else at all. Lance and I had been such a short time together. We hadn't had any time to find out the ups and downs of marriage but I think we would have made a success of marriage. We planned to have quite a large family. I'm very fond of children. Oh, I would love to have had a family. That is a great sadness, a great sadness. And really, although I've met up with a number of people, [there's been] nobody that I felt I would want to embark on – the older you get the more hazards you see attached to marriage.

At the time it was totally intolerable. I said I couldn't take any more, I had to have a more active war. I went for an interview to go to the Supreme Headquarters of the Allied Expeditionary Force [SHAEF] and I was very fortunate to be chosen.

It was an exacting job. I was responsible for a hundred FANY drivers. One hundred individuals! The FANY Driving Company was the plum of the women's unit. They were splendid, but they took a bit of looking after: a FANY is a great believer in calling a spade a spade and if they didn't like anything, they said so! We were part of a Mixed Transport Company, because in 1941 when conscription came in it was decided that the FANYs could no longer work as an independent voluntary organisation and we were seconded to the Auxiliary Territorial Service, but we kept our identity by having 'Women's Transport Service FANY' on our shoulders. We were stationed at Bushey Park [which was] very Anglo-American. We were the target for the V1s and the V2s: you could hear them coming and you could see the flame, but you never knew when they were going to cut out. We had twenty-six in and around the camp, on one day. There was a look-out whose job it was to announce the arrival of a flying bomb. He'd say, 'Flying bomb! Take cover! Take cover!' –and you could hear him taking cover! We would just get under our beds and put our tin hats over our faces, so that whatever else got bashed up, our faces would be all right. We could sleep like that – and we did.

We had a women's camp with a thousand women in it, of which a hundred were FANYs. The American women, in their opinion, were in the front line of the War. Serious stuff this. They'd come with garments for every occasion: when attacked in battle, when off-duty – they had the most remarkable quantities of garments. The Americans kept sending television crews over [to film] their first brilliant women overseas and we kept having to parade. If they'd been within a hundred yards of a bomb they were awarded a Purple Heart. They used to line up splendidly in one of their garments and generals used to come and plant these Purple Hearts on them. I'd say to my FANYs, 'For God's sake look interested, because you'll be on television and our Anglo-American relations will be strained if you don't.'

When the time came to go to France, [the men] went ahead with the heavy transport vehicles and left me with all the staff cars to follow in due course. I was given all sorts of map references with which I'd got to get down to Winchester with my hundred drivers and despatch riders. When we got to Winchester, which is the staging camp for Southampton, there was an American Heavy Duty Transport Company who'd been there for a week or so, waiting for transport, who weren't allowed to leave the camp. The sight of a hundred women appearing on their doorstep was too good to be true. It was fairly hectic! I kept saying, 'I think we'd better get down to the dock,' and they'd say, 'No, no, no, you can't do that.' Then they said an Italian Truck Company was coming and I said, 'That's it! Get us down to the dock!' Which they did – but they didn't say we were women, and when we got down to Southampton it caused a considerable upheaval because they'd no rules and regulations [for women] or any special accommodation or anything. Everywhere we stopped, you see, they thought they were in for a good night out. It was very tricky.

An American Liberty Boat was the next one to go out. It was already scheduled to have on it a Coloured Truck Company, and of course they said we couldn't go with the Coloured Truck Company. I said, 'I don't see why not. Their trucks are going to go in one hold, our cars are going to go in another hold; they're going to go aft, we'll go for'ard.' I had to sign an indemnity that it was entirely my responsibility if there was any incident between the Coloured Truck Company members and the FANYs. Having got so far as that, they then vouchsafed the information that it was standard practice for the crew to let off steam by going and getting dead drunk in Southampton. I went to the Military Police and said, 'Would you please come and sit on the top of the hold when [the crew] come back? I can't deal with really drunk men. What about you doing this for us?' So when the crew returned drunk, the Military Police sat splendidly there, guarding the English womanhood – and at the turn of the tide we set off. The captain's idea was that as I was the only officer about, I should share his cabin. He was very fat and very drunk and I said, 'No, no. Not on. We can't do that.' He got very cross about that, and all the girls were giggling.

We got to the other side and at the next high tide we got ashore. The weather was disgusting. It was very muddy and very wet and the sides of the road were mined, so that whenever you wanted to spend a penny, you had to put up four blankets on the very edge of the road and just hold them up. This was the Red Ball Route – we were the first women to go on the Red Ball Route.* When we got to the Falaise Gap, the whole town had been completely razed to the ground by us and the Americans, and [the townspeople] were all living in the cellars. They were told a bit ahead that we were coming, and they tore off lilac branches and put them on our cars and trucks. There was an English governess who had married a Frenchman and she came with two gladioli. It was very touching. We were the liberation! When we got to our meeting point, it turned out be the local undertaker's. We'd been nine days on this journey, and everybody had been in their clothes for nine mornings, noons and nights, sleeping very uncomfortably. They really were very tired by then, so I said, 'Come on! Those of you who can get into the hearses, do so!' So they got into the hearses, and slept there side by side.

We finally landed up in Versailles, a day late, with every vehicle covered in mud, and lined ourselves up outside the palace – nobody knew we [were coming] until we got there. We were in Versailles for the best part of a year, living behind Versailles in these cottages with Aladdin's lamps. The condensation ran down the walls: you had to put your clothes under your mattress to keep them aired to wear the next day. The girls were staff-car drivers, so they couldn't go anywhere

* *A direct route through the Falaise Gap and up through the Bulge used by troops returning from the Front.*

unless they were driving an officer – and the men couldn't go anywhere without a FANY because there weren't any other drivers for staff cars. It was a monopoly in its way. [The job] did require a certain amount of diplomacy: Monty was absolutely against women drivers and Eisenhower was very pro women drivers.

The FANYs gave me access to a man's world, an entirely man's world. One knew the other women's organisations, but our paths didn't cross. We had nothing to offer the regular women's services, we being neither fish, fowl, nor good red herring. Yes, it was always talking to men, never to a woman. A number of people would say, 'Not a woman at any cost,' but you were briefed with something they wanted and in the end they might have a try.

While I was with SHAEF, I had the opportunity to spend three days up at the Nuremberg Trials, listening to the people who were going to be tried. I was told very few of them were German, they were European. I wouldn't like to put a name to them, because it's thoroughly uncomplimentary, but these were the dregs – in any civilised country they would be in a mental home, they were just brutish. I suppose it was only those sort of people who could do the kind of jobs they were asked to do. I was at the trial of a doctor. It was a camp which became notorious for turning the skins of the prisoners that they were experimenting on into lampshades. This was one of the things which was actually discussed during the time I was at the trial. This doctor's wife was very fond of him and wished to say what good things he did, how he used to have these very civilised concerts, with the orchestra taken from the prisoners in the concentration camps. It was awful really, you could see she was condemning her husband rather than saving him. The laboriousness of translating from German to English and back again, the slowness and meticulousness of that sort of justice, I found it a horrible experience.

It came to the stage when the Headquarters were reducing staff and I was posted to Brussels to run an Ack-Ack Company of three hundred women, Auxiliary Training Staff, not FANYs.

Ack-Ack were women's gun emplacements in defensive positions, they weren't drivers at all. They all came from in and around Liverpool and to be abroad was a major thing. I must say, it was one of my really interesting experiences – and my vocabulary increased no end! These girls came from very tough homes. None of them ever had a bath, ever. Most of them always slept in their clothes – it was something about decency. I couldn't get them to get their clothes off to begin with to put in the weekly laundry. Of course, they used to go hedging and ditching: the men used to fill them with Dutch gin and shove them into a hedge or ditch. They never knew anything and got no fun out of it at all. The men would just fill them with this wretched stuff. It was maddening. 'Never knew any more, ma'am. Don't know how it happened.' We had what was known in the army as Para Eleven for when they were pregnant. I always remember one little thing saying, 'It's all right, it's just lucky my mum didn't sell the pram.'

In 1946 Sheila Parkinson was released from service and in 1947 she went to work in the headquarters of the Women's Voluntary Service as regional organiser.

Part of the organisation was [run by] seconded civil servants, all women. It was an eye-opener to me that all these women did such remarkable work, a couple of million of them: the unsung heroines of the war. It was often said that Lady Reading was the female Churchill – and she was. She was the most remarkable woman and she held the loyalty of a great cross-section of people. She didn't suffer fools gladly at all, but she had a delightful sense of humour. I enjoyed working with her. I was seeing the [volunteers], who came into London from the various centres, about what they were doing and what they might do next. When the Hungarians came over, for example, there was a great demand for blankets and food and clothing, and the Regional Organiser was responsible for co-ordinating this throughout the country. It was a very interesting job, but it only carried a bursary of five pounds a week and I had to find something that was going to put a roof over my head.

So in 1949 I went to the Kuwait Oil Company as their personnel officer. It was an Anglo-American company and the Americans [had] poured a great deal of money into building a town completely from scratch. Ahmadi, it was called, eleven miles from Kuwait Town. My first job was recruiting all the nursing staff for the magnificent new hospital they had built out there. We also had two schools [in Ahmadi] and again I recruited the staff, with professional advice. They all had to be single women, aged between twenty-five and thirty-five, both the nurses and the teaching staff. My commitment was to find the girl with the personality for the very restricted life in an oil town. Everything was free and everything was magnificent, but after a time it palled, just driving from your home up to the Club; there were few outside activities, unless you enjoyed things like sailing or swimming or tennis. But the salary offered was good, and the [idea] of this absolutely magnificent hospital and a much more free and equal social life was a great attraction. A lot of quite unsuitable people applied thinking that this was going to be a wonderful opportunity for finding a husband, but it was not so. The problem, which I made abundantly clear to them, was that there were very few single men.

I was also in liaison with the women down in the town, the wives of the sheikhs who were in harems. They were very much kept in purdah at that time, but I used to go and visit them. It was fashionable for the Kuwaiti sheikhs to marry someone from Beirut, [which] meant that there was French blood in those girls, and they wore these glorious, very expensive French creations from Beirut. Oh, they had the most glorious clothes and glorious jewels. But when they went out they had to go veiled: they'd appear on the plane to Beirut completely veiled and doing the correct thing, then they'd vanish into the Ladies immediately we landed, whip the whole thing off and underneath was this gorgeous garment! But they were very delightful people, a highly sophisticated, amusing lot who spoke excellent French. If one could enthuse them with a few ideas, they were the best way of getting things changed. They had far more to do with what happened in the country than most people gave them credit for.

I used to go out to Kuwait every year to see how [the staff] were getting on, and talk to the people for whom they were working. Kuwait at that time was a brand new thing. It wasn't a stable community because it was just growing so fast. [Everyone was] in some way involved with oil, whether it was the distribution of oil, the finding of oil, or the building of this new town. All the dogsbody work was done by the Indians, the Sudanese, the Eygptians. They're suffering from that now, of course: that's why it's taking Kuwait so long to get back to normal. The electricity's not working, the water's not working, and the Indians, the Sudanese, the Egyptians have all gone. The borders are nothing but old oil drums on a piece of sand. Well before the days of Saddam Hussein the relationship with Iraq was an erratic uncertain thing. The Gulf War was only the beginning of what's going to be a continuing horror.

I left the Kuwait Oil Company in 1963. I was beginning to get stale and I thought I would go out and see what the employment world was like for somebody in their early fifties. I saw advertised a job as registrar in the John Lewis Partnership. I did that for a year and I was based in John Barnes, which no longer exists, in Swiss Cottage. I had a team of about seven people working for me and was responsible for about three hundred staff, male and female. My army experience of general admin and admin of women was an advantage. Once a month I had to put in a report to Head Office on the things that were happening in the shop. I now look on anything to do with people who work in shops with admiration. The people that one had the greatest sympathy for were the department heads because they had to justify the sales turnover. To hear these people getting up and saying, 'I bought in a thousand purple gloves, which haven't sold and therefore I'm minus point something down on my sale . . .' It was the first time I'd come across a world in which a proportionately large number of people were having psychiatric treatment – because of the stress of the job. It was also the first time I'd come across what it's like for people [living] on a very small amount of money. If another shop offered you another fifty pence a week, you moved, life was so tight. The men had their collars turned, their cuffs turned . . . they were very hard-pressed to run a family and keep their clothing up to an acceptable level. It was a life not of hardship, but of grinding carefulness.

As registrar you were looking after the welfare of the entire staff. In a rather surprising way, you were even able to report on the managing director: if I thought there was anything that came in his sphere which wasn't working, I was meant to talk about it. It wasn't an enviable post, it was a lonely job. You knew everybody from the man who drove the van to the managing director, and that was as Spedan Lewis intended it, but there wasn't anybody to pass the time of day with.

Since the War, Sheila Parkinson had remained involved with the FANYs on a voluntary basis. As she put it herself: 'Once a FANY, always a FANY – providing you pay your subscription.' At the time that she retired from the John Lewis Partnership, the head of the FANYs was in poor health and looking for a replacement, and in 1964 Sheila Parkinson was invited to take over as corps commander, a post she held until 1991.

I went from being a backwards FANY to corps commander in one jump. You either sank or swam. The traditionalists were highly alarmed [by my appointment], and it will seem strange to anybody who knows the structure and general administration [of the] army that somebody like myself, who was just a FANY with no rank at all, could go to being corps commander. But I was around, and I was established in London, and there was no other obvious person and no very good reason why I couldn't do it. The FANYs in 1964 was at very low ebb: they hadn't got an objective, they'd got very little money and they were [about] to have no accommodation. The FANYs is now very well-respected, financially sound and has proved itself. I think I can take a certain satisfaction from that.

The FANYs has given me twenty-five years of an enormously interesting life and it's given me the good fortune to meet a great cross-section of people whom I would otherwise have had no possible means of meeting. On behalf of the FANYs I have met the most amazing people – in the police world, the army world, the parliamentary world. We have a finger in a lot of pies, by virtue of the unique skills that we've got. My deputy corps commander, for example, spoke four languages.

The FANYs we recruit now range between twenty-five and thirty. Many of them are secretaries, a fair percentage are graduates, a fair number are entrepreneurs: interior decorating, cordon bleu cooks, graphic designers. There's an architect, a couple of young barristers, a fingerprint expert from Scotland Yard. There's somebody who runs her own electronics firm. They're all in full-time jobs, therefore the training is done in the evenings and weekends. The obligatory training involves radio/telephony, city documentation, navigation, and first aid. The Royal Army Medical Corps does the first aid. Then we have a course in shooting – the Irish Fusiliers always, slightly ironically, taught us shooting. They learn how to strip and reassemble their rifles, and during the autumn they have a shooting competition. Then we've got a unit who teach them the defensive element of unarmed combat; three or four of them have [avoided being] mugged because they knew how to defend themselves. They take part in 'Survival Weekends' when they are taught how to light a fire without any matches and so on. The annual ten-day orienteering camp is another optional extra. They're sent out on a night-reading exercise on lanes with no signposts. You've got to be able to use your compass and read your map. It's not just getting from A to B; there are always hazards, you can very easily get lost. It's a bit of a challenge and it's good for the initiative. To be taught initiative and self-reliance is the basis of the whole thing. Nowadays there are so few opportunities for finding out what you're capable of. It's a missing thing in today's life, a challenge.

The principle [of the FANYs] remains unchanged: you've

got to be competent, you've got to have initiative, and you've got to have a sense of humour. It's merely applying them in different ways: into the First War with horses, into the Second War with transport, and today it's communication – a result of [our] work with the Special Forces [during the War].

There's about a hundred and ten London FANYs working today and about five hundred country FANYs [who were active in] the last War. They pay an annual subscription which gives us the income to do our training. We send out about six hundred *Gazettes* to twenty-two countries. You name it, there's a FANY sitting there. The oldest is a hundred and three, and she pays up every year. She's the third one to reach a hundred. Several of the First World War FANYs lived well into their nineties. They led a very structured life: they were brought up by nannies, they weren't indulged, they were disciplined, they played a lot of games and were made to walk a lot. I don't think the ones now in their seventies will live as long.

The First World War lot achieved remarkable things. The military medals are the outward and visible sign of that. They were sitting there in 1907, arranging flowers and waiting for holy matrimony, but they were a bunch of very determined women and they had been brought up to be independent. The Guards down in Pirbright taught them to ride and to look after their horses, and the Royal Army Medical Corps taught them first aid, and when war was declared in 1914, these women went and said, 'Here we are.' The War Office said, 'For God's sake, stay at home. We've got nurses, we don't want you.' The Scots woman who was leading us then wrote to the Queen of the Belgians and to the Head of the French Red Cross and they wrote back saying, 'Come at once.' So they went, and out of that group of three hundred and forty FANYs, sixteen got military medals, the first military medals awarded to women in the First War. In the Second World War, we got three George Crosses and two George Medals.* We've now served in three wars and we're the most decorated unit – there isn't an

---

* *Two of the George Crosses were posthumous for girls who were killed in concentration camps; Odette is the living one of the three.*

army unit that's got more decorations, by size, than we have. In army terms, the FANYs have got a very distinguished record.

And they're not just a PR exercise, they're really needed. If there is a disaster in the City [of London], we have a commitment to the City Police and a call out system: we say that we will be staffed within an hour and a half. The first disaster was the Moorgate tube disaster in 1972 when we were able to provide for the police secure, uninterrupted communication between the scene of the disaster, the three designated hospitals and the headquarters in Bishopsgate, when all the public lines were blocked with anxious enquiries. The team did that for three days and four nights, working in six-hour shifts over twenty-four hours, with frantic people ringing in from all over the world about their relatives, wanting to know what was happening.

The FANYs also played a vital role in communications in October 1988 when a hurricane unexpectedly hit London, and in 1989 when the Marchioness *party boat tragically sank on the Thames, again working closely with the police from the outset. In 1982 they were approached by the army to help on their communications side. And on a lighter note, the FANYs have provided all the communications for the British Horse Society one-day events since 1967. In 1977, in recognition of her work with the FANYs, Sheila Parkinson received an OBE.*

In the last ten years my near relatives have died and it is my intention not to be beholden to cousins, not to impose on them. Five years ago I started looking for a retirement home, which I've now found. It's got a high percentage of people from a service background and I've been on the waiting list for four and a half years because there's such a long queue. You've got your own flat and you're left to fend for yourself; if you're in need of help it's there. I intend to travel, as soon as I get down there. I budgeted that I can do it. I'd like to go to India and to Peru. I've always enjoyed travelling. If you start when you're young, you see for yourself: people in their own countries are quite different. It makes reading the papers greatly more interesting. Having seen and sat and talked to and listened to people in their own countries has given me an opportunity to make perhaps slightly better informed ideas of what is happening in the world.

Looking back, I was very fortunate to have those two or three years before I went into the army in Palestine and Kenya. [It was] an important happy-go-lucky bit of life which had a great bearing on how [I] look at life generally. I come from North Country stock and army stock; I think I've got a degree of determination and I'm blessed with an ability to get on with most people. I like people. One of the things you learn is never, never to make your decision on a person's character on just a first acquaintance, because hidden beneath that you will find all sorts of interesting things. My religion is Church of England; not Evangelical, not High Church. I feel that there are many routes to God and people should choose the one that they've been brought up to or have learnt about. I have the greatest respect for Muslims and Hindus: those people are living a life of religion quite as full of merit as anybody who is a Christian. I do believe there's an afterlife and I think reincarnation is of great importance. In one life, no way can you have done either sufficient good or sufficient bad to merit sitting in green fields and pastures. I feel you come back to learn a particular aspect – patience is what I'm learning in this one.

HILDA BROWN

Hilda Brown was born on New Year's Day 1917 to nonconformist missionaries, both of whom were trained as scientists. One of five children, she spent the early years of her life in China, her upbringing nevertheless 'as English as was possible'. She was educated in England, first at Walthamstow Hall, Sevenoaks, and then at the London School of Economics. When the Second World War broke out she was working in Ireland, but left her job to return to England where she became a factory inspector in the Black Country. She remained with the Factory Inspectorate until shortly before the birth of her first child in 1947, although the War prevented her from qualifying formally. She returned to part-time work as personnel manager for a small pharmaceuticals firm when her children were still small, and later taught economics and business management, introducing courses at both Slough and Hendon to prepare college students for membership of the Institute of Personnel Management. Since retiring, she has become involved with the Fawcett Society.

Like her parents, Hilda Brown has had a lifelong concern with creating a better society and has endeavoured to combine this with leading as full a life as possible whatever the circumstances. Her life has not been without its difficulties: her eldest brother was a prisoner of war in Singapore and died a week before VJ Day. In 1960, she was suddenly widowed and left to raise two children singlehanded. Her brilliant younger sister, after becoming the first student to take a degree in Chinese at Oxford, married a Chinese fellow student and went to live in China, enduring a four-year imprisonment between 1968 and 1972. Since then Hilda Brown has visited China on many occasions.

While she is still involved in campaigning for political and social *change, Hilda Brown balances her life with such diverse pursuits as bell-ringing, piano-playing and learning Chinese. She has two grown-up daughters and three granddaughters.*

The interview took place at her home in London in 1991 where the warm and serene atmosphere made a welcome contrast to the damp, cold day outside. She expressed surprise that anyone should be interested in her story.

I was born in Tientsin in North China. My parents were missionary teachers and they met in China. They were both Lancashire people. He was a very deep-thinking person and rather reserved and shy, whereas my mother was rather sociable. She probably courted him, rather than the other way round. He proposed to her on the Wall of Peking, apparently, so their wedding cake was iced with the Wall of Peking. My mother was an unusual individual. She was the first woman to get a degree in science at Manchester University, I suppose at the beginning of the 1900s, and had been a science teacher in England. She went to China with the London Missionary Society just before the First World War. My father had already gone in 1908. He was also a scientist. He showed brilliance as a mathematician at school, but he wanted to be of service to society, so he studied chemistry at university – he thought that would be more useful than mathematics – and became an industrial chemist. When this opportunity came to teach chemistry at the Tientsin Anglo-Chinese College, a rather prestigious missionary foundation, he applied for it. As a Christian, he was very concerned about the standard of living of peasants in China, especially North China where you can't farm for about six months of the year because of the climate. He was then Professor of Chemistry at the main university in Peking, the Yenching University, but felt it would be more useful to teach economics, so he converted and became Professor of Economics. He founded the Chinese industrial co-operatives as a way of assisting farmers to get out of debt, to produce more effectively and to raise their standards of

living. It was a very Christian and democratic way of
managing through mutual help systems. With the liberation
under Communism, they were scrapped in favour of the
commune system, but there is some return now to the ideas
that he promoted.

It was such a privileged childhood, even though we were
missionaries and salaries were low compared with business
people in China. Looking back, one can see how separated
even missionary families were from Chinese people. Our
upbringing was as English as it could be made: we celebrated
Empire Day, 24 May, we would go to the British Embassy at
Christmas, we mostly had Western food. The one Chinese
dish that we had as a treat from time to time were those boiled
dumplings with minced meat and cabbage inside which are
called *jiaozi*. We did live in a Chinese-style house, round a
courtyard. We had at least three servants: a cook, a coolie who
pulled our rickshaw, and a nanny, Nai-Nai we called her.
Foreign women would be expected to: you would lose face
terribly if you had no servants.

Nai-Nai had partially bound feet and she [found] it difficult
to keep up with us. My naughty little brother used to rather
play on this, running away from her. I can remember hearing
the little girl crying next door, she was about four, and my
mother said, 'They're binding her feet.' That was still being
done, although it was supposed to be banned [in] 1911.

In the summer when it was too hot to stay in Peking,
mothers and children went to the seaside where the Missionary Society had built houses for the mission families. Our
father only joined us for a short part of that time. It was so
warm you could stay in the sea all day. My brothers got up
games of Robin Hood, so, of course, I was Maid Marian.
There were quite a number of children of various ages there at
the same time. We could run wild. There was this occasion
when Eric Liddell, whose parents had one of these mission
houses, had come back to China having just won the gold
medal at the 1924 Olympics, and he saw us running races on
the beach. He said he would race with us, and we all set off,

and I can still see him now, almost running on the spot, and just winning the race in front of the fastest of us.

We came back from China in 1926 when I was nine, because of the fighting, and I started at Walthamstow Hall, the mission school, as a boarder. I went to school in Peking, but it was always intended that we should come back to school, so we didn't learn Chinese in China, to our regret now. We came back on a steamer and that meant six weeks of travel. My mother had us five children and she got my elder brothers and myself to help her with the ironing on the boat. She would give them a little pocket money for doing the ironing, but I said, very proudly, 'I will do it for love.' I realise now my mistake! [As a child] I had the misfortune of being rather good and well-behaved. I was regarded as Little Mother. I didn't realise at the time that being kind-hearted and obliging is how women get imposed on.

Through my school years, I felt that boarding school was home. We stayed with our guardian in Sevenoaks during the holidays, or visited our aunt or other relatives. The school had fairly advanced ideas about allowing girls to grow up with privacy, and instead of all sleeping in dormitories we had our own cubicles. And the teachers were quite inspiring. I can remember the history teacher's eyes flashing as she talked about Garibaldi and the Italian Risorgimento, and about the French Revolution, when 'it was bliss to be alive, but to be young was very heaven'! There was a real feeling of family at school because the parents often knew each other on the mission field. There were two girls whose parents had been married with my parents in Tientsin, a joint wedding. When later we sent our daughters to that school, the head had been in the sixth form when I was at school, and the housemistress had also been an old girl.

School seemed like home. It was a life quite separate. My parents seemed very far away, very remote. Of course, we were in regular contact with letters and it was always a great thrill to get letters. My mother was a very good correspondent. I never got very close to my father, [he] being this rather

1a Helen Brook, aged five, with her mother at Pett Level in Sussex in 1912

1b Helen Brook in 1936.

1c Helen Brook at the seventieth anniversary of the East Street Clinic in 1991.

2a Lucy Faithfull (*front row, centre*) with the
Senior Girls' Club at the Birmingham Settlement in 1932.

2b One of the tasks of students at the Birmingham Settlement
was to collect money for the Provident Bank. Lucy Faithfull
is pictured here collecting in Brearley Street in 1932.
These back-to-back houses were later demolished.

3a Josephine Barnes receiving her doctorate from Oxford in 1941. She was only the ninth woman to do so.

3b Josephine Barnes performing a caesarian section at University College Hospital in 1943.

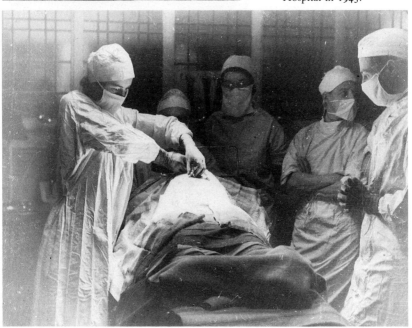

4a Sheila Parkinson at the
Buckingham Palace Investiture,
November 1977, having been awarded
her OBE for services to the FANYs.

4b Hilda Brown
with her husband
and younger daughter
in 1951.

4c Hilda Brown, aged twenty-two, with the Civilian
Anti-Gas School during her time as welfare officer
for Crosse and Blackwell in Dublin in 1938–9.

5a Jean Graham Hall, aged eight, on holiday in Bognor in 1925.

5b Jean Graham Hall (*third from left*) in procession to Croydon Parish Church for the Mayor's Service in 1985.

5c Mary Smith, on behalf of the Peabody Trust, handing over a contribution for the modernisation of the Southall Day Centre in May 1990.

6a Livia Gollancz in 1950 during her time as principal horn for the Sadler's Wells Opera. This was her last job as a professional musician.

6b Livia Gollancz became director of the publishing firm Victor Gollancz Ltd after her father's death in 1968. She is pictured here in the firm's Covent Garden office in the early 1970s.

7a Una Kroll (*second row on left*) on the Cambridge Women's Swimming Team in 1945, during her time as a medical student at Girton College. The following year she captained the team and was awarded a half blue.

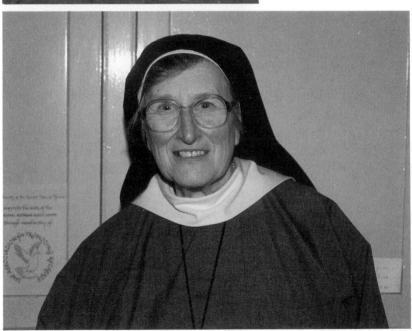

7b After the death of her husband, Una Kroll joined Tymawr Convent in Wales in 1990 as a novice sister.

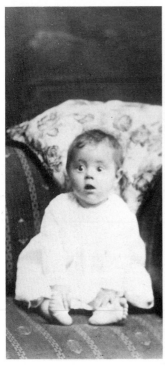

8a Betty Boothroyd
at her home in Dewsbury,
West Yorkshire,
in early 1930.

8b In May 1973,
aged forty-four,
Betty Boothroyd won
the West Bromwich
by-election, a seat
she still holds today.

8c Betty Boothroyd
made political and
feminist history in 1992
when she became Speaker
of the House of Commons,
the first woman to hold
the post in Parliament's
600 years.

reserved person and away so much of the time. He was pioneering many things in China and very absorbed by his university work, so he was very often in China while my mother spent quite a number of those years with us in England, unlike most missionary mothers. My mother wasn't someone who [you] could really share your worries or inner ideas with, because she was very ambitious for all of us. Looking back, one can see that there was pressure to do well. My mother took the view that we should all get a degree and be prepared to take up some career. I have always been very grateful that she did assume that the daughters would have this as well as the sons. It's certainly an insurance if one is left on one's own, as I was later.

The school supported various good causes like the Childrens' Country Holiday Fund and the Peckham Street Settlement. [The settlement] ran a week when middle-class children were to go along and see what life was like. I represented my school and then had to go back and give a talk. Was I only fourteen? That was when I really began to move into the idea that we needed to change society. It was the sight of the slums and realising these girls were earning their living at that age. Certainly I had a social conscience by the time I left school.

I went to LSE [London School of Economics] in 1935. It was a very exciting time; in fact, I couldn't imagine that real life existed anywhere else except in London. How could one dream of living anywhere else? So much was going on. The Spanish Civil War began in 1936, so one was thrown very quickly into the politics. I remember being told by somebody that LSE was a 'hotbed of communism' and what a dangerous thing for a young girl from boarding school to go there. But I survived. I shared a flat in Wapping with a girl in my year whose brother used to read Marx's *Das Kapital* on his way to work and had it in a brown paper cover so that it wouldn't show what he was reading. That was the kind of feeling.

I've never been aggressively political or extreme, but my views on life did develop during the time I was at LSE. There were three professors whom I particularly admired. One, for the way he gave his lectures, was Harold Laski who lectured us on politics. The main one was R. H. Tawney who lectured in social history and was a Christian Socialist. He helped to unveil the injustices of the life of the poor. He had met my father when he went to China to look at the agrarian society there, so I was invited to tea at this great man's house in London. Again I just didn't feel I was quite as grown-up as I'd like to have been for the occasion. Dr Eileen Power was a beautiful lecturer, it was a pleasure to listen to her. Both she and Professor Tawney lectured on economic history and helped to fashion my view of the need for socialism and political change. I threw myself into the various societies: the Student's Union, the Cosmopolitan Club, the Student Christian Movement. I helped campaigns for election of some of the Socialist candidates. And I certainly grew up, in the adolescent sense, at LSE. I began to meet men for the first time and be taken out. I was very shy of men. I wasn't quite sure how to approach them. I remember my mother saying, 'Just be yourself,' but one isn't quite sure what oneself is at that age.

In my third year at LSE I took an unofficial course in labour management and worked for a while at a settlement in East London. I couldn't see what I was going to offer these girls who were so much older in maturity and outlook on life; I was not in the position to tell them anything about life. I also arranged through my elder brother, who was an industrial chemist, to go for a month to be a factory hand. Factory girls now would be too sophisticated to accept you [as one of them]. I helped pack choc-bars on a conveyor belt. I was not at all nimble, and I remember the supervisor saying, 'What's she doing at the end?' You had to make sure that all the bars that hadn't been packed before they came to the end, didn't all fall off into the sack, you had to have got them into the boxes. I was put [back] down the line. One of the girls said, 'You should be a telephone operator, you speak so nice.' I stayed with one of them in the East End – and that was also a revelation: of getting into this bed with her, these rather grubby sheets, getting up in the morning, not having any breakfast, off we went. I felt I was in grave danger of picking up all sorts of infectious diseases. Certainly my relatives were.

While I was at LSE, I was still thinking in terms of taking up some profession that would be of service to society. That had been so much in my own background and upbringing. I decided that my contribution to society would be to help the lot of the women working in factories by going into personnel management. When I completed my degree a post was advertised in Dublin, at a factory run by Crosse and Blackwell's, and I went to an interview in London and was appointed.

Dublin was a capital city and yet it was like a village in some ways. I was the welfare officer at this factory, interviewing girls to take them on. I was supposed to make sure they didn't arrive late in the morning and I had to go round the factory talking to the supervisors, and finding out whether the girls were working all right. I say 'girls' because there was still a marriage bar and you couldn't work once you'd got married – as applied also in most factories in England. They were mostly round their twenties. My age didn't matter: the fact that I was English gave me status in the factory. We had a social club, and I remember one male factory worker very bravely asked me to dance and shaking all over with the temerity of it! I had a very happy time there. It was only a year and a half, because then the War had broken out, and I felt I would be more part of the war effort if I went back to England.

I started in Walsall in Staffordshire, on the edge of the Black Country. It proved to be a fascinating area in which to learn about factory inspection. At the beginning of the War there were premises which could have come out of Dickens's time. But because more and more women were being recruited with no experience, more care had to be taken. Much better lighting was brought in, for instance, during the War, and better facilities. You trained on the job, what we called 'rabbits', little jobs, to get used to going round. One gradually got the idea of what to look for. The more experienced inspectors would handle the more dangerous factories, the chemical works and power presses. The District Inspector of Factories was in charge of the district, and the junior inspectors divide the territory and go round to see that the Factories Act is being applied properly. That covers safety, health and employment. The biggest aspect was safety of workers but there are all kinds of premises, some that have no mechanical power, so there wasn't the same safety problem, and the bits of the law that mattered were to do with employment and facilities – proper washing and lavatory facilities and so on. One of the great attractions was it was not a nine-to-five office job. You went out on your own and planned your programme for the day. We used to do night inspection as well.

You learnt, as they say, on the job. You were thrown pretty quickly into taking the responsibility. It did mean that you immediately had the full-blown powers of an inspector, the right of entry; the employer could not keep you out. I remember on one Sunday inspection, going into a factory where the women were working and should not have been. While I was busy taking statements from them the manager came storming in, but I just calmly went on with my job. When we did take them to court, he actually said how he appreciated that I'd dealt with it in such a professional way. You just have to know you're right and not be intimidated. Intimidation was one thing, another was that they keep you at the factory gate while they rush around and put the guards on the machines. You have to go unannounced, and try and find things as they really are.

I did find visiting factories very interesting. Iron foundries, glass-making, power presses . . . I was in for six years. And it was a well-paid job for a woman. Equal pay had not come in for women, there weren't many well-paid opportunities, and a woman with a degree would tend to go into teaching. This was better paid than teaching, and certainly suited me a lot better. And it being wartime, one felt one was taking part in a national effort, this was something which needed to be done: it was providing a service to employers, it wasn't purely a policing arrangement. You were influencing them, not just taking them to court. I found it a very exciting period of my life. I was young for one thing, and so were a number of the inspectors. We had this status and responsibility: employers treated us with great respect. [Being] outsiders, the inspectors formed a very close-knit community and we had plenty of social life among ourselves. We used to pool petrol, which was rationed, and go to Snowdonia, four or five of us, all young people, unmarried. It was a very exciting time.

It was there that I met my husband who was also an inspector in that district. He was [later] appointed to run a research project out in Buxton at the Safety in Mines Research Station and I was sent down to Richmond in Surrey. That separation was when we realised we wanted to get married and stay together. Because of the shortage of inspectors during the War, I was able to say, 'I'm leaving Richmond to get married. Can you find a district for me up in Derbyshire?' So they fitted me in up there – most unusual for the civil service to be so thoughtful. The marriage bar was removed during the War, so I carried on as an inspector. Prior to that, some women inspectors did live 'in sin', as it was called, so as not to be disbarred from [their] career. We lived in Matlock, so that he could travel to Buxton on the train and I could travel to Derby where my office was.

It seemed the natural thing, to get married. I was rather modest over my chances. I'd always thought it very unlikely that I would find anyone who wanted to marry me, but it was what I'd hoped to be able to do, so I didn't need much persuasion! He was thirty-five when we got married and I was twenty-six. He'd been a reserved man whose interests had been playing the piano and reading, and he saw himself rather as a confirmed bachelor. It was a shock when he found himself with two children and so on! He had been brought up by his aunts and I'm afraid I didn't really live up to his expectations, or rather his experience, at first. I was no cook – naturally, that was my domain, cooking. It all seemed a great labour.

Fortunately, he had his midday dinner at work, which was common in the North, and during the War, so I hadn't to worry quite so much about the evening meal. Even peeling potatoes for two people seemed to me a tremendous undertaking. We did have a cleaner in Matlock. She used to arrive in her fur coat, she was much better dressed that I was! She was glad to have this domestic job to save being sent to a factory to work. So she did the cleaning, but she didn't do any cooking.

We'd been married three years before we decided to start a family and then I gave in my notice as an inspector. My husband felt he was quite incompetent when it came to babies; he just assumed that women were competent and had hidden reserves of energy, and left it to me. But he became much more of a modern parent than would have seemed possible initially. He adapted very well to bathing the babies and so on and became much more involved with them as they got older. He would read to them and play nursery rhymes and music for them to dance to before bedtime. He was good at those things, but I don't think he ever changed a nappy.

I did remain a Christian until after I was married. My husband had been brought up in a religious family, but by the time I met him he was not a churchgoer or believer. And gradually I questioned it in my mind and lost faith. At school I had been very devout and, of course, as children we believed in God. My parents had tremendous faith and felt they were doing God's work, but they didn't preach. They believed that it's how you live and 'by your fruits shall ye be known'. I remember my mother saying, 'I don't want you [just] to believe what we believe. I want you to find out for yourself.' Which for a missionary is quite an unusual approach. I went to LSE a very dedicated Christian, but it was [there] that I met my friend, Betty Scharf, who had been brought up as a Humanist. I'd never met an English person who had not been brought up as a Christian before, so this was quite revealing. I suppose you grow out of it: if you start to think about faith, what it consists of and what it's based on, you start to question it. I had this idea that ethics was the important part, rather than how one expressed one's faith. I think that goodness has always been the hallmark for me; how you lived was the important thing.

I began to get a little restive. I was getting on, because my first baby was born when I was thirty, and I was wanting to do something to use my background and skills. I heard of this organisation based in Manchester set up to find part-time careers for women graduates, and wrote to put my name on the list. The first job that I was offered was teaching arithmetic at a technical college in Stockport for day-release students. It was only one day a week for two hours. But that was the start of other things. The next job was as a personnel officer at a pharmaceutical company at Hazelgrove near Stockport. I went for an interview, and I had very much the qualifications they wanted, but when I got home, I rang up and said, 'No, I couldn't take the job, because of holidays.' The works director said, 'Well, how much holiday would you like?' Which took me aback. I felt I couldn't ask for more than a month, though that still wouldn't cover [the children's] holidays. I developed myself in that job, as well as developing the job. I was forty, and the only woman on the management team. I did the job for three years, 1957–60, on a part-time basis, which was unusual then.

Then my husband was transferred south. Both the girls were then at boarding school, so it meant I was free, and I was going for an interview for a new town development housing supervisor, something of that kind, on the day that he died.

It was such a shock. It came out of the blue on his way to work. Shock cushions you for a while. I didn't get my full energies back for a whole year after. An aunt of mine said he would have been pleased to see that I was trying to cope and keep things going, and that, I suppose, was my response, really: that having the children, I must make life as normal as possible for them. I was glad they were at boarding school, which was easier for them than to have a single parent family. If they'd just been at home with me, I would have leant on them emotionally, much more than I would have done with a husband. But it's the lack of companionship that is immediately so shattering, and, of course, the loss of sexual satisfaction, which we'd always enjoyed so much. But that wasn't the biggest loss by any means, it was this not having anyone to talk to and share things with. I started turning to my various friends for company and for holidays. At work I felt fortunate that I was single not because of a divorce, but because I was a widow. It did make it easier to hold up my head. I knew I hadn't been neglected or walked out on. And I'm so thankful that I have children, which at the time made life important and worthwhile, and who are such a comfort and such good companions now.

There's no replacement, you never get back what you've lost, but I've filled my life with all sorts of interesting things. When you're married, you're so busy contributing to the home and the family, it's very difficult to find time for outside things. Your focus is much more on the present circumstances. But after I was widowed and began to wonder what the rest of the world was doing, I became more politically active. I've always had that socialist inclination, and believed that the government ought to control private interests for the public good. When I was on my own, I could do things which I wouldn't have wanted to take the time to do if we had been together: going to meetings and classes. Belonging to women's groups, which provides a network of friendships and relationships, is particularly appealing to women who are on their own. It's much harder for a married woman to have the time or the inclination to pursue things which would be separate from her husband.

My husband died in 1960, and I had to think about full-time work. I started teaching at Hendon technical college, now Middlesex University, the same year. It kept me very occupied and my previous experience of personnel management and factory inspection, and of the part-time jobs I did when I was still in Buxton, was so valuable.

One of the very first [part-time] jobs was giving lectures to supervisors from ICI quarries. They were concerned with lime processing and quarrying, a completely male activity, so it was a great shock to see a woman, but I managed to present to them some of the modern thinking on human relations in management. I always remember one of them saying, apropos treating people as adults, 'Well, if you're not shouting, they don't listen. They don't think you're speaking [to them]. You have to shout.' There was such a gulf between how things were practised in the old days and these modern ideas of management.

The other [part-time] job was interviewing women shift workers about the effects of shift work on social and domestic life. Shift working was something the government wanted to introduce much more widely, to create greater productivity from the limited machinery we had after the War, get more out of the capital. I had to design my own research programme and I found that interesting.

There was great sex discrimination when I first went to Hendon. The head of our department was a very autocratic gentleman; the women teachers had the secretarial girls and the men did the technical things and management. I was the only woman appointed to the management group. One day the head of department passed the classroom where I was talking to the supervisors and heard a burst of laughter, so he threw open the door to see what improper things were going on, saw me just standing in front of them, everything was quiet and proper, so he nodded his head and went out again. The women had [a separate] staff room and one time I was in the men's staff room when this head of department came in, and he said, 'What are you doing here?' I said, 'I have to consult my colleagues.' 'Well, don't do it again,' he said, and walked out. That was how it was then. It's changed, of course, since more women have come into management teaching and the secretarial courses have gone and the degree courses have come in.

Another thing we did was to put on courses for the officers as they were demobbed after the War, to help them to decide what jobs in Civvy Street they should take up. I had to go and talk to them about industrial relations, because that was something completely outside their army experience. That was rather alarming at first – these men in their fifties, brigadiers, and majors, all sitting there. To them, industrial relations was subversive. Shop stewards and union people were seen almost as enemies of the country. I rather enjoyed establishing an authority with these officers. I remember saying once, 'I'm going to read something to you. I don't expect you've been read to for a long time.' It was about Lord Shaftesbury introducing the Factories Act and the state of the employment in those days. I found it quite rewarding to meet people with such a different outlook and gradually come to terms with them.

With the introduction of the diploma courses in personnel management, Hilda Brown was invited to set up a course at Slough College. For five years she was senior lecturer at Slough, teaching economics and running their personnel course. She then returned to Hendon to teach industrial sociology on the business studies degree course.

There was increasing pressure on people at that time to have post-graduate qualifications, and I was persuaded to enrol at the LSE to do an MA, under the supervision of Nancy Seear, now Baroness Seear. I had started some research in Walsall for the Foundry Industry Training Board, who wanted to have some idea of the backgrounds of foundry managers. I was looking at what was happening in recruitment into management. Traditionally in England, the foreman or supervisor is somebody who does well on the shop floor and is promoted and doesn't go any further because he's a working-class man who has no education. He had the craft, but not education. But after the War, with the eleven-plus, theoretically the best brains were chosen to go on to the grammar school, and people then would be qualified to be managers. I wrote a paper on it and gave a talk on my findings to the Foundry Industry Training Board, but it was not a large enough piece of work and never finally took off as an MA or a PhD.

When I was coming near to retirement I joined the Fawcett Society, because I was very impressed by what the pioneering women had done to achieve the vote for women. One realises these things have to be fought for. I've become more convinced as I have become more involved that women are disadvantaged in the world of work and in their status in society; their needs are not taken into sufficient consideration. I've found it very rewarding to work in the campaigns to improve opportunities for women. And that's been quite time-consuming in recent years. I helped in a survey of opportunity for girls in the Government's Youth Training Scheme, showing that they missed out on the really worth-while trainings. I did a study on women in part-time work – their lack of protection from unfair dismissal; lack of redundancy payment if they are dismissed; lack of protection for pregnancy dismissal. Often they don't get company benefits like holidays and sick pay; they're treated as marginal labour at minimum cost to the employer when in fact so many of them depend on the money they earn. This seems quite an unnecessary form of discrimination. Then there are the Positive Action Awards, set up to bring to public notice anything that is successfully done to positively advantage women. One award was for getting girls into science, one was for training for women returners, another was for eighteen- to twenty-five-year-olds who missed out in proper education and training earlier. It's been a very worthwhile activity, and it's taken a lot of work too.

Since I retired I've become more and more involved with China. I got my O level in Chinese while I was still working, and I've now taken the A level course, but I haven't attempted the examination. Piano lessons and Chinese lessons have been two of my busiest things. I went for my first skiing holiday in March, and I've taken up bell-ringing – I rang my first peal when I was seventy, which takes nearly three hours. There is a shortage of bell-ringers nationally, so I go every Sunday morning and get called to ring for weddings on a Saturday. One is a much slower learner when older, but it takes you out of yourself. You're so absorbed that even if you're very tired, you feel relaxed afterwards.

I've had a very fortunate life. At every stage there's been good things: having such unusual parents who gave us every opportunity educationally; being born abroad, which made one's life different from other people; a loving, close-knit family. Even the fact that we were boarders and not with our parents had many compensations. My childhood experiences were marvellous; they were a good foundation for life. Being at university at a time of great social change, of political excitement, was interesting too. And it was a very happy time when I was married. My husband and I shared values and enjoyed so much together. Even after I was widowed, and had to create a new life with these two children, I was young enough to start again, and I got tremendous satisfaction in finding that I could hold my own with male colleagues at the college, and establish something of a reputation in running these courses.

It's hard to reconcile oneself to living alone. Solitude is not part of human nature really. I did have a man friend for a short time, but it turned out he was married and I wouldn't have wanted to break up a relationship. I should feel very sorry if I'd never married and had children, so that is something to be proud of, pleased with. Having children gives you a future in life. So these years also, since I've been on my own, have had their satisfactions. I wish I had been more confident when I was younger; timidity has made life poorer than it should have been. So many opportunities and friendships were lost from lack of confidence. I still lack it, but at least there is a bit more knowledge of self. I'm a little more sure of myself than I was! I realise now that one needs to relax and enjoy the artistic and pleasurable things, not strive so much. I don't expect to go to the top, and I'm quite happy not to. I remember at school one of my friends saying she didn't know whether she should buy scented soup, because it wasn't necessary – these were the things that used to worry us: how pure and Christian should you be? Well, I've come to the conclusion that life should be much more balanced between self-seeking and helping others. I certainly don't aspire to changing the world any more.

JEAN GRAHAM HALL

Jean Graham Hall was born on 26 March 1917 in Inverkeithing, Fifeshire. After school in Surrey, she studied social work at the London School of Economics, and during that time she lived and worked at St Margaret's House Settlement, Bethnal Green. Both the LSE and the settlement had a profound effect in shaping her social and political attitudes. In 1937 she joined the Birmingham University Settlement, where she eventually became sub-warden. She left in 1941 to become the secretary of Eighteen Plus, a youth experiment, and ultimately to train as a probation officer. After six years' probation work in Gosport, Fareham and Croydon, she decided to take a degree in law, and in 1951 began her pupillage in the Temple. Unusual and disadvantaged in being a woman, left-wing, non-Oxbridge and trained in social work, she overcame the odds. She was the first woman president of the Gray's Inn Debating Society, and secretary of the Society of Labour Lawyers. In 1965 she was made a stipendiary magistrate and in 1971 she became a circuit judge.

There are currently 480 judges in England of whom twenty-seven are women.

A committed socialist, Jean Graham Hall has worked consistently throughout her career for the rights of women and children. She chaired a Government Committee on Statutory Maintenance Limits from 1966 to 1968, which resulted in there being no limit set to the amount a woman could get from her husband in the magistrate's courts. She has also written a number of influential legal books and articles. She was a pioneer of family courts and has co-written books on child abuse, crimes against children and expert evidence. In 1992 she finally retired from the bench, but not from legal and social work.

She is currently working on the problem of international child abduction and is still lobbying for the creation of family courts. She is involved with the International Federation of Women Lawyers and is a patron of the Multiple Births Foundation. Her hobbies include theatre, travelling and seeing friends, and she likes nothing more than a 'well-put-together lecture with a discussion afterwards'. She never married and has no children of her own, but is an enthusiastic great-aunt and godmother.

Jean Graham Hall lives on the outskirts of London within view of the site of her old school, now a block of flats. The interview took place at her home in December 1991 after a lunch of homemade lasagne and strawberries.

All my family were in some way connected with paper. My paternal grandfather had started off, as my father did, in a small shop in Edinburgh, selling paper there. My maternal grandfather had been the head foreman in a mill in Mid-Lothian. Overnight there was a mill fire and he lost his job, so that very morning after the fire, with his wife and four children, one of which was my mother, he went to Inver-keithing, and that's where my father and mother met, at the Caldwells Paper Mills in Inverkeithing. The mill is still there but I believe the name has changed. He had some executive position and my mother was his secretary.

[We lived in] a mill house called Umbella, it was ten minutes' walk from the mill, ten minutes' walk from the school and ten minutes' walk from the station. Opposite was a bowling green, which my brother tells me has shrunk in the years. I can remember the bowling green. And I remember us having the first wireless in the town, before 1924. And I can remember going to the cricket pavilion as a child, when my father was playing for the mill. My mother [didn't] have any [help] in the house. It wasn't a question of affording it, it didn't come into our world at all; we didn't live in that kind of world.

I never think of ours as a loving, close family, but clearly we were. My mother was always there when we came home from school. It never occurred to me that she wouldn't be. And when my elder brother, Robert, and I were at the primary school, my father used to come home from the mill for lunch every day. Later I wished they had shown more physical affection toward me, more touching, cuddling, [but] that wasn't the Scottish way of doing things at all. I'm always sorry about that. But we must have been fairly family oriented. My aunts lived in the same town, as did my grandma, and they used to come and see us every day. Their brother lived nearby in Rosyth and my father's relatives were in Edinburgh, which was only about thirteen miles away. So in the early years, we saw a great deal of our relatives.

My mother had a gentle temperament. My father used to say that he'd chosen the best of the three sisters. She was a tenacious woman. She left school, as he did, at fourteen, but she could write a beautiful letter. It was from her I learnt how to write letters of condolence to people. She simply wrote from the heart, in rather a pretty, easy-to-read handwriting. As she got older, she learnt how to enjoy other things, like reading Trollope. She was a woman who never thought of being other than devoted to her house and her children and didn't consider it a burden either. The great trauma for her was when we came to England, to Sanderstead. My father was promoted to be the representative of the mill in London. I was seven, my brother Robert was nine and a half, and Graham was three and a half. That was a tremendously traumatic experience for her. She might as well have been going to the Arctic Waste. But my mother wasn't the kind of person who would moan or do anything of that kind. She just decided to get on with whatever she had to do and made a life for herself and us as well. It was a marriage that was solid, lasting. It never occurred to them to do anything except make a good marriage. In the world they lived in they just expected to be married and manage and have children and be ambitious [for them]. It was [a marriage] really deeply rooted in normality.

I have my father's temperament. Much more volatile. My younger brother has it too. My father was for his wife and his children. He enjoyed the company of his children. I remember when he bought us all bicycles. Just my elder brother and I were going to have bicycles, and he took the three of us along to the railway station, and my younger brother said, 'Oh, look, Dad, there's a third bicycle just my size!' and my father said, 'Really? Well, why don't you try it.' He'd bought three, you see; he liked doing that kind of thing. Within the limits of their budget, they certainly did all they could for their children. [They] believed in a good education; that they did give us. [I had] a normal happy childhood. It's no good saying I had a marvellously happy childhood, nor a very unhappy one, neither would be true. It's stability they gave the three of us, and I'm more conscious of it now than I was then.

Throughout her teens, Jean Graham Hall became increasingly concerned about social injustice and increasingly determined that something should and could be done about it. Although she was studying for a teaching diploma in dramatic arts and elocution, she decided that her real ambition was to become a social worker. Using the logical approach that would stand her in good stead throughout her career, she determined the course and the place of study. Her father, however took some convincing.

He wasn't keen for me to go to university, especially not to the London School of Economics, but I was determined. I wanted to study social work at the London School of Economics, no other place would do. [I wanted] to change the world and have a place where everyone had enough to eat, and everyone had a doctor and all those simple things which people certainly did not have in the early thirties. I agreed with my parents to finish off my other qualifications so that when, as my father saw it, I fell away from my – he would have said, 'socialist views' – I could do something reasonable, like teaching. My mother persuaded him to pay for one term, saying, 'The girl deserves as much a chance in life as the boys, and she works hard and she's quite clever.' Having persuaded him, he walked with me to the door [of LSE]. I'm not sure he kissed me, but he certainly made it quite clear he wanted me to do well. Any night that I was late, he would walk the dog down and meet me [from the station].

He had to turn his whole ideas round to accommodate me and my views. He had to accommodate the fact that the girl was the one who had not only ability, which the boys had, but some determination and stickability. I was going into worlds that they'd certainly never been into. He and my mother didn't encourage me to do any of the things that I did, but when I had made up my mind what I wanted to do, and made it clear, then they would help me. They could see that I was keen to study, keen to get on, keen to conquer the little world in which I was doing things. Other girls [at school] had as much talent as I had, and probably more, but I was able to channel it: I could always see the immediate goal, everything I had to do next seemed very obvious.

The social science department at the LSE was not at all politically oriented, but there were very strong political influences. Miss Eileen Younghusband at the LSE was one of the great social work teachers of all time and had a tremendous influence. Aneurin Bevan, Sir Austen Chamberlain, Laski, Ginsberg, Tawney: I heard all of them speaking while I was at LSE. I've always loved the teacher, the guru, the one who is going to tell you things. At St Anne's College in Sanderstead there was a woman called Miss Skinner who taught me elocution and dramatic art. She had a great influence. I remember Miss Skinner writing in my autograph album, 'Genius is an infinite capacity for taking pains,' and this I decided was correct. I was eighteen when I started at the LSE and [still living] at home, and I must have been, in their terms, fairly left-wing. [There would be] discussions that ended in shouting sometimes with my father. I had ideas he didn't always want to accept, but he enjoyed the arguments, I don't think either of us would have missed [them].

During her time at LSE she spent two months living at St Margaret's House Settlement, Bethnal Green, in the East End of London. As part of her social work course she also visited the area regularly.

That was a new world opening out to me. It was a world I'd never known, couldn't believe it existed this way. You'd find a mother who just couldn't go to the doctor, she didn't have the money, the father would go because he was the wage earner and he'd got to be well. If there wasn't enough food to go round, the mother didn't have the food. There were people in real poverty in those days. I wanted to do something that was worthwhile. I'm not sure exactly what motivated me. I didn't go [to the settlement] with ideas, I got the ideas when I was there. Hearing Mosley speak, seeing the terrible poverty: thirteen people to a room, one tap [for the whole landing], unbelievable conditions I'd never seen before . . . I just wished to be part of the process by which things were fairer. I was very keen on equality – egality's always seemed a marvellous idea – and I realised there were some people who had to be helped enormously to get started. We took some of the children to the Zoo on the tram. They hadn't been on trams before and some of them never to the Zoo. I'm sure there were lots of other people doing these kinds of things, but they were important to me.

It was where I lived and what I saw that made me aware. In elocution classes I was aware of wonderful poetry and how that could express things that I certainly couldn't, beautiful ways of putting things, and the rhythm of words, but it wasn't anything to do with social class. In Bethnal Green I could see that some people simply did not have the same chance as others. They just did not have it. It's quite a set-back to one's idea of life to go to your first interview in the East End of London in a very nice navy suit with a hat to match, and see children without any shoes on. I had no time at all in those days for, as I saw them, toffee-nosed public school people. Miss Kelly, the warden of the settlement at St Margaret's, would say to me, 'Hall,' – she always called me by my surname – she would say, 'Hall, sometimes you know you must give other people the opportunity of giving, and you must learn not to think you can do everything for them.'

In 1935, after LSE I went to live in Birmingham at the

University Settlement. I was the club leader to begin with, ran all the girls' clubs, ran the camp in the summer: I had to take examinations in camping. I had to go to the Guides and learn how to camp, how to strike a bell tent. I wasn't very good at the cooking and I never had the right knickers. Later, I became the sub-warden at Birmingham, under Molly Batten. Some of the people at the settlement had deep religious ideas, and we had prayers before dinner every night, but I was conscious of *social* influences: these awful back-to-back houses with the girls never being able to wash properly; one lavatory for five houses. It was a time of terrible unemployment and the girls used to come back from work and give their fathers pocket money. It was dreadful. Terrible conditions. I don't know what I thought I had to give them, but the girls taught me so much. They were rough, wonderful girls. We used to have a netball team and they used to play in hair curlers on a Saturday afternoon because we had the dance at night. We used to go through Birmingham with their hair in curlers. They taught me about gaiety and life, and they taught me to dance! And when the clubs were over at night, we would sit down by the fire and have a cup of cocoa and discuss the world. It was a great experience. I used to get a bus from Birmingham centre out to the settlement and the bus conductor would repeat the words above the door, 'Birmingham Settlement, Service Above Self.' You'd have to crawl off the bus with everybody looking at you. One of my brothers said he'd got real respect for me when he realised where I was living, but I never needed any respect, I was happy, I just thought this was the centre of the universe.

Whenever you do something you find it isn't the ultimate answer; your ideas change, so you must try something else. It had gradually dawned on me that group motivation wasn't enough and I must try and do things individually. So [eventually] I applied to the Home Office to be a probation officer. We had a three-month course and an awful lot of lectures about sex. Oh, dear, dear, dear! We used to go round to the pub at night and you could scarcely hold anybody's hand in the dark it so overwhelmed you. They made us totally uninterested in the subject personally. I was the best qualified of the group, because nobody had a Social Science Certificate except me. I'd realised by then that if a woman wants to get anywhere, she's got to be better qualified than anyone just to get started.

> Her first job as a Probation Officer was at Gosport and Fareham in 1945. Her work there as a guardian ad litem in adoption cases became a lifelong interest, and she later lectured on the subject for the Home Office and wrote documents for the Department of Health looking into adoption procedures. In 1946 she left Gosport and for the next five years she was a probation officer in Croydon.

We had a lot of teenage girls who were on probation for something like theft, handling stolen goods, assault. That was just the sore on their personality, if you like, their real problems were much deeper. They were rejected, often by their parents, and you really did see how much childhood [experiences matter]. I also had to do a certain amount of conciliation work and divorce. It was much more difficult then to get a divorce, the grounds just weren't there. Often the solicitor just couldn't see a way legally. I'm [not whole-heartedly in favour of easy divorce], I would like to see far more done in the way of reconciliation. And certainly I would like to see far more conciliation, making suitable arrange-ments about the children in particular. We don't spend nearly enough money on that. The people who cannot bear divorce are the children. No question about that. The child wants the parents to be together. I don't think they notice the quarrelling and the arguments and the unhappiness. Sometimes the parents can get on quite well when they're separated and satisfied, but you're never going to satisfy the child, ever. It seems impossible to make them feel other than deprived and upset. As people often make a mess of their second go, it does seem a pity that more effort isn't taken over the first. Australia and New Zealand, places I know well in this respect, make much more effort than we do here. A skilled counsellor can have an enormous effect.

During six years as a probation officer, she realised that 'casework wasn't the complete answer to the world's problems', and began studying at night for a law degree at the University of London. The plan was to go into the Home Office Inspectorate. She completed the degree three years later in 1950, by which time she had begun to think about a career at the Bar. A firm believer in the power of qualifications, she decided she had better take a second degree in law. Despite her highly untypical background – a career in social services, left-wing, not a scrap of Oxbridge education, and a woman to boot, in 1950 she made the first steps towards becoming a barrister.

One of the students from the law course took me along to the office at Gray's Inn and I spoke to the secretary. 'Who's sponsoring you?' [he asked]. I said, 'I haven't got a sponsor.' 'You must know somebody, some eminent member of this Inn?' 'No, I don't know anyone except the student that's brought me.' So they took me down to one of the Masters of the Bench and he kindly signed my forms, crossed out 'Him' and put 'Her'. I didn't know anyone. I only had that one sponsor.

I never thought of it as a man's world when I went into it. It wasn't until I got to the Bar and actually started to try and practise that I realised it was a man's world where it was a disadvantage to be a woman. Up till then I'd been in a social worker's world where the women were the best qualified, even as probation officers. When I first started I had great trouble in getting pupillage. If you've been to the Cambridge or Oxford College, or your father was a solicitor, or your uncle was at the Bar, you could get someone to get you into chambers. But I didn't know anyone; I didn't know how to set about it. [When] I got a pupillage in the chambers of Fred Lawton, who later became Lord Justice Lawton, it was made absolutely clear to me by Mr Lawton and by his clerk that I could stay six months and not a day longer. Some chambers would not take women in [at all]. The clerk would say, 'We've only got one lavatory, you know.' I learnt to say, 'Well, I can wait till the others go. I'm not in all that much of a hurry.' Sebag Shaw, later Lord Justice Shaw, and Lord Justice Lawton and Du Cann, the old Duke, they had women pupils, but there were very few. I knew about two other women. We were very dependent upon the goodwill of a few men to begin with. I remember one saying to me, 'Well, you're in your thirties now, you're not a flibbertigibbet coming here to look for a man.' They thought some women were going to the Bar just to find a suitable husband. As if there were any!

I flourished nevertheless, and enjoyed it. I wanted to hold my own. I [still] had to do finals and my Bar exams and I only had enough money for my pupillage. I took out my super-annuation as a probation officer and I did other jobs, market research, all kinds of things. When I was at the Bar and hadn't got any money, I was lecturing part-time at the polytechnics. That's how you learn your law, by lecturing. I'm grateful to at least two chaps, because I certainly wouldn't have studied so hard if I hadn't been personally unhappy. It was [the time] of one of those great unhappinesses of my life. I studied in the first instance because I was unhappy, work was a consolation, and then I got to like studying. Of course I minded terribly when I had [no children] and wasn't going to have any and thought the world had come to an end, but if you're studying you really don't have time for anything else. I wasn't aware of [competitiveness]. All I [was] conscious of [was] the next logical step. I was allowed one shot on the target, like a cowboy: pull a revolver from your hip, one shot on the target and you were home. I knew I had to do well; you were not allowed many chances.

When I came to the Bar, five solicitors said they would brief me – they'd known me as a probation officer. My clerk would really rather have given the work to somebody else who was more competent and I remember going in there one day, and I must have been in a real temper, and banging my hand on the table, and saying, 'Look Edgar, you're doing this to me because I am a woman, because you're afraid. It simply isn't fair. I'm going elsewhere with my five solicitors.' Goodness knows where I was going to go! He didn't want to lose them, so he said, 'All right, Miss Hall.' But I wasn't all that competent. You can't be competent just on one or two cases, you've got to do them endlessly. But there was one firm who kept briefing me when I lost cases. One of the solicitors said to me, 'I will tell you why: because you lose them so well.' He said, 'If we thought we were going to win this case, we would give it to somebody of a different level. If we thought it was a possible win, we would give it to another person. We give you the hopeless cases.' I said, 'Well, I've won two.' He said, 'That's when we made a mistake in giving them to you.' I hadn't realised it was an asset to lose them well.

And sometimes some man wanted to be represented by a woman; they saw [you] as more sympathetic. It wasn't true either way. Nobody I ever represented in my mind was ever guilty. I always thought my clients were innocent. I always saw the point of view of my client and then did my best to put it. The best advocate – and I don't mean me – doesn't really know the client very well. I think women sometimes make a mistake in becoming too allied to the client personally. Your legal adviser is also your substitute mother or surrogate father or whatever, but [it's] much better to have an advocate who isn't so kind and nice. I don't think I was ever the great advocate. I was a good representative, but never the great advocate.

[Most resistence to women came from] the solicitor that didn't want to brief you. If you won, that would be all right, but you only have a fifty per cent chance, often less, and they were afraid that if you lost [they would] have to explain to a wretched client who's on [their] back that it must have been because it was a woman. The fewer reasons they had to explain away the better. Now it isn't like that: there are a number of competent women as solicitors and at the Bar and you don't have to explain it.

I never ignored the solicitors' clerks. They were the sources of your income. They would be the ones who'd give you the small briefs. There'd be a dozen [briefs] that they could hand out, and they would give it to the person they quite liked and who didn't make them feel like nobody. (The arrogance of some young barristers really had to be seen to be believed.) I don't think you have to have a track record of high success, strangely enough, but you have to have some sort of empathy. It won't do to treat the client, whoever it is, in an arrogant fashion, because the solicitor's bread and butter comes from them.

I was doing anything and everything, anything I was given, criminal work mostly. I was regarded by a number of people as wholly incompetent, I think, and they were right. You only become competent through practice and I didn't have enough practice. One day I met a chap at some party and he offered me a job as his private personal representative for £1,000 a year. I said, 'I don't do any typing,' and he said, 'Oh, I don't care. You could run my office.' It was a vast sum of money. I went home and I thought to myself, if I'm worth £1,000 a year to him when I don't even know how to type, I'm not going to do it, I'm going to stick where I am, I must be worth more.

She became the first woman President of the Grays Inn Debating Society and President of the Society of Criminology. She also became increasingly involved with politics and in 1955 stood, unsuccessfully, as the Labour candidate for East Surrey. For eleven years she was secretary for the Society of Labour Lawyers and helped write the legal manifesto for the 1964 Labour Government which led, amongst other things, to the abolition of capital punishment, the creation of the ombudsman and the Law Commission, and raising the age of consent for homosexuals to twenty-one. She describes Gerald Gardiner, chairman of the Society of Labour Lawyers and later Lord Chancellor, as one of her great heroes. When in 1964 the Labour Government was elected, Jean Graham Hall was asked to be a stipendiary magistrate.

I was asked if I would go to the Lord Chancellor's office [to be] interviewed. They told me that the salary was £6,500 a year.

The proper answer to give would have been, 'That's just peanuts to what I'm earning,' but I told the truth. I said, 'I've never earned that much in my life.' I was given a chance: three weeks at Tower Bridge on a sale-or-return basis. They sit for years as deputies now, but not then. So on 5 December 1965 I became a metropolitan stipendiary magistrate and started with enormous pride at Bow Street. You've no idea what you're able to do until you get a chance. The chief magistrate was Sir Robert Blundell. They had a great discussion [about] what loo I should use. Somebody suggested that I could use the women staff [lavatory], but Sir Robert said, 'She's one of us. We won't need to use it at the same time as one another. She can use the same one as I do.' I loved him for that. He had no views on women at all, certainly wasn't *for* them, but once I was in, there was absolute equality. I was so nervous when I was sworn in I could only put about three words together. There hadn't been a woman stipendiary for twenty years, since Miss Sybil Campbell. They were very good to me, the staff, the police, the probation officers, my colleagues, they all wanted me to be a success. I remember one day a man had no money to pay the fine and I didn't know what to do; the jailer stepped forward and said, 'May I suggest one day in default, ma'am?'

I thought I would be a magistrate forever. It was so interesting; it was life itself. I remember looking out of the window one Saturday morning and I actually saw a policeman catch a man. That man was before me in the morning. Within three hours the man had committed the offence, been arrested, charged, come before the court, dealt with, and out. You don't see that nowadays. I would have liked to have been a stipendiary magistrate for longer, I hadn't finished learning, but the Beeching Report* came in and I was asked to be deputy judge at the Quarter Sessions. I sat for eight days before I was appointed. (Now, of course, they have to sit for about six years before they're appointed.) I hadn't been in the

---

* *The Beeching Report on British Railways, published in 1963, which recommended that the railways should be allowed to shed loss-making operations.*

Quarter Sessions for five years, not since I went to the [stipendiary] bench, and I didn't quite know how to do it, but I found Judge West-Russell's notes of what to say to the jury and I read them and adapted them, and I still use them now. That's still the skeleton of my summing-up for the jury. If I use it properly I never go wrong. The Quarter Sessions then became the Crown Courts, and so I became a judge by Act of Parliament. I was sworn in at an annexe of Croydon in one room and immediately sent into another to work. I was so overcome by what I had to do, I hadn't got time for pride.

[Since retirement as a full-time judge, I've enjoyed] being a deputy these last two and a half years. I just like to do something different from last week or month. Week before last I was doing a criminal case. While the jury was out on a robbery, I changed the Crown Court into the County Court, closed it and did a defended custody. I just said, 'This is a County Court. I am now in a divorce hearing.' The judge is a judge and [you] should be able to do anything that comes in front of you. Certainly if you want to be a judge today, you want to be all-purpose. I am aware of the power. I must have it, and I'm going to be obeyed. The other day one of the doctors wasn't going to come to the court, he didn't think it was necessary, so I said to the Crown Prosecution in open court, 'I'll issue you a summons now. If he doesn't answer it, it'll be a warrant.' The court was not going to be defied. That is power, I suppose. And I suppose I do like it. I like to do what I can. But I'm not aware of wielding power. If you ask me in the criminal process what do I like best, I like the trial: all the time you're deciding whether this evidence can be let in; all the time you've got the summing-up you're going to do to the jury. It is absolutely engulfing. The day passes. You don't even know it's begun.

Somebody reminded me the other day at some farewell do that I was the longest sitting woman, and the oldest, and the first to have sat continually in criminal work with a jury. I'd never thought of that. I certainly would never be where I am now [without the support of a number of men during my career]. Never. The women have been individualists. At one time it was suggested we should have a set of women's chambers, but we were determined not to do that, not to be put in a side alleyway. But then the Bar is a very individualistic profession anyway. I don't want to be a 'woman judge'. The feminist movement came after me. I like to look upon myself as a good [judge] and I don't want to be male or female in this. I want more women to be judges, but that's another matter. There are some young ones coming along who certainly will be and are good. Give them enough practice and they're as good as anyone. They don't need to be pioneers, they just have to be good. Everybody needs a role model, somebody they can look to, and it's sometimes you who have to be it, but you never know who you're the role model for. I was sitting with the judges for lunch at Canterbury last week and one solicitor, Harvey Crush, said to me, 'Do you know how I'm here? Because of you.' I said, 'I don't remember meeting you before, Harvey.' He said that in 1984 he was robbed and his case came up at Croydon Crown Court, and when he'd given his evidence he sat and listened. I was presiding and he thought, 'Oh, I rather like the way she's doing it, it looks easy, I think I'll be one.' He applied for the papers and became an assistant recorder. He said it wasn't as easy as it looked!

The Bar opened my mental horizons. As a social worker I had read everything and could do everything. I was not personally stimulated, no good saying I was, but I was among good people. When I got to the Bar, I wasn't always among good people, but I was among people who could stimulate me, and have continued to do so.

I'm retired from the Bench but I've got other things I'm going to do. There's a Five Year Plan. I don't say I'll achieve it all, but I can see that I will achieve some. I'm interested at the moment in international child abduction, so I'm doing a background paper, then [we'll try to] get the International Federation of Women Lawyers interested and get it internationally done. In doing all that you have a dinner party, you have a chat, you go to the library, you've got coffee and home-made cakes with one co-author, lunch with another. It's all good fun.

I'm not worried about retirement. I've got a lot to do, more travelling, more visiting. I've written a great deal – they're not great books, but they're known in the world that matters to me, which I mind about. I want them to be well thought of – and I suppose I do still want to write the one pamphlet that changes everything. I really still believe that one more pamphlet will help to change things. Not in a great big way, no more of that, but in the reform groups. We still haven't got family courts, and that's got to come. I don't want to waste my time. One good cause does tend to lead to another and it's a great comfort to have something to turn to; maybe that's why I'm always thinking up another new project.

I don't feel a workaholic, but I find it's a natural thing to do. I have worked ever since I was twenty, never been out of work for a day. I know that I have inner drives of which I'm not aware; I know I have an infinite capacity for taking pains. Everything I've done seemed logical, what happens next. It's all seemed very obvious that that's what should be done next. I can see my weaknesses. I can see that other women were better looking. I can accept all of that now – didn't care for it quite so much then – and I've not fought as hard as some women to get their men. (I don't think it's always been worthwhile in the end, when you saw what they'd got.) I've tried quite hard – it's not trying any more – to come to terms with myself, find happiness or fulfilment in myself. I don't always succeed all the time. If you can simplify the issue and come to terms with what you can't have, and not mind if other people are successful when you're not . . . I'm not inclined ever to look back on the past if I can help it. I'm only conscious that it's part of what I am, and it's no good regretting it. I would have liked to have been the chairman of an enquiry on child abuse. And in my heart of hearts I always wished I had married and had children. I've felt deprived in not having them. I don't feel that now, but I have felt very deprived. It wasn't through choice; I never meant to be other than married and have children. (I never think beyond my first-born, that would have been a boy.) I think it's the desire of every woman to have children, though I know that there's some who don't. You could say that any writing that I've done on children's work is a substitute for my own life. I'm sure people would say that. There's always a half truth if not a whole truth in these things. I personally wouldn't know. When I realised I wasn't going to have any children of my own, I thought it was the end of the world, but I've come to terms now with any regrets. When you're old enough to know how to play Juliet, you're only able to play the nurse.

There are moments of pride. Managing those days, a morning, any morning, any Saturday morning at Bow Street, the centre of the world, I was proud of that. And I suppose I am proud of having one Government report that was put into operation. That is a matter of some pride. There *are* moments of pride. I have taken pride in my work. 'Proud of' – funny thing, I really can see so many things that *haven't* yet been achieved. I know I'm liked, respected, feared sometimes, by the young. People tell me I have a reputation for being fair but firm, and those are beautiful words, as beautiful as any lover can give to you. Fair but firm. Who could want more than that?

You have to be a woman of your time. Twenty years before I wouldn't have begun. Twenty years later there are all these excellent women going. You had to be just there at the right time, almost without knowing it.

MARY SMITH

Mary Smith was born on 5 January 1920 and raised in Plymouth. She recalled her working-class childhood with pleasure, telling how her father was apprenticed as a carpenter but realised his dream to become a train driver. Although her mother died when she was young, her father remarried after two years and she has always been close to her stepmother. Advised that she should not attempt university because of poor eyesight, Mary entered the field of housing upon leaving grammar school. She later did a degree in English by correspondence course. In 1967 she was honoured with an MBE for her contribution to housing.

After serving with the Crown Estate Commissioners for twenty-four years, Mary was one of the first advisors appointed to the Department of the Environment's Housing Service Advisory Unit in 1978. Although she retired in 1985, it is still common for her to spend five days a week on housing activities, being a governor of Peabody Trust and a member of the committee of management of several housing associations. She is an active member of the professional associations: a past president of the Institute of Housing and current president of the Housing Centre and chair of the National Housing Forum. She is also the author of three editions of, and a supplement to, the Guide to Housing. She is currently involved in moves to set up a National Housing Library in memory of Harry Simpson (the first director-general of the Northern Ireland Housing Executive, and subsequently controller of housing for the Greater London Council). Her long and continuing years of activity in the field have been recognised by the Crown Estate Commissioners, who have named a block of flats near the Tate Gallery 'Mary Smith House', and by the Women's Pioneer

Housing Association who have a 'Mary Smith Court' near Earls Court station. From 1976 to 1978 she was also chair of the Fawcett Society. Locally, she has chaired the Wimbledon House Residents' Association since 1989.

Mary Smith was made an honorary fellow of the Polytechnic of Central London (now the University of Westminster) in 1991 and contributed to a series of eleven lectures by the honourary fellows to mark the inauguration of the polytechnic as the University of Westminster. Her subject was 'Housing: A Citizen's Progress'.

She does not begrudge the time she gives, but will be pleased to have more time for family, friends and the garden in the future as her commitments ease.

The interview took place in 1991 at Mary Smith's home in London in a room busy with china and fresh flowers. Scheduling the interview had not been easy, owing to her many commitments, but, having made the time, she gave her full attention to the interview and recalled her experiences with a certain amount of self-conscious enjoyment. After the interview, she provided tea and biscuits and proudly produced the latest photographs of her granddaughter.

My father was an engine driver on the Southern Railway. When I was four, he was transferred from Guildford where I was born, and we moved down to Plymouth. [He had] left school when he was fourteen and was apprenticed to be a carpenter, but he'd always wanted to be an engine driver. All boys do, don't they? He was driving trains during the bombing of Plymouth. I can remember the night the Germans set light to three or four oil tanks over at Turnchapel and these tanks were all on fire – they were a target for the German bombers.

My father was one of eight and my mother had nine brothers and sisters, so there were lots of relatives. There aren't the big families now that there were when I was small. It's a pity. I think children miss out. I used to go and stay with Auntie Grace, my mother's sister, in Guildford for the whole of my summer holidays. I absolutely loved my holidays down in Guildford. I used to walk about the train on the journey there, I was so excited. Auntie Grace had an allotment; we used to spend hours on the allotment, pottering about. She [had] a great influence on me. There was a very deep affection and love there, and I think it helped me to relate to other people, it helped me to see the value of ordinary things.

As a child I was encouraged to study, definitely. I was expected to help with the washing-up, but apart from that, I wasn't expected to do a lot. My brother would much rather have been out playing football, but I enjoyed studying – that's probably why I passed all the exams. I went to the local school, Cattedown Road School, until I passed the scholarship to go to the local grammar school.

Unfortunately, when I was nine, my mother died. I remember it very well. She had been ill for a week and on this particular day I was bundled off to a children's party. I remember going in to say goodbye to her, and going off. Obviously the relatives knew she was dying but the idea, I suppose, was to get me away while all this happened. At the party I was given a balloon and one or two other things and I remember being in a terrific state of excitement to take these things back to show her. When I got home, of course, my father told me what had happened. I was just nine at the time.

For a couple of years my brother and I were looked after by an elderly couple who moved into the ground floor and then when I was eleven my father married again. I had quite a close relationship with my stepmother, who was some four-teen years younger than my father, so that I had guidance and help from somebody who was nearer my age than my mother would have been. My stepmother is still alive, she's ninety. My father used to drive the engine between Plymouth Friary and Turnchapel and he used to hold the train up while my stepmother came running down to catch the train. She was always late. They set up a friendship and eventually married. She was a widow and had a little boy, David, who was six when she married Daddy. So there was then my brother, Les, and David, my stepbrother. My brother died about three years ago, but David is still alive.

I'm eternally grateful to my stepmother that she accepted what my father had already accepted: that a girl deserved as good an education as she could get. In those days a lot of ordinary working-class people didn't think that way. The assumption was, 'Oh well, the girl'll marry, so we don't want to bother.' My father had always decided that even though I was a girl I should have the best education they could afford and my stepmother supported that. I owed them a lot.

I didn't do too well [at the grammar school] in the beginning, because I was very short-sighted and couldn't see the blackboard. My mother had decided that no way was she going to have this little daughter wearing glasses. But when it was discovered that I was short-sighted, my stepmother and my father decided [I'd] got to be able to see and I was given glasses. I remember I cried and cried when I first had to wear them. But once I could see the blackboard, I took off! I was what is known as a swot. I did very well in exams: I got a School Certificate with honours and I got a Higher School with a matric. exemption, which would have enabled me to have gone on to take a degree.

My father and stepmother would've somehow or other scraped to get me through university if this foolish eye specialist I saw at that time hadn't said it would ruin my eyesight. It was as a result of that, that I didn't go to a university. Quite ridiculous, looking back. The headmaster [of the grammar school] was a very enlightened man and believed in equal opportunity, and in our library we had a lot of careers pamphlets. One of the pamphlets was about housing management and I decided to go into a career in housing. In those days, of course, women didn't get into top jobs. It was unusual. We're talking about the 1930s. The headmaster got in touch with a Miss Maud Jeffrey who was the agent for the Crown Estate Commissioners [then the Commissioners of Crown Lands] and very famous in the housing world, and when I was seventeen I went to London as student secretary to Miss Jeffrey. I remember it very well: the first job I had to do was to make ribbon rosettes for Mr Morrison. He came and opened a block of flats in London and I had made the rosettes that the visitors wore.

I stayed with the Cumberland Market office of the Crown Estate until 1938, and then went off to Lincoln for six months to do housing training in a local authority office. I was paid about a pound and I had to make it up from my own savings. I had something like twenty pounds by the time I left school and I thought I was rich: twenty pounds was a lot in those days. I drew on that money to keep myself going. It wasn't until the War came in 1939 and I went to work in Plymouth that I got paid [a proper wage], and then it wasn't all that much. I was living at home, so it wasn't so difficult; I wouldn't have been able to survive [away from home] on what they paid me.

That was my very first housing job. I managed a housing estate for Lord and Lady Astor in Mount Gould in Plymouth. I was given the job of property manager, looking after this little estate of ninety-six houses. I must have been nineteen. It involved going round and collecting the rents, taking rates from tenants and looking after the maintenance: the houses developed very bad cracks along the back walls and we had a lot of damp penetration. That estate would now be called social housing. The rents were, I think, eight shillings and sixpence a week and I used to collect them door-to-door. Now, no one collects because it isn't safe, but in those days, we walked about with the rent bag round our waist. You were supposed to keep the bag under your coat, but half the time we didn't, and never thought anything about it, never thought of mugging or anything. Completely different from what housing managers have to face these days. We had several eccentric tenants, a family of gypsies, for instance, but we didn't have the hooliganism and the viciousness you get now.

Another part of my job was welfare work. This was Plymouth during the War, so a lot of the men were away and there was quite a bit of welfare work, making sure that the wives were getting all the benefits to which they were entitled.

One of the jobs that Lady Astor gave me was to form a 'Tidy Club'. The idea was that we ran classes and clubs for the youngsters and got them to run around the estate and pick up all the litter. I used to run clubs for the children, and for the wives. I did quite a bit of community work. You did get to know the families very well, and if there was anything wrong you could get help quickly. In the old days of housing management, you certainly wouldn't have these awful cases of children lying starving in back rooms, because housing managers would have picked that up long before.

I was then studying for the Royal Institution of Chartered Surveyors exam in housing management and I completed that in 1940 and got the Octavia Hill prize for the highest marks of the year. I told you I was a swot! I stayed [in Plymouth] until 1942 and then got a job as an assistant housing manager with the Cheltenham Housing Corporation. We were well into slum clearance in those days. Quite a few of the estates had slum-clearance tenants on them [who] had been moved out of sub-standard property and put into very nice three-bedroomed houses with gardens. Many of the tenants had never had houses with modern amenities, so again there was quite a bit of welfare work to do there. We were responsible for the repair of the property: if a tenant drew one's attention to a leaking roof or a leaking WC pan, any defect, we would inspect and then give the necessary order to the contractor. We were all qualified by a Royal Institution of Chartered Surveyors qualification, so we understood building construction, we understood drainage and sanitation. Although we were young women, the contractors appreciated [that] we did understand what we were talking about. If there was anything seriously wrong anywhere, you got out your bicycle, no cars in those days, and just dashed away and had a look. In all weathers, snow, rain, everything, yes indeed! It was a part of the job. But it was very enjoyable, and in those days you could reckon on finding the housewives at home, certainly on a Monday they'd be there doing their washing. If a tenant wasn't in, she'd leave the rent somewhere, either under a mat or on top of a gas meter, or there'd be a key on a string. You'd just put your hand through the letter box, and draw out the key and let yourself in. Very often tenants would leave you a teapot and you [could make] yourself a cup of tea. Nobody would do that nowadays, nobody would allow somebody to walk into their house.

We also did requisitioning. If a property was empty, we had special requisitioning notices and we used to have a taxi and get to the house, run like mad up the front path, put this notice on the door and then run back to the taxi, because you didn't want anybody to catch you doing it. The other thing we had to do, of course, was fix rents. We had a differential rent scheme, as against the rent rebate system now. You worked it all out very carefully – I think it was a fifth of tenants' income – and you checked with the employers and if the tenant's income went up or down, you altered their rent. It was a very satisfying job as well as being very interesting. I thoroughly enjoyed it. I loved it.

Housing managers in those days were rather paternalistic and there has been criticism about the early housing managers, but we're talking about a different society and various sorts of people. In the very early days quite a lot of the housing managers would have had private incomes and perhaps did regard the tenants, not exactly as stupid, but a different class. By the time I got into it, that was altering: after all, my father was an engine driver, I hadn't any sort of private income. The Octavia Hill system of housing management in which I was trained was very good indeed, but it was slightly patronising. Octavia Hill would certainly have regarded the people she was dealing with as a different class from her own; working-class, maybe even less than that. Although this criticism of paternalism can be levied, one's got to remember that the people we housed were having enlightened management for the very first time; they were having people coming round who were prepared to look at a leaking WC pan or a dripping overflow pipe, whereas the old estate agents had simply been interested in taking the rents, and repairs were just neglected, which was why housing was in such a bad state. We all thought we were really doing good things.

During my time at Cheltenham, a friend put me in touch with Douglas, who was in the Air Force, and we kept up a long correspondence and when he came home he came to see me in Cheltenham and we eventually married in 1947. Even when I was nineteen or twenty, very few of us had had sexual experiences. I had boyfriends in [my] teens: you went to the pictures and you held hands and you'd kiss goodnight in the back lane, and it was all very exciting, but at no stage would we have thought of going to bed with a young man. I don't know whether it was fear or what. These days, fourteen-, fifteen-, sixteen-year-olds are in steady relationships, aren't they? I think the whole fun of it has gone. I can remember when I was first kissed behind a cricket pavilion. My daughter would pooh-pooh that. The attitude's completely different now.

We were all set on getting married; we used to go to the British Restaurant for lunch, and usually the topic was the boyfriend. Once the men came back, a lot of the women left to get married. Of the people I worked with in Cheltenham, all except one gave it up. Dilys stayed for about twelve months and then married and went up north and had a family. Later she went into teaching, she didn't go back into housing. Doreen stayed for about two years and when she went back to work, she also went into teaching. Joan stayed in housing until she retired fairly recently. Ceridwen stayed in housing for a long time, but eventually married a factory inspector, so she went out. The manager, Bridget, she stayed for several years and then married and eventually went to South Africa. The person who replaced her, Peggy, stayed for some time, but then she went north to look after her father and she went into teaching. Not many of them actually stuck to housing. Not very many of them were so career-orientated as I was. I married, and *didn't* leave housing. That was the difference.

After we married, I went to live in Bath, because my husband was an architect there. Our first flat was a one-bedroomed flat with shared facilities. I didn't work for two or three months, and then I got a job with the Ministry of Supply, looking after an estate at Woolavington near Bridgwater and an estate at Bradford-on-Avon. I travelled backwards and forwards between the two and stayed away one night a week. These were all prefabs attached to a Ministry of Supply factory. The men were coming back after the War and people were looking for property. It was really something to get a prefab. They had beautiful kitchens and most of them had small gardens and, to the wives, they really were a dream. When you finally allocated a property, it was really very satisfying.

We left Bath in 1951 when my husband got a job in London. We moved to Coombe Manor, which is now the Victoria Nursing Home, and we had a top-floor flat in this old manor. It was very nice indeed. Douglas was studying for his architectural examinations and I decided to complete my degree. I took a correspondence course and eventually got a BA Honours in English. I did my RICS, my technical surveyor's qualification, by correspondence course too. I've always enjoyed studying. I've got a photographic memory and that's a great asset. If you can actually visualise what you've been reading, you're streets ahead.

I was then asked if I would take on a post with the Crown Estate Commissioners as an assistant housing manager. The Crown Estates are mainly around the royal parks: Regent's Park, Vauxhall Gardens, Eltham Palace, Victoria Park. I looked after the Millbank Estate. I was assistant housing manager of that estate, then housing manager, then senior housing manager, and finally the chief housing manager. And because I was there for over twenty years, I got to know the tenants very well indeed. Very often I could see a baby born and eventually be housing him or her! It was very good. When I went there first, [the properties] were mainly tenement houses, many five-storey houses, and they had shared bathrooms, and shared WCs. Again, you went and visited applicants, checked their housing needs and what size accommodation they wanted, and eventually let a flat to them. There was quite a lot of welfare work to do. One had to keep full records, and when people's families increased, you moved them to larger accommodation. We had a system whereby we housed sons and daughters of tenants. That meant that you'd got whole families on the estate, and when children came home from school, they could go round to grandparents, or if they got up to mischief, there was an uncle around who'd cope with them. They don't do that [sort of allocation] on estates now, it's considered unfair.

When the Crown Estate Commissioners decided to develop the estate, my job – by that time I was the chief housing manager – was to start decanting people, clearing streets, so that redevelopment could go ahead. If you go to that estate now, the whole thing's been swept away now, it's all been redeveloped. We used to take our sandwiches over to Bessborough Gardens: well, you take your life in your hands to get across that main road now. It's completely different. It was very much a community. We had quite a few corner shops, milk dairies and groceries. It's mostly offices now. That estate illustrates, very clearly, how society has changed completely.

I stayed with the Crown Estate Commissioners a long time, twenty-four years, and thoroughly enjoyed it. People did stay: the working conditions were very good and we didn't have any political interference at all, which is what bugs so many housing people now. The board gave the housing managers a great deal of autonomy; you were able to make decisions. And if you went to any of the commissioners with any sort of plan, it was listened to. We all got maternity leave: I had six months on full pay and six months on half pay. Or at least I could have had, but I didn't take it, I only stayed away three months, if that. It was a very, very good office. And when I was there it was all women managers. There's a man now in the job that I had, but we were all women managers then.

Housing management was very much a woman's field when I went into it. We were the professionals and the men let us get on with it. Of course when I started the men were at the War. That's needs must: the men were away, so the women did the work. But after 1974, when there were the changes in local government, highly-paid jobs in housing were created and the men took the jobs. Women are often mainly concentrated in the clerical and typing grades. We haven't had another Evelyn Sharp.* When I went to the Department of the Environment in 1978 it would often be automatically assumed [out on a visit] that I was there to take the notes, until I asserted myself as one of the advisors. Unless you are assertive or aggressive, men still tend, as they did then, to think, 'This is the little secretary come along to take the notes for the men.' When housing management was a fairly low-paid job, then the women were there; once it became a big job and the salaries went up accordingly, the men took the directors' jobs. But one mustn't get strident about these things, otherwise you get labelled as the witch that keeps on about equal opportunity! The women's libbers didn't do themselves any good by being so strident. Such a lot these days is done by compromise. I couldn't say that I ever experienced discrimination, but I can still see quite a bit of prejudice against women. It is sad to think that the housing management profession was started by a woman, Octavia Hill, and the Society of Housing Managers was originally the Society of Women Housing Managers, and yet the number of women directors of housing these days is about six or seven. Not many. It's rather sad.

I really only got interested in the Women's Movement after I'd been to public-speaking classes at the Fawcett Society in the 1950s. I was beginning to be asked to give talks on housing and women in housing and I felt that I really didn't know much about public speaking. I remember the first time I went to talk about housing, and I think I had to take about six aspirins before I could get there. I was terrified! So I went and joined the Fawcett Society and went to their classes. Public speaking is very, very useful. In housing, women haven't really asserted

---

* *Renowned for her activity as speaker and demonstrator in the militant suffrage movement, 1905–18, and later as a speaker in humanitarian and international causes.*

themselves, haven't gone along to branch meetings of the Institute of Housing in large numbers to speak up for themselves. It's important that women can put their points of view over, and be articulate, but a lot of women lack confidence. If they're coming back to work after ten years bringing up a family, they need some guidance, they need their confidence building up.

Douglas knew from the time we married that I intended to go on working and [he] was extremely supportive. He was very willing to take his share in the cooking and looking after the house. If the wife does work, that is the only way you can have a satisfactory life together. It was a very good marriage. Very good indeed. He was very supportive. He became secretary of the local architectural 'chapter', so we used to go to a lot of RIBA do's. The Royal Institute of British Architects has that very nice building in Portland Place, and we used to go to a lot of lectures and dances there. We had a lot of friends, particularly in the architectural world and my housing people. We used to walk a lot. I went down to Plymouth quite often when my father was alive. We went abroad whenever we could afford it. There was always something going on.

For a long time, I didn't want to have children. It was only, well, I suppose I was about thirty-five, when I thought, 'Time's getting on a bit. If I'm going to have any children, I'd better try.' It took us seven years before I did finally conceive and I was forty-two when I eventually had Fiona. In those days there was quite a bit of criticism about women with children working, and quite a few of our friends certainly didn't agree [with it]. I had one friend, particularly, who was quite open about her disapproval. But I was determined to do it and I don't think Fiona suffered. We had a nanny living in – that takes a bit of getting used to – and I always had the full support of my husband. I think it would be very difficult to combine the two, a full-time job and a family, if you didn't have that. I always intended to work and be independent, and fortunately I went into a profession where women were needed and there was always an opening.

In 1966, when Fiona was four, Douglas died. He had the third coronary and just collapsed. It was dreadful. It took me about four years, really, before I could come to terms with it. I got terrific claustrophobia: I couldn't go in a lift or anything, it was dreadful. I also kept getting these panics. I would be sitting in a tube, and I'd have to get out because I couldn't stand it, and I would say to myself, 'This is ridiculous. There's nothing. Everybody else is sitting in the tube.' When I went to Expo in Canada in 1967, again I had the most terrible claustrophobia in the pavilions, and these terrible panics at night. But it's something one can't explain . . . reason doesn't come into it. I had that for about three years but I gradually got myself over it. It was a terrible shock, when he died, yes, awful. But having Fiona, I more or less had to get on with it. I would have had to go out to work anyway. This is one reason why I'm so keen on equal opportunity for women: because if I hadn't kept up my career I'd have had to rely on State assistance and I would have had to give up the house – in addition to all the grief.

I didn't remarry. I did have another relationship for about ten years, but I didn't consider remarrying. By the time I'd accepted the fact that Douglas had gone, and by the time I felt I could even look at another man, by that time Fiona was nine, and it would have been extremely difficult to have brought another man in. I've had various men friends, but I really haven't considered marrying again.

In 1967 Mary Smith was awarded an MBE for her work for the Crown Estate Commissioners. She went with her stepmother and daughter to Buckingham Palace for the presentation. She accepted the award not only as a tribute to her profession, but also as recognition of the significant contribution of women in the field of housing. Her reputation as a spokeswoman on housing issues continued to grow and people began to listen to what she had to say.

For ten or twelve years, I had been writing the leading article for the magazine *Housing* [under the pseudonym, Oedile], and

I'd said over and over again that the Government ought to have more housing management expertise: they'd got sociologists, they'd got armies of architects, but they hadn't got a single housing manager there. Well, in 1978, they set up the Housing Service Advisory Unit and when the jobs of housing service advisors were advertised, I thought I ought to apply, and I got the first of two. So in 1978 I left the Crown Estate Commissioners and went off to the Department of the Environment. There were 160 staff of the Crown Estate Commissioners and when I went to Marsham Street, there were some 3,000 staff. The change was absolutely total. It was an administrative job. I didn't have actual practical management of estates. Part of the work of the Housing Services Advisory Unit was to facilitate a close relationship between central and local government. I and the other advisors and the director of the unit used to travel around the country visiting local authorities, finding out what they were doing on their estates, looking at their housing management and generally advising. The travelling got a bit onerous, but on the whole I enjoyed it. I enjoyed the feeling that I was at the centre of things, and I enjoyed meeting everybody.

I was appointed by the Labour Government in 1978. Peter Shore was Secretary of State and Reg Freeson was Minister of Housing. Then in May 1979, Michael Heseltine and John Stanley came in. Since the Conservatives came in the whole housing scene has changed drastically. When I was first at the DOE there were big local authority estates. Then, in 1980, 'Right to Buy' came in and now about a million houses have been sold off in the public sector. The emphasis is on housing associations taking over the management of local authority estates, rather than on provision by local authorities. Completely different from the sort of management when I went into the DOE. A lot of the housing managers' time now is taken up consulting tenants, forming tenants' associations and providing tenant management boards. There's a swing between more money going into council housing and more money going into private sector building. All round the country you can see these private estates, and a lot of them are standing empty. I am concerned about the spec-built estates: I think we're going to have a lot of housing problems later on.

The whole job has changed, the whole housing scene has changed. It's changing all the time, that's what makes it so fascinating. When I began, rent collection was the corner-stone. It gave you an entry into the houses, and it enabled you to check on maintenance as you went round the estates. I stopped my staff collecting rent in the Crown Estate in 1970. After the building of flats [in the] 1960s, housing managers could easily have been accosted on the landings and there was nobody about to take any notice. It's not only that society has changed, the structure of housing has changed too. These streets in the sky are absolute traps. Provided blocks of flats are properly managed and properly furnished, they can work, but in this country, a lot of mistakes were made, particularly putting families with children up on top floors. They weren't managed properly, and they weren't maintained properly.

I went to visit Stockwell Park in Brixton when it was first opened. On the face of it that was a lovely estate, with water and bushes, but intensive management [was dropped after a time] and, with such high density, you have difficulties if you don't have proper management. The streets in the sky just didn't work. The people don't seem to come out of their flats and talk. When they lived in a terrace the doors would be open and they'd be out on the landing stone and in the back garden. Put them in a block, and you don't find them coming out and talking in the corridors. I don't know why, but they don't. You go and collect rents in Mary Smith House (the Crown Estate house that's named after me), and people say, 'I never see anybody from morning till night.' Now, if they'd have been in their house, they'd have gone down the front path and leant over the gate and had a talk to somebody passing by. There are tremendous problems in managing high-rise [estates]. I can see how it happened, but I find it very, very sad. A lot of the criticism of local authority management of estates is due to the fact that the managers weren't properly trained.

But proper management is expensive, and local authorities haven't got the money to do it all.

I regard good housing as an essential, the same as health and food and education. It worries me that there still isn't an overall housing strategy. Although the Government talks a lot about providing affordable housing, there's no definition of affordable and there still isn't a strategy whereby everybody who really needs housing gets it. Which is why we've got this rising homelessness. If you don't manage the homeless problem properly, you're just building up more and more social problems. I would like to see more money given to local authorities for the homeless. It offends me, all these kids begging on the stations with their placards. I'm appalled at all these people sleeping in cardboard boxes. We really ought to have a complete drive to get homeless people into proper housing accommodation, not just putting them into disused hospitals and schools. It costs money, of course, it's very expensive, but that's what it wants and that's what I'd like to see. I think we want more of the gross national product going into housing. At the moment, the Conservatives have cut down on the amount of money given to local authorities to build and with the funds so cut, the crux of the problem is that there just isn't enough housing.

Housing ought to rate higher on the agenda. One of the reasons why I wrote the *Guide to Housing* was because the general public know so little about housing. The *Guide* shows how housing policy has changed and it shows how housing is [directly] influenced by politics. If you ask any-body in the street, 'What's a housing association?', they don't know. Yet look at the amount of public money that's being poured into housing associations. There have been surveys in the papers in which the general public put in order of priority what they consider important, and they talk about health, they talk about education, they talk about transport, but they don't talk about housing. Housing doesn't appear at all. People ought to be interested, but they're not. With owner occupation running at seventy per cent, the majority have got good housing, but we've still got a lot of people who aren't well-housed.

> *Since retiring from the DOE in 1985, Mary Smith has remained very active in the housing field. She is a governor of the Peabody Trust and a member of the Council of the National Federation of Housing Associations, which represents all the housing associations in the country. For seventeen years she has chaired Women's Pioneer Housing, an organisation founded in 1920 by a group of single women who pooled their resources and bought property and which now owns nearly 1,000 units. She is also deputy chair of the Committee of Management of the Hanover Housing Association, a national body with 13,339 properties (rented and leasehold) across the country, set up in response to demographic change to provide sheltered housing for the elderly. She is characteristically alert to the wider implications of such housing schemes.*

Most housing associations now are having to look at how they deal with elderly people. People are living much longer: one of the things that does strike you when you go around sheltered housing schemes is how many people there are above ninety. Good thing, but it does have to be taken account of in a housing policy. Some of the sheltered housing schemes are very nice indeed, and if you could do it for all elderly people, yes, but there may be an argument for saying, instead of providing such super housing for twenty-four people, why don't we spread it out a bit more thinly and improve the ancillary services for a lot more. The other thing people argue about with sheltered housing schemes is that it makes elderly people more dependent. I don't know about that. I've never found that tenants themselves feel that. I think it depends on the individual. In the last few years, the trend has been for 'stay put', whereby older people are helped to stay in their own homes, and there are quite a few initiatives now to encourage people to stay in their own homes, which is a good thing. My mother, as I say, she's ninety, she wouldn't go into a sheltered housing scheme; she won't even put out an 'H notice' that

Plymouth provide if you need help. It depends a lot on the person.

I've lived in this house for thirty-one years. Really it's much too big for me, but I'd hate to give it up. I suppose one day I'll have to go into something smaller. There is quite a community feeling around here. I know all my neighbours well and if I go down to the village, Wimbledon Park Village, I know I'll meet people I know. That's one reason why I would be very reluctant to leave here.

I shall go on working in housing. When I was coming up for retirement in 1985, I thought, 'Goodness me, I'm going to be stuck down in Wimbledon, pulling up the weeds in the garden,' you know, and I said yes to everything that was offered. I rather took on too much and now I find I've got a tremendous amount to do. But it's probably a good thing: once you retire, it's easy to stay in bed and get up late and watch the telly and generally vegetate. I've never given myself any opportunity to do that. The only thing that does rather worry me is Alzheimer's Disease. I've seen friends who were as active and probably more alert mentally than I am deteriorate into senility. There doesn't seem to be anything you can do to prevent it. I don't like to think too much about that. I do think sometimes I'm a bit too busy, because I would like to go down and see Fiona more than I do. I still find there are some weeks when I'm doing housing every day, rushing about. I'm off to the Scilly Isles to have a look at a Hanover Scheme, I'm going to a housing conference in Torquay, you know, I'm on the move. But it keeps me active, keeps my brain going.

As you get older, as you see that the number of years are getting less, you do tend to think about [death] a lot more than before. I'm not really a religious person. I don't go to church on Sundays. I worry at the Church's attitude towards war. In 1940 I remember I went and had a talk to the local vicar about it, because it worried me to be in church and to hear them praying for our servicemen who were busily killing off Germans. I never really got a clergyman who would talk to me seriously about it. I was equally worried over the Gulf War. I could quite see that we really hadn't any alternative, but I was worried. When you look at the dreadful things that happened to some of the Iraqis, I don't know how you can really reconcile that with Christian beliefs. I don't know. I think about it a lot.

I'm content now. You don't have the same peaks of happiness that you do in earlier life, but I'm very content. I can decide, more or less, what I'm going to do and I'm financially independent. I'm not well off, but the house is paid for and I get a reasonable civil service pension. My greatest claim to fame, perhaps, is the *Guide to Housing*. It's now in it's third edition and I have just finished writing a supplement to it. And I was very proud that I became president of the Institute of Housing, because they still are very much male-dominated. But my proudest thing was having my daughter, Fiona. Definitely. Having my daughter. What was so tragic was that having waited all that time, Douglas died when she was four. He was absolutely over the moon that he'd got a little daughter, and then for him to die like that, when she was only four, it was really very, very sad. And my father had died in the December, so he didn't even know I was going to have Fiona and he'd been so keen for me to have a daughter. They were two nasty blows that fate gave to me, but there we are. I'm very happy that Fiona's qualified and that she's got a little girl, dear little thing, she's fifteen months. Fiona used to say to me when she was sixteen, 'You shouldn't have children if you don't intend to stay home and look after them,' and I used to say, 'You wait until you're qualified and see what you feel.' And now, you see, she's working four days a week as a pharmacist and the baby goes in a nursery. So opinions change. Fiona used to say, 'You had to do it,' because her father died, but I say that's not true, I intended to go on working whether Douglas had died or not. The whole sad business reinforced my ideas of equal opportunity, that women should have the same opportunities. Because you just never know what's going to happen in life, do you?

LIVIA GOLLANCZ

Livia Gollancz was born in London on 25 May 1920 into a distinguished family. Her great-grandfather, Samuel Marcus Gollancz, was a rabbi who like thousands of Jews of that generation emigrated to England in the middle of the nineteenth century. Two of his three sons were knighted later in life: Hermann was a famous theologian, Israel was Regius Professor of English at Oxford. The third, Livia's grandfather, was not so academically minded: apprenticed to a wholesale jeweller, he spent his life in trade. He had three children, of whom the youngest, and the only boy, was Livia's father Victor, who was to found the publishing company Victor Gollancz Ltd, and the highly influential Left Book Club.

Livia's maternal grandmother's family, the Solomons, were artistic. Her great-uncle, Solomon J. Solomon, the portrait painter, was a Royal Academician. But it was in the feminist movement that they shone: her grandmother was an active suffragette, all of whose daughters were taught to drive, and Livia's mother made her own contribution to progress by becoming one of the first women to study architecture at the Architectural Association.

Livia was intensely political in her youth, a keen member of the Left Book Club from its inception in 1936 and a member of the Young Communist League. She joined her father's publishing company at the age of thirty-three and after his death in 1967 she took over the running of the firm. However, music rather than books has always been her great love and prior to publishing she had a distinguished career as a professional musician. She played principal horn in a number of eminent orchestras, including the Hallé, Covent Garden and Sadler's Wells, and she worked with many of the great *conductors of her generation, including Beecham, Barbirolli and Boult. At one time she considered training to become a doctor, but she was unable to provide the proof of matriculation required for entrance into medical school, having spent the money for her School Certificate, at the age of sixteen, on tickets to the opera.*

While her enthusiasm for politics did not survive the Second World War, her love for music did. She still plays the violin and the viola, as well as singing. In the early 1950s she took up walking and in 1959 she went on an all-women expedition to the Alps with the Ladies' Alpine Club. She still walks, both in Britain and abroad. Two of her four sisters are still alive and they keep in regular contact. She never married and has no children.

This interview took place in January and February 1991 at her home in North London.

My mother's parents lived just round the corner from us and we were in and out of each others' houses all the time. We went there for lunch almost every Saturday, a big family lunch where my grandmother sang Hebrew grace and everyone joined in. She would start off, and she always sat with a particular expression on her face, with her chin on her hand and her eyes looking up to heaven. My grandmother [had been] a suffragette. She looked rather like Mrs Pankhurst, and they would swap clothes after meetings sometimes, and Mrs Pankhurst would leave by the back gate in my grandmother's clothes, whisked away by my grandfather in his motor car, while my grandmother, in Mrs Pankhurst's clothes, would allow herself to be arrested at the front gate by the police. She was [also] arrested in her own right and went to prison, and so did my eldest aunt, Gertie, Gertrude Salaman as she later became. My grandmother died in about 1950 in her ninetieth year. She loved travel; she travelled to all sorts of places. She went in an aeroplane for the first time when she was in her eighties.

[Her] family had been in England since the fourteenth century. They were tanners in Bermondsey, and had a tannery

just under London Bridge station. My grandmother told me
once how exciting it was, when she was a child, when they
moved house to a crescent off the Old Kent Road, with a little
lawn and a few trees in front of it. This was really going up in
the world, from living over the tannery in Tooley Street
which must have been awfully smelly. Her mother, my
great-grandmother Helena, had come from Prague, possibly
from Vienna, I'm not quite sure, one or the other, and was a
very enlightened woman. She had fourteen children and they
were all taught to paint and to play the piano and sing. The
idea was that they wouldn't have to be house servants, they
could be governesses, because they could paint and play the
piano. One of [her children] was Solomon J. Solomon, the
artist, who was very famous.

My grandfather was a rather dapper little man. He really
wanted to be an engineer, but he was apprenticed into the City
when he was young. I don't exactly know what his job was,
but he went to the City every day, and sometimes he made a
lot of money and sometimes he lost all his money, so the
fortune of that family fluctuated quite a bit. He was mad about
engineering and collected model railway engines. He built a
railway round his garden. It had a gauge of about a foot, and
rolling stock of about two foot six long. When my mother was
a child they could actually ride in it. He had a collection of
model engines [which he] lodged at St James's Park station. I
think they've now been sold to a private collector, but they
were kept there for a long time, and as a result my grandfather
had a free pass on the underground.

They had eight children: Gertie, Ethel, Albert, Lina,
Mother, May, Lilly and Joe. Six girls and two boys. And after
eight children in about nine years my grandmother shut her
bedroom door on my grandfather and there weren't any more
children.

My mother was a very intelligent woman. She could have
been clever academically, but she hadn't been to university.
She'd had a reasonably good education at St Paul's School,
then she went to the Slade and studied painting, and she then

decided that as a painter she could only earn her living by teaching and she didn't want to teach, so she got into the Architectural Association in 1917 as one of the first four women students. She had only just finished her studies when she married my father. At home my mother always did things like mending the fuses. She drove the car, my father couldn't drive. She did all the gardening; he never did a thing. He used to go round occasionally and dead-head things, but that was all. She had live-in help, so that she didn't do the cleaning, and she didn't cook until after the Second World War. Later on she had to learn to cook, which was something that women weren't taught to do as they are now. [She was a powerful influence in the family] and yet when she married my father she realised very soon that she would have to take a back seat, because he had such a strong personality. She played that part very well. She was wonderful, a lovely person. I think he was unfaithful to her about twice, but she was sensible about that. She was very sensible about everything, including her relationship with my father. She was sensible about giving him just exactly what he wanted, which was a wonderful home background, which he needed; making him feel that he had something that he could depend upon utterly, but that wasn't going to cramp his style. She devoted herself to him, utterly, sometimes I think to the detriment of the children. She was a good mother, but she had a curious air of detachment. She always said that her children were unique individuals and she didn't want to impose herself on them, impose her own views and that sort of thing on them. She felt that she should learn as much from them as they could from her.

They were always out in the evening. My mother used to have a sleep every afternoon so she'd be fresh for the evening. They went to a lot of concerts, [and] the opera in the summer, and they were very keen bridge players. My father loved being with people, where he was always the centre of attention. They did entertain quite a lot, and they sometimes had very grand parties in the house. My mother was always putting on evening dress. She was a wonderful dressmaker. She made clothes for us too, but when we were children there was a seamstress called Miss Boutelle who would come for three or four days and make new clothes for the entire family. My mother would buy a bolt of cloth and give it to Miss Boutelle and say, 'Make dresses for all the girls,' so we would all have the same dresses. I wasn't terribly interested in appearance. It was the mind that mattered to me.

My parents never went out on Friday nights. They always had dinner at home on Friday night. They would light the [Sabbath] candles and bless us, and instead of having a high tea in the nursery the older children would come down and have dinner. The two generations kept fairly separate lives, we really only met them in the morning – when they were getting up we would be running around, getting in their way – and in the evening before we went to bed. Right up till I was fifteen or sixteen we had high tea in the nursery [except] on Friday nights. On the Saturday we used to attend synagogue children's service. We would always walk home through the park, prior to having lunch with my grandparents, and Mother would tell us stories about the suffragettes. We wanted to hear about suffragettes more than any other stories that [she] told us. She used to talk about Emily Davidson stopping the King's horse in the Derby, and somebody else handcuffing themselves to the railings outside the House of Commons, and [how they] got into the House of Commons air ducts and started shouting, 'Votes for Women.' I'm sure she told us the same stories over and over again, but we never tired of them.

After lunch on Sunday my father would read us a Sherlock Holmes story [or] a bit from the Bible, and very often bits from the New Testament. He thought they were good for us morally. The only time my father ever went to synagogue was on the Day of Atonement. He would walk about the streets and if he passed a synagogue he would go in for an hour, any synagogue he passed. I don't know whether he ate or whether he fasted. Mother was much more Jewish. She came from a Reform Jewish home and it stayed with her all her life (although once the War started she never went to synagogue again). My father came from an orthodox home, and revolted from it completely. He had flirted with Christianity when he was at university, and towards the end of his life he was very much the darling of a lot of Catholic priests who were trying to convert him, but they wouldn't have stood a chance really: he was emotionally completely Jewish. Rather like my father I feel emotionally Jewish, but I haven't set foot inside a synagogue [for over] fifty years.

I was the eldest of [five] sisters and was very much the responsible person who helped with the younger children. I accepted it. I've always accepted my duty; that's why I carried on with the firm, really. [As a child] I was fiercely independent. I was very forthright in everything I did. I had masses of very thick hair and it stuck out in all directions; I used to put a hairband round it and it stuck out all round behind the hairband. I always thought I knew best, always wanted to have my own way. I wouldn't do what I was told, I would always question everything and think everything through from first principles. To a certain extent my parents had brought me up that way. I never liked school very much. I didn't like being told what to do. I wanted to work everything out for myself and just do what I wanted to do. I wasn't really very happy until I got to college and was studying music. Really I'm a natural musician, and if I'm not doing that, or not doing something which complements music in my life, I'm frustrated. All the time I was working in the office, from 1953 until last year [1990], I couldn't give my full attention to it, and it made all those years seem in retrospect less important to me.

My life was politics and music. When [the Left Book Club] started I was sixteen and I threw myself into it with great enthusiasm. I used to go and act as an usher at meetings and I read a lot of the books and used to go out on demonstrations. I was well to the left of the Left Wing at that time. One really felt that one could influence the future of the world in the thirties. We used to go on demonstrations, shout, 'Save Czechoslovakia, Save peace,' all this sort of thing. I was very keen, and I really felt that I was doing something that was significant by going on demonstrations and making my voice heard in this way. When Ribbentrop signed a pact with the Soviets in 1940, I felt absolutely devastated. I'd been totally in favour of the Soviets and totally against the Nazis. I felt so let down that I dropped politics altogether and I've never really been very political since. I learnt very young that even the best politicians, once they've become prominent, lose many of their good qualities. I became pretty cynical about them at quite a young age, before I was twenty.

Politically I suppose I was influenced by my father, but music comes on both sides of the family. My mother's family have musicians in it and my father's family were basically rabbinical and of course they had to sing quite a bit in the services. My great-grandfather had a very good voice and my [maternal] grandmother fancied herself as a singer. [She used to sing Hebrew grace at lunch on Saturdays.] We had a gramophone at home and when I was very small I used to dance round the room to certain pieces of music and I always had a very good sense of rhythm. I started learning the piano when I was about six with a piano teacher who came to the house and taught me and any sisters who were old enough. I was tried out on the violin, but I didn't take to it, I was slightly embarrassed by the sensualness of it; the very fact of making a vibrato on the violin I found embarrassing. So much so that I didn't want to go on with it. This was at the age of seven. I was afraid of these feelings that it evoked in me, probably quite sensibly so.

When I was ten I [went to] Kensington High School [which] had the most remarkable headmistress called Ethel Home who was extremely keen on music and thought that all children should learn music. For twenty minutes before the mid-morning break the whole school [was] reshuffled according to our musical ability and we all did aural training for twenty minutes. I was put in a very low group for aural training, almost at the bottom, and my sister Diana, who was eighteen months younger than me and much less good at the piano, was put in the group below the top. So I went and saw [the headmistress] and I said, 'I'm much better at music than my sister and you've put her into the group below the top. I think you ought to swap us round.' She didn't swap us round, she left Diana where she was and put me in the top group. That was the beginning really. I knew from then that what I wanted to be was a musician.

My mother gave me a front-door key when I was twelve and let me spend my pocket money on going to concerts and the opera, and I used to go to a great deal. In those days, in the early 1930s, Covent Garden just had a short summer season, there wasn't any opera there the rest of the year. I would bicycle up in the morning before seven o'clock from Notting Hill Gate to Covent Garden and put down my stool and pay the man sixpence, and that was [my] position in the queue for the gallery. Then I would bicycle home, go to school and, if it was an early opera, I'd go straight from school by public transport to Covent Garden to claim my stool, half an hour before the doors opened. It was all rather time-consuming, but cheap. The tickets were half a crown and you paid sixpence for your stool. My parents let me do that all on my own, they were really very forward-looking.

At St Paul's I started learning the viola and when I was fifteen I decided that I wasn't going to take my school certificate because I wanted to go to the Royal College of Music and study the viola. But I desperately also wanted to learn the horn. I always wanted to play the horn. I loved the sound of it. We used to go to the Robert Mayer children's concerts at the Central Hall, Westminster, and at the beginning of the season each instrumentalist would give a little solo on his instrument and I thought the sound of the horn was wonderful. My two favourite pieces of music were the Scherzo from Beethoven's Fifth Symphony, and the first movement of the 'Emperor' piano concerto. Both had prominent horn parts and I would always pick out the horns. My mother, [who] was very keen that I should do my School Certificate, said, 'If you get through the exam we'll buy you a horn.' So I had some coaching in maths and I got through the exam and we went out into Soho and we bought a horn for five pounds. I went for my entrance examination for the Royal College of Music later in the summer and played 'The Bluebells of Scotland' on the horn, and was accepted as a second study horn pupil, and a first study viola pupil. I was sixteen. By present-day standards I was barely adequate.

While I was still at college the War started. I'd left home [by then] because I didn't get on terribly well with my father and we were having too many rows at home. There was a terrible shortage of horn players, and I just got pushed into professional work. I didn't apply or anything, they came to me, said, 'We Need You.' I had my twenty-first birthday away on tour with the London Symphony Orchestra. Moïsevitch, the pianist, who was on tour with us, heard it was my birthday, and invited me and some of my friends to join him for a drink – he was a great drinker – and tried to drink us all under the table. Some of my friends got a bit tiddly, but I managed to remain reasonably sober and get us back to our digs afterwards.

[Playing in orchestras throughout the Second World War] was very exciting. I was doing the thing I wanted to do most in the world. And it was great fun; one usually had a jolly time with orchestras. We got taken to all sorts of places that other people wouldn't have been able to go to. I remember going to the Isle of Wight, for instance, and we went over to Belgium and Holland, playing to the troops. One did a lot of travelling and made quite deep friendships. I remember being in Middlesborough once when it was blitzed and the gasworks was hit, and watching this gasometer burning from our hotel window. There were certain things that only we had experienced that did draw one together. By and large the feeling in a touring company is pretty close anyway. I enjoyed that very much. It was one of the things I was sorriest to lose when I gave up professional music. But one took [these friendships] entirely for granted, and very often they just evaporated when that particular job had finished. Perhaps I was just unfortunate in that, because some people did form very close and lifelong attachments, but not many people; mostly the sort of attachments you make in that sort of life are just for the time being. [It was a] gypsy existence. I enjoyed it. I was young, I was in my early twenties and it was great fun. One didn't have time to think about the pros and cons of it.

In 1943 Barbirolli came over from America to take over the Hallé. I heard that he was stuck for a first horn, and someone said to me, 'Why don't you phone him up and ask him if you can have the job?', so I did, and he said, 'My dear, how much do you want?' I asked for £2.00 a week over the union minimum for principals out of town, and got the job. He was a wonderful man to work with, because he didn't spare himself at all. He worked himself as hard as everybody else, in fact harder. He would have the strings in the morning, the wind in the afternoon, and everybody together in the evening, so he would work for nine hours and we'd only be working for six. He shared all our trials and troubles on journeys. There was no thought that he would be travelling first class and we would be travelling third. He travelled in with us always, and if we had to sit or stand in a luggage van with draughts coming up through the floorboards for a journey [on a] cold night, he would be in there with us.

I was first horn in the Hallé for two years and then Barbirolli and I had some disagreement. [At that time] the Hallé didn't have an orchestral committee, the orchestra didn't have any say, [it] was simply run from above. Some of us who were a bit bolshie, as I was in those days, got together and formed ourselves into an orchestral committee. We didn't have any power, and I don't think we could do anything, except possibly by personal influence, but it was very much disapproved of. In addition to that we'd been playing a lot of very classical music and his approach to classical music was to slightly romanticise it, to play it with a bit of rubato, not absolutely square and classical, whereas in those days I was a terrific purist of classicism. One day Barbirolli said to me, 'I sometimes feel that you're not very happy with the way we make music.' And I, with the audacity and stupidity of youth, said, 'Yes, I sometimes feel that your approach to classical music is rather too romantic for my taste.' Really I should never have said such a thing to him. It was symptomatic of my upbringing: I had to think everything out my way and ultimately I couldn't help telling him so. He took it marvellously at the time, then a couple of days later he called me in and he said, 'Well, you know, if you feel like this, perhaps we should go our separate ways.' I was very sorry about that. I didn't want to hurt him, I was very fond of him. I think he was very sad about it too.

I got a job in the Scottish Orchestra as principal horn for a couple of years, then went to the BBC Scottish, and then, in the summer of 1947, Covent Garden were in need of a principal horn, and rather foolishly I applied for the job. I did an audition and passed it with flying colours, but if you've never played in an orchestra pit you don't know how difficult it is, and when I got into the pit I found the music was over there, and the conductor was over there, and the light on the music stand was dreadful, and the singers kept pulling things up, and I couldn't see the conductor properly, and I didn't know the operas, and really I had no right to have taken that job. The main conductor was a man called Rankl and he didn't like women much anyway. After a few weeks, when I'd mucked one or two things up, he said, 'Well, I won't have her playing for me any more,' and my contract wasn't renewed. It's quite true that some players who had gone off to the War were coming back and wanting their jobs back, but I thought the Musicians' Union ought to have done something for me, so I applied to them and said, 'I think I've been wrongly dismissed.' They wouldn't do anything for me and I felt sure that was because I was a woman.

Different orchestras behaved differently to women. As far as your playing was concerned [you] were equal, but you weren't always equal in the way you were treated from the point of view of pay or jobs or privileges. In the Hallé they depended very much on women because there were so few men around. Women were treated very well there, very much on merit, performing merit, and very much appreciated. Certain London orchestras I'd been in, both before and after my time with the Hallé, [did not give] women all the privileges that men might have been given. We were all paid union rates so no one was paid more than anyone else, but if there were extra jobs going for people to bump up in amateur orchestras or local orchestras which were short of certain players, these jobs were usually given to the men. Film sessions and that sort of thing would tend to go to the men. If there was a choice between you and a man as a player they would probably take the man. [You] accepted it. You just considered yourself jolly lucky for what you got. I suppose fair enough – if the men had families to support they needed more money really. It was a social thing more than anything else; the men were usually the fixers and they preferred to take men rather than women. They could go and have their boozing together and that sort of thing.

In the late 1940s I got in with the people doing the music [at] the Old Vic Company. We did Michael Redgrave's *Hamlet*, Laurence Olivier's *Richard III*, all sorts of well-known actors and actresses. It was absolutely the top thing in London. There were two horns on the books, which gave us a chance to do some freelance work, and [in 1949] I was doing an out-of-town job in Manchester when I got a phone call from Michael Mudie, then principle conductor of the Sadler's Wells Opera. Their first horn had suddenly, I don't know what happened to him, he'd collapsed, gone off, died, I don't know, but I got an SOS from Michael Mudie, 'Can you come quickly!' They were in Hull or somewhere, it was a terrific journey across the North of England [and] at the end of the week I joined them as principal horn. Michael Mudie was a wonderful conductor. He unfortunately developed disseminated sclerosis, and, alas, by the mid-fifties he could no longer conduct, but he was the best English conductor of his generation. A really brilliant conductor. I was lucky, I played for all the good conductors of my day, Barbirolli, Beecham, Malcolm Sargent, Adrian Boult. I had a very good innings.

[After two years as principal horn at Sadler's wells] I began to get trouble with my teeth. I have rather thin enamel on my teeth and [it] began to wear away from horn playing. I was born soon after the First World War and probably in those days one's mother wasn't given extra milk to drink, and her diet may have been poor, I don't know, but anyway, I've always had bad teeth, and they began to be affected by the horn playing. I started having to have them stopped across the front but the dentist wouldn't stop them both at the same time, so sometimes I would end up blowing out of my mouth in one direction, and then it would get worn down on the other side, and he would build that side up . . . It was just becoming too nerve-racking to play first horn, so I moved down to second. I stayed for another two years and then the trouble with my teeth became so bad that I realised I'd have to give up playing. I didn't know *what* to do. At that point I ran into my father. I said I was in this dilemma and didn't know what to do, and he said, 'Come into the firm! We'll give you a good time!' So in 1953 I went into the firm.

I'd got to the point when I thought, 'Well, the horn isn't the be all and end all of life. It isn't even the be all and end all of music.' So I didn't mind giving it up [but] I didn't really want to join Gollancz. I was like a drowning person grasping at a raft. I [had thought about becoming a doctor but I] could see that medicine was going to be a very long haul and be very hard work and I thought, 'Well, if he wants to pay me to go and work in his office, why not?' I had to get used to working regular hours, and I had to get used to working social hours instead of antisocial hours, and I had to build up a completely new lot of friends, because all my old musician friends were still working antisocial hours and I found I was drifting away from them. It was four or five years before I built up a new circle of friends. I originally thought, 'Perhaps I'll stay a few months,' and then I remember discussing it with a friend and saying, 'I suppose if he's given me a job I'd better stay a couple of years.' I didn't expect to move up in the firm at all. I didn't expect to be made a director or anything like that; I didn't expect to do anything except a bit of filing.

I went in right at the bottom, learning general office procedures, typing the labels for books that were going out for review. I couldn't type, only with two fingers, I never learnt to type properly, I'm trying to teach myself now. After three or four weeks [my father] decided that he needed a typographer. He'd been doing all the typography himself, and he decided he would make me into a typographer. He sent me to see the head compositor who was in charge of doing our jackets, and he told me what instructions a printer needed – all our jackets in those days were typographical – then my father sent me home to his flat with the spring list and a pica rule and some large sheets of paper and he said, 'Do a layout of a full-page *Times Literary Supplement* advertisement, writing all your own copy for our spring list.' So I did, and showed it to him, and he thought the copy was OK. So he had it set up in type, and it more or less fitted the space. After that I did all the jackets and some of the advertisements and when my father went away I would do all the advertising. Then he started me on reading and writing reports, and then writing jacket copy, and after a couple of years, I suppose, he let me edit a book. The first book I did was called *Journey into a Fog* by Margaretta Berger-Hammerschlag. It was her reminiscences of having come to England as a refugee. He would give me one book at a time to look after. Then he put me on the board, and I started going to production meetings and all the general discussions that go on in a publishing office. Gradually over a period of ten or twelve years, he taught me the whole business.

He could never have taken me into the office if I hadn't had that fifteen years as a professional musician, when I got my corners rubbed off me. We just wouldn't have got on at all. As it was we didn't get on that well, although we did understand each other. I'd learnt to respect him more, having been out in the world for a number of years, and he respected me more, so we got on much better. I mean I did sometimes get cross with him, and I would show him my displeasure by walking out of the room and slamming the door, and he would accept that and for that reason we got on all right. He took it very well and we always made it up. He very rarely showed displeasure of me. Once I'd gone into the firm he was remarkably patient with me. He was a wonderful teacher, he really loved teaching people. He'd been a schoolteacher at Repton and he started the Left Book Club in 1936 because he wanted to teach people and make people think for themselves. I'm quite sure that his early influence on me was to make me think for myself in every possible direction.

Then in 1967 my father had a stroke. Before he'd had his stroke he had gone on an extended holiday and left me in charge of the office for nearly three months. I really became a publisher during those three months, and consolidated all that I had learnt. He came back in August and he had his stroke in October, so I simply took charge again. He died in February and from then on I ran the firm. Certainly there were one or two people who rather resented my rise, and when it was perfectly obvious that he was favouring me and beginning to look upon me as his successor, that caused some problems. One or two people left because they didn't want to work under me, but other people made a very big contribution. Everything was very well organised [when I took over]. It all worked extremely well, marvellous filing systems, you could find anything, everything was very efficient, all the chase-ups were done at the right time. I didn't want to upset that and change things. I was very keen on changing things *gradually*, just changing one thing at a time. [My father had] run a very close-hauled ship, in which he made all the decisions. He had control over absolutely everything. All the strings in his hands. I tried to do the same and it didn't work; I had to learn how to delegate and I was never a very good delegator. I learnt to in the end, but it took a while. Until he died, I just looked after odd books really and then I took over the thriller list and quite a lot of his authors: Ivy Compton-Burnett, all the thriller writers, Michael Innes, Edmund Crispin, Anthony Price. I discovered Anthony Price. I encouraged him to write his first book and looked after him ever since. I also looked after some novelists, Terence de Vere White for instance. I did all the books about music, all the books about mountaineering and walking.

[With the increased responsibility after my father's death] I did various time-saving things: I grew my hair so as not to have to bother to go to hairdressers; I used to go every weekend to my mother's country cottage because it gave her a focal point for her life now she no longer had my father to cook for, and it gave me a chance to do office work at weekends. I was doing all the jackets and writing the blurbs and I would work the whole of every weekend. She would look after me and I would just work. And [during the week] I never came home before seven o'clock in the evening. A lot of the work was very interesting. When I realised I was going to have to retire I felt quite devastated and wondered how I would do without it. It's been much easier than I expected!

[When I took over, Gollancz was almost entirely staffed by women.] My father found it difficult to get on with men. There were a few men, mainly in top jobs and in the accounts department, and the packers of course. Women [have the advantage of being able to] come in as secretaries, and learn the job as apprentices. People used to come and see me and say, 'How can I get into publishing?', so I'd say, 'Learn shorthand-typing, get a job as a secretary to an editor and look upon it as an apprenticeship.' And in most cases I think those that did got on well. Certainly in our firm almost all the promotion was done from within and after I took over I very much pursued a policy of promotion from within. I had good people there who had been doing secretarial jobs and knew the way the firm worked, and I didn't want to have to teach anyone else how it worked. We did have some sort of rule by which [women] had a certain length of maternity leave and then they had their job back if they wanted it. But that's fairly recent; in the earlier days that just didn't arise. There were only three or four of us high enough up in the company for it to apply to. It just didn't arise. A publishing firm is like an hourglass: if you don't get through the little gap into the top bit, you leave at the gap anyway; you take a step sideways into another firm. But once you've got through the gap and you've got into the upper echelons then you've probably got past the age when you would want to be having a family anyway. Most people by the time they'd been promoted didn't have children. They either didn't marry or they didn't have children.

We worked nine till six; the whole firm worked nine till six in those days. We had a fortnight's holiday a year, and an hour for lunch. We didn't pay any overtime. Of course there were always people who would work late, but they didn't work late if they didn't want to . . . You get that in publishing; you get people who are so interested in the job that they'll come in on Sundays and work. They're not interested in being paid for so many hours, they want to do the job properly. I don't know about other firms, but it's still true in Gollancz. You go there at seven o'clock at night and you'll find at least half a dozen people still working in the building, if not more. You go in on a Sunday and you'll find two or three people in there.

We had shareholders and we had to pay dividends [but] we tended rather to ride roughshod. Provided we could pay dividends to the shareholders we didn't want to make more money than that. Keep ourselves going, pay dividends as necessary. Otherwise we were quite prepared to lose money on the odd book. [Competition from large conglomerates made] things extremely difficult. I admire [the women's presses] very much, but I don't know how they can manage to compete. The smaller you are the worse your cash-flow problems really, and because you're small the agents aren't too keen on selling you books and therefore want the highest prices if they're going to sell you their books. Equally, the booksellers don't consider you're very important if you're only small, so the big conglomerate booksellers pay you last and make great demands in the way of returns' policies and that sort of thing. You're pretty well caught both ways. You have to be very inventive and try to find new authors who are not too expensive, and of course, as soon as you make a success of an author you lose them because you can't pay for their next book because their agent wants so much money. There is no reason why agents shouldn't help an author to keep a good relationship with his editor. When I came into publishing, agents were much more like that. Agents used to honour the clauses in the contracts which gives the publisher the right to consider the next book. They would let the author write the book and then they would take it round to the publisher, and if the publisher made a reasonable offer the agent would be happy. Now the author writes an outline and the agent flogs it to several publishers at once, so obviously the agent is preventing the author and editor making a good relationship. The agent has his eye on his own rake-off, he wants to get the best possible advance for his authors, to pay his own rent, therefore the agent is always keen to use his authors as a means of pitting publishers against each other to get the biggest possible advance from a publisher, and isn't so particularly interested in retaining an author–editor relationship. I think agents are at fault there, they don't see that relationship as part of their job. I formed very good relationships with several of my authors. Anthony Price has been very, very faithful to me, and we've been very good friends for many years. J. I. M. Stewart too. [But] we lost a number of writers: they had perhaps started with us without an agent and then they went to an agent and the agent started putting the price up and we decided that we couldn't do well enough with them and lost them. So one way and another you have to be on your toes and you're always losing out, but somehow you keep the business going.

I began to think in terms of retirement when I was about sixty-seven and in fact I retired three months before my seventieth birthday. I'm still officially a consultant for the firm and I go in about once a fortnight, but I have virtually stopped doing any editorial work. Three or four years ago, when I saw retirement looming, I started having lessons on the violin, and since I've retired I've been doing a great deal of chamber music on the violin and I've been playing the viola too. One three-hour session a day is as much as I really want to do on the viola.

The violin is much lighter and smaller, not so heavy to hold up, and physically easier to play. I don't mind how much violin playing I do. I started having singing lessons when I was forty-six and I [still sing]. I don't have lessons very often now, but my last teacher taught me a way of getting my voice into order that works so well that I can really just about manage without. During the 1970s and early 1980s I was doing a great deal of amateur operatic and I loved that, it was great fun. I was enjoying very much the acting side of it. When I was young my sister Diana wanted to be an actress, so she was always the one who did any acting at home in charades and things, and I didn't want to compete with her; but when I came to sing and wanted to use my voice in opera, I found that I was quite a natural actress, and it all came quite easily, and I was effective on the stage. I'm [also] very keen on walking. I usually go [on holiday] with a commercial party or a walking club group. Sometimes I go just with a friend, but you've got to find exactly the right person to go with, particularly at my age. Most of my friends have given up walking by now, or they've had so much knee trouble or back trouble that they don't want to walk more than, say, an hour or two a day, whereas I can still walk for five or six hours a day if necessary. Last year I went to Nepal and Crete and Switzerland and Scotland. It was my first year of retirement and I slightly overdid it. Certainly my knees thought I'd overdone it! This year I'm not going to do so much. There are still places that I would like to see: I'd like to go walking in the north-west Himalayas. I want to go to southern India, but that won't be walking, that will be just sightseeing. I'd like to go to the Sahara. I'd like to see that.

I play the violin, I dig my allotment, I try and keep my garden tidy, though I find I spend more time on the allotment than I do in the garden. I shall go on singing for as long as I can, but obviously there'll come a time when my voice won't respond as it is still doing. I hope to go on living in this house for a long time. It has advantages which I thought of when I bought the house, in that it has a bathroom on the ground floor as well as one upstairs, so that if ever I get so crippled that I can't go upstairs I can collapse onto the ground floor and have someone upstairs keeping an eye on me, looking after me. Not having any children, I won't have anyone to look after me in my old age unless I pay them to do so. One must think about these things in advance. I don't want to be a burden on my sisters, or on my nephews or their wives. I very much [wanted to be a mother], but I had a hysterectomy when I was forty-six, so that put paid to that. I mean, I probably wouldn't have been a mother anyway. I do regret not having children. There have been important relationships from time to time, but I am the sort of person who needs a good deal of time to myself too and one of the inhibiting factors for relationships has been that I have always been aware of wanting to hold back something just for myself.

When I was in publishing I spent all my time reading manuscripts, most of which were declined, and I never had a chance to keep up with books that other people were publishing, or even read classics from the past, so now I go to a literature discussion group where we read a book a fortnight and meet and discuss it. I don't find the time on my hands at all, I keep very busy and seem to be getting busier. I don't think there'll be any problem about filling in my time for the rest of my life.

[I'm proud of a few things I've done in my life.] This perhaps may sound silly, but there's a very difficult fourth horn part in Beethoven's choral symphony, slow movement, and in 1941 when I was twenty-one I played the fourth horn on the last Friday night of the first Proms season at the Albert Hall. The last Friday was always Beethoven's Ninth Symphony and the fourth horn part was usually taken over by the first horn because it's a big solo part, but I told Henry Wood, who was conducting, that I wanted to play the fourth horn part, and he let me play it. That was quite a thing. Mind you I did crack one note!

Selling the firm in such a way as to satisfy the main shareholders and at the same time not having lost a single job: I was very pleased with that. But it's very funny that the whole of the publishing thing has just really gone from my mind. Subconsciously I must have absolutely hated it. I'm not really a booksy person.

UNA KROLL

Una Kroll was born on 15 December 1925. Her ancestry includes archbishops, egg merchants, doctors and spies, and spans several countries including Italy, Turkey, Germany, Latvia and Russia. At the outbreak of war in 1914, her maternal grandmother fled on foot across the wastelands of Russia to Latvia. This same grandmother was later to die attempting a similar trek in 1939, when she fled from Latvia into Germany. Una was the result of a passionate romance and a 'marriage of convenience'. Her father was an occasional visitor in her life rather than a reliable presence and she was brought up single-handedly by her mother.

She won a scholarship to Girton College, Cambridge, and went on to train as a doctor. She completed her medical training at the London Hospital and was about to begin specialising in neurosurgery when she received a calling to the Church and left to become a nun. This began a lifelong tussle between medicine and religion, which in large measure she managed to combine. In both fields she experienced the full weight of male power, authority and prejudice. While working full-time as a GP, she took up the cause of women's ordination and throughout the 1970s and 1980s she was a vociferous and tireless campaigner for women priests. She became a deaconess in 1970 and was ordained a deacon in 1988. She has written several books, including Transcendental Meditation – A Signpost to the World *(1974),* Flesh of My Flesh *(1975),* Lament For a Lost Enemy – A Study of Reconciliation *(1976),* A Spiritual Exercise Book *(1985),* Growing Older *(1988) and* The Healing Touch *(1991).*

Una Kroll describes herself as 'an incurable idealist both in my

*medicine and in my religion', and this streak of courageous
unconventionality can be seen also in the extraordinary story of her
marriage to Leopold Kroll, a celibate priest of thirty years and a man
twenty-three years her senior, with whom she had four children.
Since her husband's death in 1987, she has largely withdrawn from
public life. In 1990 she joined the Convent of the Sacred Cross near
Monmouth as a novice, where she lives and works, now a professed
sister.*

   *The interview took place in a simple and peaceful guest room of the
Tymawr Convent over two days and between services in October
1991. The tranquillity inside was matched by the autumnal stillness
outside.*

My mother was born to an Italian merchant and a very staunch
English lady in the middle of Russia. She came from a
distinguished clerical family in England, two members of
whom were Archbishops of Canterbury. My father had a
similarly chequered ancestry. He was the son of British
parents who were egg merchants, and they, too, in the spirit of
adventure prevalent in Britain in those days, emigrated and
landed up in Russia. My father was a great traveller and so was
my mother, they both spoke many languages. They were very
cosmopolitan their whole lives.

   My father became a British intelligence agent during the
First World War. He worked with people like Philby and
Burgess and McClean. He knew all those people. I was very
influenced by his sheer courage; he was a man who knew the
depth of fear, and because he knew the depth of fear he also
knew somehow the secret of managing to combat it and get on
with life, which he did. It wasn't romantic; it was extremely
painful. My mother was my father's courier in the First World
War. She was in constant danger too. Her last mission was to
carry out the crown jewels of a branch of the [Russian] royal
family that did escape. The British Government flew her out at
the last moment and she came home sitting on the crown
jewels! They'd met and fallen in love in Italy. It was a mad

romance and they conceived me. They married before I was born to make me legitimate, but already by the time I was born their marriage was breaking up.

My father left when I was eighteen months and I met him only twice during my childhood. Once, when I was eleven, when he told me that he was married again. I desperately wanted my father and mother to be together again and I saw myself as the reconciler, so this was an enormous disappointment to me. Then, for my eighteenth birthday – my father was a valiant showman – he took me to Claridge's for a birthday lunch and we had lobster. I've never eaten lobster since. He told me that not only had he been married since my mother, but he'd been married before and I had two half-sisters. It was a terrible shock. I was very religious at that age and it meant in my eyes that I was illegitimate and that his marriage to my mother had not been a real marriage. All my illusions about him disappeared. Later on I remember seeing all the medals he had from the First World War, the DSO and an MC, there were three rows of medals which he had for bravery of various kinds. But it wasn't until after the Second World War that I got to know him, when my own children were born, and I began to discover that a lot of his wayward-ness had come out of the period of his life when he'd lived with death round the door almost every day. It was a reaction to his undercover work, to living a double life all the time. He drank too much, he lived too fast, he never gave himself time to stop and think what he was doing. I was older then and I could understand what living under those conditions of fear and daily danger does to people. As a child I didn't understand any of that.

My father was an immense influence in his absence and I romanticised his existence. My mother would never speak of him. I was not allowed to go to my father's family, except once when I was about five or six. I remember my paternal grandmother tried to tell me my father was a good man, but I knew differently from my mother. It wasn't a happy time. My mother was extremely poor, living from hand to mouth, dependent in part on my father's sister who was very good to us. She often took us in when we had no money at all.

I grew up in a Russian émigré colony in Hampstead in London. I spoke French, English and Russian fluently: Russian at home, English at school, and French in the Russian émigré community. Hampstead was full of people living in exile who had been important people in their own country and who now found themselves destitute. I remember as a child sitting curled up in a chair, listening half the night to their conversations. These were [my mother's] friends, the people she really owed loyalty to. They also were very poor. The silver teapot would go down to the pawnbroker on Saturday nights and come back whenever they could afford to retrieve it. They had a sweat workshop making clothes, and my mother worked on sewing machines. I remember going down to these basement workshops in a big old Victorian house in Hampstead, inhabited by a lot of people struggling to make a living, working half the night to sew clothes for very little money. They managed with a blend of gaiety and tragedy. A couple of them committed suicide because they just couldn't bear it any longer.

When I was five, my mother couldn't cope with me and I was sent to Latvia. My aunt put me on the boat and said if I was unhappy I was to send my mother a picture of a ship. Unfortunately she forgot to tell my mother. I repeatedly wrote my weekly letters home with a ship and of course got no answer. I spent a year in Latvia as companion to a girl whose father was in the diplomatic service and was also a spy. It was a very unhappy period of my life indeed. There was a lot of physical cruelty in that family and sexual abuse, it's a very dark period of my history.

I came home when I was seven and we settled down again in an attic flat in Hampstead. My mother was extremely unhappy. One night she tried to kill us both. I remember her closing up the windows and putting the gas on. Unfortunately, or fortunately for me, she hadn't got enough money; we woke up in the morning with the most ghastly headaches.

It was a terrible time: she used to beg for my school fees. But she was a fighter. She was like a tigress with a tiger cub. She was fiercely defensive, and I think that's what kept her alive. I can't think what else did. She was very attractive, half Italian, a very beautiful woman. I was like a pale, dull shadow compared with her. She was determined that I wouldn't starve through lack of education. When I was four she hit me on the head because I wasn't reading fast enough. And if I was bad or naughty or whatever, she'd go into withdrawal silences for days and that would put me into a complete panic. I was passionately adoring of my mother, fiercely loyal to her, but also frightened of her.

I wasn't a very good child, I was rude and awkward and difficult, an impossible adolescent. I was always outside the headmistress's office. Soon after the beginning of the war, my mother and I left London and went to Malvern. I spent about nine months at Clarendon School which was run by Plymouth Brethren: you didn't cut your hair, you wore long skirts, never went to parties, never went to the theatre or a cinema. It was when I was at Clarendon that I decided I'd be a doctor.

At eighteen Una Kroll won a State scholarship to Girton College, Cambridge where she read natural sciences and won a half blue for swimming. In 1947 she went to the London Hospital to do her medical training. In that year all previously 'male only' teaching hospitals were obliged to take a ten per cent quota of women students. Una Kroll was one of the first women admitted in this way. As a woman medical student she encountered open hostility from both doctors and nurses and was treated with contempt or flirtatiousness by male consultants. The biggest compliment of the day was, 'You've got a male mind.' The absence of womanly female role models and the blatant discrimination angered her, but her dedication to medicine remained intact. In 1952, having completed her training and survived two years on house, she received her calling to be a nun. Despite fierce opposition, she left medicine to become a nun at a convent in Malvern. But here too she found herself in a

*world dominated by men in which women were second-class
citizens.*

I was professed on 14 September 1955. As a sister in simple
vows, I promised to stay for three years with a view to staying
for life. But towards the end of my noviciate, I was in two
minds as to whether I ought to go on or not. I saw an
unhealthy love of power in the Church. The rules were made
on the whole by men to hold down women. Certain things
were taken for granted that I couldn't take for granted. As a
nun you had to be dependent on people who might be much
poorer than you. I didn't find that easy. I didn't find wearing a
habit and being taken to be a holy person easy, when I knew I
wasn't holy. I was worried about our separation from
ordinary people and wanted to find ways of living more like
ordinary people. I cared deeply about that. I was looking for a
different style of being a nun. But almost as soon as I was
professed I was sent out to Africa to be a doctor and a nun in a
place called Bolahun, a village deep inside Liberia.

I adored Africa. It fulfilled my passion for medicine and for
serving people. But I was unusual for my time. Missionaries in
those days were convinced that Western ways were the best. I
didn't agree. I didn't say, 'I'm a Christian, I'm better than
you.' I went to be with people. I learnt the language, I learnt
the customs, I worked with one of the witch-doctors. I have
always crossed boundaries, and crossing boundaries means
that you enter into other people's shoes and understand life
from their point of view. Africa was no different.

The convent was about half an hour away from the main
village, in a clearing with tin roofs and mosquito nets, and a
bath outside, and latrines. You had the convent at one end of
the village, the monastery at the other end, a big church in the
middle and schools. I worked in the hospital, mostly looking
at wounds, treating sleeping sickness and malaria. We had
very little to treat them with. When you find yourself as the
only doctor in the middle of a jungle, scientific training really
goes by the board. You improvise. We had a heap of

hypertensive drugs sent to us from America which I used to use as placebos. I also did surgery. All I'd done until then was take out appendixes and a few hernias. I had three weeks' surgery training at the London Hospital, again in my funny old clobber – I was so ashamed of being in that peculiar disguise, but still I did it. When I got out to Africa, right from the beginning I had to operate on enormous hydroceles [water in scrotal sacs]. The men used to come in with them on a wheelbarrow, it was so dreadful. It was a regional thing. Female circumcision was practised too. I knew I couldn't alter the custom, but I used to supply disinfectant or advice which helped to save some lives. The women wouldn't have a man present at childbirth, so a lot of them also died in childbirth. As a woman I was allowed to attend the birth and I began to treat the infections and so give them live babies.

I quickly became very popular with the Africans, but it got me into a lot of trouble – missions are no different from anywhere else, jealousies arise. When the Father doctor came back, I saw a golden opportunity to set up a surgical clinic. If I'd have been wiser or older I probably wouldn't have done it, but I was young and inexperienced and enthusiastic and I didn't handle the diplomacy side of my job at all well. If somebody needed an operation I would operate and I wouldn't be up at the convent at mass, which I ought to have been. The priest would bring me communion and I'd go on operating. To me the whole thing gelled, but to other people I wasn't being a good nun. Nobody knew if I was being a good doctor or not, because nobody understood what being a good doctor was about.

I wasn't popular with the mission doctor or the male establishment on either side. I was in Leopard country [an area of Africa where local communities were 'ruled' by a group of widely feared witch-doctors and other powerful 'Leopard' men] and I undoubtedly offended some of the Leopard men, the witch-doctors. One man was bitten by a snake and he came in desperately ill. I was trying to save his life and my dresser said to me, 'Don't do it, the Leopard men are against him.' And I said, 'That's rubbish,' and I did rescue him, but three weeks later he was dead, mauled by a leopard. It was probably a human leopard, but he was dead all right.

Anyway it all began to go wrong. The mission began to rumble and want me to go home and in the end there was a big blow-up, with the Africans petitioning the Superior of the Order in America not to send me home. The Superior at that time was a man called Leopold Kroll, who had worked in Africa for over fifteen years and had been at the mission, and was very respected. So in February 1957 he came. I was very much in awe of him. He was the boss of the whole thing, and had a lot of power. He listened to what everyone had to say, and then he said to me that I should go home, that he didn't think I'd got a vocation to be a nun. I was still very sold on being a nun and I was very angry.

Just about that time one of the local witch-doctors fell ill and the mission sent me out to see what I could do. When the Superior said, 'You must go home,' I said, 'But I've still got this man who's very ill; it would be irresponsible to just leave him. You've got to give me longer.' I kept him alive for a bit but then he died, and that night I fell very ill indeed. It's difficult to describe, of what nature, but I had a breakdown. Africa is a place of intense psychic energies. What I think I experienced was the intensity of people's hatred, not only the hatred of the white people, but also the hatred of the black people. I had crossed boundaries, not only by empathising with people, but I also crossed boundaries between good and evil. Leopold was a man of enormous wisdom and he really defended me from the encroaching anger of these two different groups.

With the Superior of my Order, Leopold watched over me and cared for me from February to May. I recovered, but I was still quite poorly. I'd already determined to leave; I didn't really see how I could go on. Plainly the pull towards medicine had grown very strong, and the religious life as lived at that time wasn't really compatible. I thought I'd come home, spend the next year trying to reorientate myself and then maybe go and put some of my ideas into practice. But in the event it didn't happen my way.

Leopold felt he couldn't leave me because I was still unstable and not well, so he was going to deliver me home to Malvern. On the way we stopped in Paris. He stayed with his brother and I stayed with my mother. And during that period in Paris we decided to get married. It was contrary to all our ethos; it was contrary to *everything*. It was a mad arrangement. Before we made the decision, we went to the Sacré Coeur to pray. I was the one who was less sure that it was right. Leopold seems to have been convinced. And that was the first time we made love – we thought we'd got to do something to be sure that we were not going back! We came over to England and had to wait three weeks before we got married. They came from America to try to persuade my husband to leave me and go back with them. And they came from the convent. It was an incredible three weeks.

I'm not at all sure that I was in love at the time we were married; I was in love very shortly afterwards. But at the time I was too ill to actually be in love with anybody or anything; I was still really in a world of cosmic good and evil, I wasn't really on this earth at all. Leopold did go through a lot of agony about it, but by the time we married he seems to have been convinced. I think he was in love with something he saw during my illness, when I had to be watched and guarded and nursed; the experience was spiritually very intense. He knew the power of evil in Africa and what it could do to a person, psychologically; we'd both seen people killed through fear. We were both crossing barriers: cultural barriers, he was American, I was English; age barriers, he was fifty-five, I was thirty-two. When these people came over to try and get him back, I left him with very open hands. I was the harlot and they didn't talk to me, they just talked to him. He was very cross about that. I think if they had talked to me I probably would have left him. But they didn't – more fool they!

He was a very strong man. I guess he was also the father figure that I had wanted when I was young and hadn't had. He was to me a spiritual father, a father figure, and an immense lover. I wasn't in love with him when we married, but within a very short time, because we had such a struggle beginning our marriage, I was in love with him, and that began a thirty-year partnership which survived all kinds of traumas, and which was marvellous right the way through for both of us.

Leopold had been a religious for thirty years when he married me, but he was never allowed to work as a priest again. Attitudes in the Church were very savage. The Archbishop of Canterbury said he would never work again, and he didn't. His Order wouldn't release him from his vows for over twenty years, they expected him to divorce me and go back. When he was restored to the priesthood after eighteen months we thought that was the end of it, but they have a system of black-spotting people. They didn't tell us for fifteen years and we didn't know, but we quickly realised that if were going to live we would have to live on my salary. Having been a very respected member in his own community, Leopold suddenly found himself unemployed, at the bottom of the pile, not respected, and struggling to get a job. It was very demoralising; it was dreadful.

Almost from the beginning we had to role-reverse. The day we got married he was suspended from his priesthood and we had nothing except fifty pounds which a patient had left me. We survived with a series of local jobs. I got a job working for a Jewish doctor on the North Circular Road. I worked on Friday nights and Saturdays. I was pregnant at the time. My first child was born in 1958 and I had to work right up until the time I went into labour, because women doctors didn't have insurance at that time: the moment you got pregnant, insurance companies wouldn't cover you. We had to raise money to get a mortgage, and in those days you had to do it on your husband's income. It was very hard. We survived really because Leo managed the role-reversal so well, not without pain for him, not without pain for me. But right from the beginning we were partners.

I then got a job in another practice with a slightly larger

house in St Paul's Cray in Kent and my third child was born there in 1961. Six weeks later my mother came from Paris and she lived with us until she died. Through her illness I developed a very great love for her which I think I hadn't had, or maybe I'd lost. We talked about feelings and we talked about her death, and I was able to ease her pain. And I think that I was able to ease also some of my own guilt. It was one of the best experiences of my whole life.

So from 1961 through to about 1967 it was a very quiet and steady life. I was discovering the joys of general practice, and also the joys of being married, having a family and bringing them up. When my youngest daughter was born in May 1964, my father paid a visit to our home. My mother was very ill by then, she was clearly dying, but there was a kind of tenderness and softness between them which was lovely for me to see. My husband was also ill with a double hernia and had to have an operation. I was running to see her, and on the same day going to the hospital at Orpington, and at the same time trying to run a practice.

When I look back, I think how did I do it? But then I see so many people living lives of equal difficulty, so in a way it's given me a lot of understanding of what ordinary life's about, and how tough it can be and how good it can be. We were experiencing in practice what we believed in theory we *ought* to be experiencing. The actual living-out of it was both a discipline and tough, but it gave a lot of stability to our marriage. There seemed to be some point to our struggle – we just weren't always sure what it was !

I was a fighter. By that time I was the fighter. I was aware that I was fighting for my family's survival, and that was all I was aware of. I was very like my mother. Whatever people were throwing at me, I coped with. It was an instinctive reaction, but I couldn't actually fight for myself; I had to have either the underdog or my family to fight for. I remember feeling at one time quite bitter and angry about the harshness with which the Church had treated us, but I suppose because I was religious, seeing oneself as part of the whole of humanity, helped me to channel my anger into concern for other disadvantaged people.

The beginnings of my vocation were around. I remember the first time I expressed the desire to become a priest, a woman priest. I remember saying to my husband, 'I don't see why women can't be priests and I very much feel that I myself am wanting to be a priest.' And I remember my husband's laughter, and my husband's friends', about the idea of females who were priests. I can remember that laughter now, it echoes in my head. And for eleven years I didn't say another word. The laughter silenced me and I didn't say any more. I had no confidence in my own goodness at all.

I was ten years at St Paul's Cray in Kent and I took to general practice like a duck to water. I had a large mixed practice; mainly the people were poor. We were all deeply committed to the National Health Service. I wouldn't take private patients at all, I never have done. One of the strongest forces in my life is the commitment that everybody should have the best possible treatment. While I was there a patient of mine died at the age of twenty-nine of carcinoma of the cervix. She left three small children. At that time cervical cytology was in its infancy and had to be diagnosed before it was too late. I was so angry that I decided that other women mustn't die if I could help it. So I went to King's College and got myself trained and set up my own cytology service within the practice. My husband and I used to sit up at night and count cells; I used to count them and he used to record them. I did cervical cytology and Well Woman breast examination quite some time before it was general custom. It was a very satisfying time of my life. I loved general practice, I didn't mind being up at night.

Gradually over the years, Leo retired from full-time work to look after the house and I worked full-time. I had a series of marvellous women as well to help with the children. But it was a struggle. I nearly had a miscarriage with two of my children, but I could not afford to go sick. Seven days after I had my youngest child, one of my colleagues got appendicitis, but we were a one-income family and the locum fees were high, so I had to go back to work. My children did suffer. I wanted to be with them but often I would have to leave them in the care of other people. They felt that I put patients first, and that's true, because if somebody called me up then I had to go; there was no question of my staying at home. If they wanted me to tell them a story, I'd be saying, 'I'll tell you a story but I've got to go and see this patient first.' That's a very difficult thing for a mother to do; it's also very difficult for the children. The thought was always in my children's head, 'Why do you love your patients more than you love us?' Of course you don't, it's just a very strong sense of duty towards people who are dying or sick.

Leo became their mother, but we learnt very quickly that we weren't interchangeable, ever. They needed a mother *and* a father. I'd still try to do the bread-making, which was my way of saying, 'I'm the mother of this house,' but eventually I gave it up: Leo was at home, no reason why he shouldn't do it. He made bread much better than I did anyway. Even so, the children would wait till I came home. He was a great friend to them and a very stable person in their lives, but they wouldn't confide in him in the way they did to me.

I didn't encounter discrimination in my practice, but they weren't very supportive either. Colleagues who didn't have children had no idea that you needed regular time off. You had to work like a man, like they did, there were no concessions. I didn't have any social life, it was just work, home, look after the kids, work. There was no going out with friends or going to the cinema.

The best of feminism and the best of societies would somehow enable both mothers and fathers to have enough time for their children, by shared jobs and things of that kind. But we haven't reached that stage. Meantime women have a double burden to bear. Children should get a reasonable amount of each parent. I don't think women should sacrifice themselves for their children. But at the same time, part of the fulfilment of yourself as a woman is to be a mother. You have to make a whole series of compromises.

At about that time a letter appeared in the *Church Times* from a priest saying how disgusting it would be to see a pregnant woman at the altar, and how obscene it would be for a woman who was pregnant to be giving the sacrament. Women were beginning to discuss their rights by that time and one thing I really loved was being a woman and being a mother. I was really angered by this letter in the *Church Times*. It linked my belief that oppression on either side is not the way to solve problems. I was very much concerned with trying to seek justice for people who were oppressed by laws in our country, including ecclesiastical laws inside their faith. I was looking for liberation for the oppressed and one way of doing that was to work for women in the Church, to show how good it was to be a woman. The two great issues in my life have been women's goals and women priests. My ordination was never a personal cause. I thought to enable women to be priests might lead to reconciliation and peace.

So I wrote to the Bishop of Southwark and said, 'I hear you've got this school to enable working men to get ordained. Would you consider a woman?' He wrote back a very equivocal letter saying, 'You're not in my diocese, you'd better go and see the right people in your own area.' I began the rounds of ecclesiastical gentlemen, who all looked at me as if I was mad and said, 'You're a mother and you've got children; what do you want?' I couldn't understand this pregnancy thing. I'd never met it before. The more I went round, the more convinced I became that it was all wrong. I was on the point of giving up, when I thought, 'I'll have a last go.' I wrote to the Bishop of Woolwich and he said, 'Come and see me.' I had expected a rather remote figure, because all the bishops I'd ever known were rather remote, you knelt down and kissed their rings and things. He wasn't at all like that; he was an ordinary, warm, welcoming person with a very good brain. And he said, 'I'm looking to expand the ordination course. You won't be ordained, you must understand that, but if you want to do it, come and see if you can.'

There were fifteen people in my year. We were all lay

people. Some were electricians, some were solicitors, some were teachers; there was a policeman, there was a probation officer, there was an artist, there was a businessman. We were all doing the course in our spare time, at night classes and weekend seminars. I had to leave my practice on a Friday night, go forty miles down the road in the car, stay for a lecture – I wasn't allowed to stay the night – and drive back again. I don't think anybody expected me to stick it. Three years, it was. I think they just thought I'd give up. Halfway through I definitely thought about giving up. They made it as hard as they could. It was like going back to the same old discrimination I'd known as a student doctor.

Right from the beginning I saw how painful it was going to be when the men got ordained and I couldn't. The first two years were fine, because we were all students together, having a terrible struggle to pass the exams. We were all in the same boat together. The crunch really came in the third year. The vicars were glad to have the men and nobody was glad to have me. There I was with two years behind me and nowhere to go. You couldn't even begin to be a deaconess, let alone be ordained.

I then got a job as a junior psychiatrist in a big London hospital and there seemed a possibility that my husband would have a job as chaplain at the same hospital. So we talked it over and decided to move. Leo was then sixty-seven. But the day we arrived there was no job for him – it was the black-spot again – and the chaplain hadn't the courage to tell us. Leo had done so much for me and I just wanted him to have the joy of a job for a year or two. But there was no job. He went into a profound depression. I'd got four children and this junior job. We stayed a year. And as a doctor I loved it; I learned a lot, it was marvellous. But it was dreadful for my family. So in 1970 I left the hospital and we moved to Sutton and we started life again. My husband wasn't working, but he did recover gradually. My children were still quite small, the youngest was about six, so they were quite a responsibility. We were much poorer; we'd lost a lot of money. I'd been a senior partner in general pratice for ten years, now I was a junior partner again, taking a relatively small quantity of money.

I still hoped to be ordained, so I went back to the Bishop of Southwark who said, 'Go and see Donald Reeves and if you can make it work, all right; if you can't, that's it.' You don't query if you've got a pistol at your back, you just go. Donald Reeves had never worked with a woman before, and he found it quite difficult, but he took me on. So in December 1970 I was ordained as deaconess to St Peter's at St Helier, Morden. It was a big church on a housing estate of 30,000 people. Donald was very kind to us and enabled my husband to be part of the team too. He was the sort of entrepreneurial type, very socially conscious, with a lot of good ideas about giving people responsibility for their own lives. I learnt an immense amount.

1972 was my turning point. Until 1972 I only saw myself as working within the local church. I had got a few women together to say why women should be ordained, but I hadn't done any more than that. In any case I had no vehicle for promulgating my ideas: women didn't speak on *Thought for the Day*; women didn't speak on *Prayer for the Day*; you couldn't preach in church or anything. It was the opposition to me and to other women in society that forced me into public life. I had no idea at all about becoming such a public figure. I simply wanted to do some church work and some visiting. I wasn't paid by the Church. I earned my keep as a doctor and I gave my services to the Church for love.

But in 1972 I went on a march to demonstrate against a move by the Government of the day to take away child allowance from women and give it as a tax relief to the fathers. I very much wanted to go as a deaconess and as a Christian, so I put my deacon's cassock on and off I went. There were lesbians, there were Communists, there were Socialists, there were Conservatives, there were grandmothers – they were all concerned about this particular iniquitous bill. I met Methodist women and Catholic women. I met Mary Stott, who was on the *Guardian* at the time. Mary and I became firm friends and close colleagues for the next ten years. And I marched.

This was really the beginning of it. I saw women's ordination as a key issue in raising women's consciousness about their goodness; this symbolic 'Keep Out' sign needed to go. I started to work politically, I started to go on marches and to be drawn into the Women in Media campaign. I was in abortion debates and working with lesbian women. I'd crossed the boundaries. I'd gone across the boundaries to the so-called sinners! I formed a pressure group called the Christian Parity Group, which consisted of Catholics, Methodists, Anglicans. We were picketing, we had an all-night vigil in St Margaret's Chapel outside Westminster, we were producing services – we'd persuade some luckless vicar to allow us to put them on in his church, all highly dramatic and symbolic! We made a television programme. Those were years of intensely active political work and also work in the Church. In the beginning we endured a lot of mockery and laughter and unkindness, but you've got to have the people who will make the headlines. Christian friends in the Church said I set the cause of women's ordination back a hundred years. Meanwhile my radical friends thought I was allying myself with the oppressor – and in a sense I was: being middle-class, being professional, being a woman, you are part of the oppressor of other women as well as the oppressed. But theologically and spiritually it made sense to me. I had learnt by that time that God and the Church are not the same thing!

I wasn't really a campaigner, I was always the reconciler, somebody who wanted to bring my father and mother together, wanted to bring Germany and England together, to bring men and women together, to bring differing views in the Church together. I wanted to reconcile them, to find a way that wouldn't involve destroying one side or the other. In the Church of England I had a foot in both camps: I was a very traditional churchwoman, with very strong views on priesthood, holding it in veneration as a typography of Christ and of God. But I was also a woman and very confident and loving of my own sex, aware of the goodness of how God related to women and how Jesus related to women. I was wanting to find a way through.

My book *Flesh of My Flesh* was written from my experience at the World Council of Churches and in my public life. I was moving in an international circle where medicine and religion and feminism came together and I was highly aware of discrimination against women. Not myself – I was a very privileged woman – but against working-class women, women who had no money, women who were sexually abused, women who were not educated, women who were sold into prostitution or sold into marriage. I wrote that book as a plea to the Christian Churches for partnership between men and women.

After the General Synod debate in 1975 when the issue of the ordination of women again came to a full stop, I went through a period of depression. I had to work with my own violent antagonism towards men [who had the power], but also with the part of myself that distrusted women as parental figures, as figures of authority, as people I could trust as priests. My way of working through the conflict was to write a book about reconciliation between love and hate, between men and women, between different parts of myself. That was when I first learnt about my own capacity for hatred and my own capacity for peace. I don't think you can work for peace unless you really know the depth of your own violence. *Lament for a Lost Enemy* is about that struggle. It's the most personal book that I've ever written.

In 1978 there was the second Synod debate about the ordination of women. I really thought the vote would go through then, but it didn't, it was lost in the House of Clergy. And I shouted from the gallery, 'We asked you for bread and you gave us a stone.' That was a very indecent thing for a woman to do. It wasn't anger. I felt that I was being told to make a prophetic statement; I remember being given the words before the vote was announced. I remember wanting not to do it, passionately.

During that debate I experienced the intensity of the hatred which people like myself were causing. As a stereotype I was terrifying to people; as a human being, I was an ordinary middle-aged mother who was a doctor. It's something that does happen to public figures; you get labelled, it's inescapable. I bore it for a long time, but after that 1978 vote I knew that the time had come to get out. I was becoming too public and wasn't giving other women chances to find their voice and their way. I was always much keener on women's ordination than on my ordination and I saw quite clearly that it was my task to go on supporting women, but not to be the Aunt Sally any longer. I was utterly convinced that if I went on being a stereotype, the woman who appears on television again and again, the woman who was talking on radio again and again, that would be oppressive to women . . . As far as I was concerned I had to get out, but a lot of people, including some very close friends, felt it was a treacherous thing to do and that nearly broke me.

I decided to leave London and in 1979 I gave up general practice. In 1981 I became a community health doctor in Hastings. I thought I was going to have a relatively quiet life and devote time to my husband who was well into his seventies by then and not at all well. But you carry your personality with you and you carry your thirst for justice with you. When I got to Hastings there were a lot of young people and no youth advisory service, so a Christian friend and I started up a little charity called the Hastings Listening Post. It was a sexual problems clinic. We were not there to impose our views, we were there to listen and elicit. My whole concept was to release in other people confidence in who they were and in their decisions. I urged them to get proper treatment and help and all the rest of it. I wasn't idiotic, but people have to find their own moral absolutes in their life. I was also part of an inter-disciplinary team of police, social workers, doctors, probation officers and teachers, working with sexual abuse. I worked for seven years in Hastings between 1981 and 1988, and all my skills in negotiating and in diplomacy which I'd had to use in political work were concentrated onto coping with child sexual abuse. Working with abused children is extremely painful and the emotional casualty rate is very high. After my husband died in 1987 I couldn't stand it and I took early retirement. I knew that without him I hadn't got the emotional support I needed to be able to do that work and retain my compassion.

I also withdrew entirely from women's ordination. I knew a lot of women in the Ministry and would listen to their difficulties and give personal support. I had a huge international correspondence with women who wanted to be priests in New Zealand, Australia, Canada, America, Europe. But I withdrew from the public scene and began to work more intensively in spiritual prayer. I went back to the General Synod in 1985, but I went back to pray and not to politicise. I went back a different woman. I had been through an extremely broken-down period where I had felt that women as well as men were not supportive. I was really not capable of uttering a word about women's ordination. I didn't trust myself. I cared about it too deeply by that time and I was too hurt.

From 1982 to 1988 I was in Chichester diocese which was terribly anti-women. The vicar in my parish was opposed to the ordination of women, but he was willing to have me as a parish visitor and casual preacher and eventually I became their deaconess. I was very happy there from about 1982 to 1988. It was a very low church, very evangelical, very traditional, very sexist. It was very, very good for me! I learnt to combine an appearance of conformity with an internal resistance. It was very good training for being here.

'Here' is Tymawr Convent near Monmouth, a Contemplative Order that Una Kroll joined in 1990 as a novice. The community consists of twelve nuns and two hermits. She describes herself as 'a subversive in a conservative context' and is searching for ways of living her present religious life. She offered these reflections on the strength of the opposition to women priests:

There is a psychological fear of women in the Church, a feeling that the Church is an area where you could go and be safe from women. When women come along, that's a threat: the men can't remain so male, nor can they be so confident in the nurturing, motherly aspects of being a priest. Undoubtedly some men see women as powerful people who can destroy them, both in society and in the Church. If a woman comes along who is powerful in healing and powerful in communication skills, a man may feel threatened. The only option then is to keep women down. A number of feminists feel that patriarchy is so embedded in the Christian religion that it is impossible to remain a Christian and a feminist. I have to compromise in order to remain in the Church; it's a constant struggle. I have to see God as not part of that oppression. My heart is with all the wonderful experiments in women's liturgy and in women's rights that are going on, but as part of an oppressive Church, I am bound to be seen as an oppressor. Essential to Christianity is to forgive your enemies and love those who persecute you, but it's not easy.

Symbolism has an enormous part to play in my life. All my forms of resistance are symbolic. One example was when I refused to kneel to take Communion. That action of standing for Communion and not kneeling to a man was immensely liberating. It took symbolic action. Christianity has a symbol at its very centre in the person of Jesus Christ, but the symbolic chap has the nature of both men and women in Him and if He didn't, I couldn't remain in the Christian Church. For me God is beyond male and female, totally beyond it, and I don't feel this person called Jesus Christ to be all-male or all-female, He's liberated from His manhood. Jesus came for women as well as for men. He had to assume female nature as well as male nature to redeem both. What Christ did not assume, He could not redeem. I believe that he assumed our total human nature, men and women; although fully male in His humanity, in His divinity He was both. It's in the Bible: 'Have I not cared for you like a mother cares for its chickens.' For me, He's both.

The women in the Bible are very important to me; they

represent what I believe is good about women. Women like Mary Magdalen, and the woman who poured the ointment out, the precious ointment, and threw it all away; the woman who'd been bleeding for eighteen years and yet she had the courage to touch the hem of the person she thinks will heal her. Those women who dare to reach out across the boundaries of respectability are very important; they're the archetype of the fierce woman who cares so much and loves so much that she dares to break the conventions and asks God for what she needs. But I wouldn't want a female God. I've been to women-only services where the God is female. If you're an oppressed people you have to assert your goodness. We create female goddesses for ourselves to assert our goodness and get confidence in ourselves. I'm sure God smiles on it, but I don't want to stop at that. I think it's phase. I've been through man-hating phases, but you can't actually meet God and go on hating; I don't believe it's possible. I remain firmly committed to a Church in which there is partnership between men and women, which reflects the partnership between the God-head and humanity.

I regret that I'm not a priest, and I regret that because of economic circumstances I couldn't give my children more time. I didn't see some things that they did, and I wasn't able to be with them in the way that I wanted to be. That is a regret, that is a very considerable regret, but by and large, I don't have many. I still hope, of course, to see the Church change its attitude to women. I realise I probably won't live to see that, but I go on with hope.

In November 1992, the General Synod of the Church of England voted 384 to 169 in favour of the ordination of women priests.

BETTY BOOTHROYD

Betty Boothroyd was born on 8 October 1929 in the town of
Dewsbury in West Yorkshire. An only child, both her parents
worked in the textile factories. Her working-class roots are not only a
continuing source of pride to her, but they have also had a profound
influence in shaping her political values and, in turn, her career. An
awareness of social inequality is integral to both her thoughts and
actions.

Apart from a much-publicised time as a Tiller Girl at the age of
seventeen and a short spell of secretarial work, politics has claimed her
attention for most of her life. She regularly attended Labour Party
meetings as a girl with her mother. A member of the Labour League of
Youth, aged eighteen, she won the National Public Speaking
Contest; the adjudicator was Denis Healey. At twenty-one she
followed in the footsteps of an uncle and ran for council, unsuccessfully.

She moved to London and in 1954, after three years in the Labour
Party Research Department, she started work at the House of
Commons as assistant to Geoffrey de Freitas, MP for Lincoln, and
Barbara Castle, MP for Blackburn. At that time, she says, she had no
personal ambition to be a politician: 'I was happy to be the power
behind the throne.' Three years later, at the age of twenty-seven, she
fought her first by-election in South-East Leicester. It was not until
1973, fifteen years and many campaigns later, that she won West
Bromwich, where she has been a devoted and popular MP ever since.
Between 1962 and 1971 she worked in the House of Lords and the
Foreign Office for Lord Walston.

Her career may have taken place within the field of politics, but it *has by no means all been within sight of Westminster. In 1956 she went with a delegation of Labour MPs to the Soviet Union, China and Vietnam; she was secretary to the NATO delegation in Paris; she spent a year in the United States writing speeches for the Republican senator Sylvio Conte, and from 1975 to 1977 she was a member of the European Parliament.*

Betty Boothroyd began to make political and feminist history when in 1974 she was appointed Assistant Government Whip. She was on the Speaker's Panel of Chairmen in 1979 and the House of Commons Commission from 1983 to 1987. She was also a member of the Labour Party's National Executive for four years until 1989. In June 1987, she was appointed Deputy Speaker, the second woman ever to take the chair (Betty Harvey Anderson, who held it from 1970 to 1973, was the first). On 9 April 1992, despite her optimism, Labour again lost the fight for government, although Betty herself had the satisfaction of winning her eleventh parliamentary campaign in West Bromwich with an increased majority of 7,830. With the Conservative victory in the General Election, her chances of becoming Speaker seemed over, but 72 Conservative politicians joined the opposition parties to secure her appointment with an impressive majority.

This interview took place at the House of Commons in July and November 1991 in Betty Boothroyd's tiny office overflowing with paperwork, where we were constantly interrupted by the telephone, Big Ben, division bells and secretaries — all the usual business of the House. Betty herself smoked with an air of imperturbable calm throughout, answering questions succinctly and without hesitation. Asked how much of her time she gives to politics, she replied simply, 'Ninety per cent – at least. It has to be.'

I came out of the womb into the Labour movement. I mean, my parents were active members, so it was always there. Politics fascinated me. But to change society was really what I wanted to do. I hated the dark satanic mills and the narrow lives and houses that people that I was brought up with had to live in. All of that made me even more concerned about changing society. But it was always there. I came from a family that was interested in politics, it wasn't something that I had to get accustomed to. It was part and parcel, like miner's coal dust that you can't scrub out of your nails. There was talk always of politics, local more than national. National politics seemed to be quite beyond us, untouchable somehow. My uncle was a councillor on the local authority, so we were always very helpful and supportive of him. Neither of my parents ever ran for the council, but I did when I was in Dewsbury, just after I was twenty-one, unsuccessfully. They were both members of the Textile Workers' Union and they were both members of the Labour Party. They knocked on doors, they canvassed for the Labour Party, we went to various meetings. My mother belonged to the Women's Section of the Labour Party, so we used to go to Women's Section meetings. We would go to Huddersfield town hall or to Leeds town hall and see the great speakers like Nye Bevan and Clem Attlee. It was a great occasion. We'd take a flask, because we couldn't afford to go to restaurants, and we'd go along with the Dewsbury Women's Section, maybe on a coach, and take sandwiches. My mother used to say, 'We'll take jam and hope for spam that we can swap around a little.' It was a very happy period.

Both my parents were in textiles. In that part of the country they all worked in textiles. People then would work from half past six in the morning until half past five at night, and on Saturdays. I remember my mother working until twelve o'clock or one o' clock on Saturdays. Women had a very, very hard, very difficult life. My father would set the boiler going to do the washing when Mother got home on a Monday night. On a Tuesday night, it would be the ironing. On a Wednesday night, it would be the bedrooms that had to be done. On a Thursday night it would be the house. On a Friday night, it would be the baking for the weekend. It was really a full-time job for women. They had a very hard time indeed. Many of them were the only breadwinners of the family. When I was a child my father spent a lot of time being unemployed. My mother used to say to me, 'You know, I am not employed for my sex appeal, I'm employed because my rate of pay is lower than that of your father's. That's the only reason.' My father used to close the door so that the neighbours didn't see him doing the household chores. A man in that generation, of that age, felt that he should be the breadwinner, so there was some shame and embarrassment about it. It wasn't until the 1939–45 War that people in those areas were fully employed, because they were then needed in textiles to assist with the War Effort, making blankets, that sort of thing.

There wasn't very much social life. Once in a while we would go to Leeds, which was the really big city for us. I remember at about half past four, we would go to a café in Leeds market where the market stall-holders used to go, and I remember having glasses of milk and lovely ham sandwiches with lashings of thick, beautiful ham in, all hanging over the sides, and lovely soft bread. So once in a while, maybe, we would have a trip like that, but not very often. In the evenings we would sit by the fire and tell stories. There was no television or radio. We had an electric meter but if we weren't doing anything there was no point in sitting there with all the electric lights on, so we would turn them off and sit in the firelight and just talk. On a Sunday dinnertime, my father would go to the local Working Men's Club for an hour. My mother would slip him a bit of money. She paid all the bills; she had boxes where she put the rent and rates and money for the electric meter, and then she'd give him a little bit of money to go off and have a pint or two.

My father was a very splendid man. We had very little money, but he was always extremely smart. He always taught me to spend that little bit more on my clothes than I could really afford so they would last longer. He didn't have many clothes, but what he had was very smart. Clothes were always brushed and hung up before he went to bed, whatever time it was – and that applies to me today. And his shoes would be stuffed with newspapers to keep them in good shape – as mine are today. All our shoes would be stuffed with newspapers. On the Saturday afternoon he would buy bits of leather from the market stalls, and on a Sunday morning the shoes would be brought out and repaired; they would be put on a last on the kitchen table, and he would hammer bits of leather onto them to make them last longer. And he would polish them: you could see yourself in the shoes that I wore. He was a very proud man.

I think they had quite a happy marriage, they were very devoted. My father married late in life and he was very much older than my mother and I think that they hardly expected any children at all. When I came along, it was quite a surprise. I was an only child and a little indulged by my father; he must have been late forties when I was born. The fact that I came along perhaps even brought them closer together. It was a very poor household, but it was a very happy one. I don't ever recall really going short of anything. If anybody went short, it was my parents. I always went to dancing class, and my father made a sleigh for me in the winter. I didn't perhaps have the very best of everything, but I never really went short.

When I was thirteen I got a scholarship to Dewsbury Technical College. I was in the commercial section and trained in accountancy, book-keeping, mathematics, French, short-hand-typing, English. My father was delighted. He felt it was the sort of education that would earn me a living. It was enormously important to him that I had a job where I could earn a living. No way did my parents want me to go into textiles. My father wanted me to have a secure job, and a secure job for him meant working in the town hall. That was security to him. Of course now I have the most insecure job in the world as a Member of Parliament!

My parents were both a great influence in so many different ways. My father in terms of discipline. I follow him in always being on time, taking care of my clothes, working in a team, being responsible to other people. My mother was not a disciplinarian. She was very quiet and she was very modest and she hadn't got very much confidence in herself outside her own home, but she was a very loving, warm person, extremely kind. I hope that maybe I've collected some of her characteristics in that way. She was a very remarkable woman, actually. I realised much later in life how remarkable she was.

My father died when I was eighteen. We were very good friends. I missed him very much. There was no other income, so my mother had to work. She worked all her life, from the age of thirteen when she left school, to the age when she retired, sixty-five or -six. She had to. [My father's death] made leaving my mother extremely difficult when I did come up to London to do a job full-time here. That really was heart-breaking. I always look back on that period and think what a very brave woman she was. She never put any obstacle in the way. I went home at weekends, and whenever I could, but she must have been very lonely, being on her own, going out to work, looking after herself, nobody to come home to, nobody to look to or to do anything for. I was probably rather callous about it, looking back. She always came to help, fighting elections, enormously supportive, on the doorstep, knocking on doors, very proud of me. She never let me know that she was proud of me, but she did say so to others. I remember in one election, just before we went to the town hall for the count, I must have been over-tired and over-emotional and I just absolutely was weeping. I said, 'I've just lost. I know I've lost.' My mother was the only one in the room, and she said, 'Oh, never mind' – she was such a matter-of-fact woman – 'Never mind. Win, lose or draw, you're still my daughter.' I mean, it was an absolutely crazy thing to say, but it wouldn't have mattered to her. She always kept my feet on the ground, you know; you never got too big for your boots as far as my mother was concerned.

My early life influenced me: the hardships of family life, of my mother, and the embarrassment of my father, left an impression. I see the real nitty-gritty problems that people come up against, that families even today have to cope with. They're not the same, but they are nevertheless enormous to them. They're 100 per cent of a problem to them. I always regarded myself as a good constituency MP because I'm interested in people and the issues that affect ordinary people, the hardships they have, the problems they come up against, the bureaucracy. I remember vividly when a teacher at school was seeking to keep me in for something I'd done wrong, I don't quite remember what it was, and I refused to stay because it was winter and both my parents were working and I had to get home to lay the table for tea and to light the fire. And there was no teacher going to keep me in after school, and deny my parents that little bit of comfort. I stood up against that and I won the battle. I explained that I'd come in Saturday morning, I'd come in Saturday afternoon, but my parents were not going to be deprived. There are times when one has to assert oneself like that for other people. I was extremely determined that nobody was going to deter me from the thing that I believed was right for me to do. I didn't really think about women's rights. I can't pretend that I did. I think of everybody as I tend to do now, as human beings. I know women's rights are a great issue and I believe in women's rights, but I can't say that I was very aware of women's rights. We were fighting as human beings, for a decent living, for full employment, for better housing, for improved education, for all of those things for all human beings.

Immediately after I left college, I got a job in the office of a local shop called Bickers. It was a grand shop. Lots of lovely smells of perfume and cosmetics and lovely clothes that I could never afford to buy. It was one of those shops where, when a customer pays, they put the money into a cylinder and they pull a lever, and it goes 'Whoop!' through the shop into the office, and one of my jobs was to check it out, stamp the receipt, put the change back in the flask, 'Whoop!' and send it back again. I started work for one pound a week and I got a fifty per cent increase the first week, so I was paid one pound ten shillings from the first week. That was the first job I had.

Then I became a chorus girl. I'd always been very much interested in dancing and I was quite good at it. I knew a girl, she was called Betty too, who lived in Dewsbury and we both wanted to become professionals. My father thought it was a dreadful idea, my mother thought it was okay if I wanted to do it. So we went for an audition and we became professionals. I was about seventeen. I danced in London and I danced in Luton, of all places. I was part of a dancing team and I liked the teamwork: you all turn your head to the right at exactly the same angle, and you all kick your left leg up at the same height and the same time. I've always been an individualist, but I'm also a teamworker – that is why I like politics; politics is teamwork, to some extent. We lived in Soho, in the Theatre Girls' Club in Greek Street. Everybody thinks if you're a dancer, men drink champagne out of your shoes every night, but we were never allowed out; we always had a matron. It was the winter of 1947 and it was a terribly harsh winter when the nation had no coal, no heating. I found it a very hard life. I enjoyed the make-up and the sparkle, but there's quite a lot more to it than just the glamour that one sees when the curtain goes up. After the show we used to take it in turns to go around the stage picking up the sequins that had fallen from the dresses, because they were hard times after the War. You used to lick your finger, and go round and pick up the sequins, put them in a box, and give them to the wardrobe mistress to be sewn back on again. I thought it was going to be terribly exciting and frightfully glamorous, but it was really just like politics: damned hard work! My father thought it was a terrible job for a good working-class girl to do and he didn't approve at all. After about six months I gave it up and came back home to Yorkshire and had a very dreary job as secretary for the Road Haulage Association. I was the only female in the office, so I was dogsbody, a 'go'n' – 'Go'n do this, go'n do that.'

I was still very much involved in the Labour Party and I wanted to work full-time for the Labour Party, so after three years with the Haulage Association I came to London to work as a secretary in the Research Department of the Labour Party in Transport House. Wilfred Fienburg was Head of Research, and Morgan Phillips was General Secretary of the Party. I thoroughly enjoyed London. I loved the people I worked with. I was doing a full-time job for the Labour Party, which I loved, and meeting people who were very like-minded. I had a great time. I was there for three or four years and then I applied for a job at the House of Commons and got it, and started work for Barbara Castle and Geoffrey de Freitas for the magnificent sum of seven pounds ten shillings a week. It was hard work, working for two Members. Geoffrey was Member of Parliament for Lincoln, and Barbara was Member of Parliament for Blackburn. Barbara was on the National Executive Committee of the Labour Party as well. I learned a great deal from both of them. Barbara was a very determined lady, extremely dedicated to Socialism and a very good person to work for. She was a hard taskmaster, very hard, but I never had any complaints. She was tremendously efficient, you knew what she was doing, you knew when you were going to see her, you knew where she was. There could be complaints laid against women employers, but I had never any complaints against Barbara. She was a good role model for any woman to follow. She took in her stride the job that she had to do here, running the Party, the NEC, running her constituency, running a home. All of that. Women in professional life always work twice as hard as a man. You do a job and a half.

I was always content to be 'the power behind the throne'; doing things for other people, getting things done for them, making their job a little less difficult. I enjoyed doing that very much. It wasn't until I'd been working with them for some years that I was encouraged to have a go at a seat myself. This was in 1957. A Tory MP called Captain Waterhouse resigned his seat in South-East Leicester and I thought, 'This is my golden opportunity.' I think I was the only person in that by-election who felt that I could win, against a 20,000 Tory majority! But there was a swing to Labour. It was an enormous constituency, agricultural. I didn't know much about agriculture and I had no idea how to fight an election, I was very amateur about it all. It was totally different from the type of elections that we fight today – and I loved it. I thought it was absolutely great. I've always loved fighting elections.

Geoffrey de Freitas and his wife, Helen, gave me tremendous encouragement and support. I shall never forget. They came up to the constituency and we all stayed in a small hotel there, and they campaigned alongside me for weeks on end. They were enormously supportive.

I fought South-East Leicester in 1957, and then I fought Peterborough in the 1959 General Election. By that time, I'd seen quite a lot of the world. I'd seen the Far East; I knew a lot of Europe. The one place I hadn't seen was America. I was very fed up with the old men of Europe in 1960 – de Gaulle, Adenauer, Macmillan – I wanted to see how things worked in America. So I got a visa and went to the States. I flew into New York, with a return ticket in my sweaty paw to come back if things didn't work out, and not very much money to keep me going. I had some contacts and had met a few Congressmen and eventually I got a job with a Republican from Massachusetts called Sylvio Conte. Sylvio was a very super individual to work for and he gave me a lot of opportunities. He rather liked my British accent, so I answered the telephone, and then I used to send out literature to his constituents. I would go through the newspapers and if you had a baby, I'd write a nice letter for the Congressman to sign and send the *Baby Book* – on how to bring up baby. If you got married it was a letter of congratulations, and you got the *Cook Book*. If you became Chairman of the Lions Club, you got a letter of congratulations and a little book about civics. Then I graduated and began writing speeches for him. I was there for a couple of years and thoroughly loved the job, liked American people, liked the standard of living: I was earning far more than a British Member of Parliament and I was the most junior in the office. And what a contrast to the facilities and the support system that a British Member of Parliament has! We had electronic typewriters, even in those days.

But Europe is my home and I'm European and I wanted to come back here, although I loved the States. Perhaps if I'd met somebody who'd asked me to marry them, maybe I would've stayed. But, again, there was my mother here, on her own.

She didn't put any obstacles in the way of my going, but I'm an only child, and I always felt the tug of her being on her own. But, over and above everything else, I felt very much a European. So I came back and had to start looking for a job. I was taken on, sight unseen, by Lord Walston, a life peer, big farmer in Cambridge-shire, member of the Labour Party, subsequently became Minister of State at the Foreign Office, and I worked with him from about 1962 until I became a Member myself. He had a big family and I became very much involved in the family. I used to go off with them to the West Indies for six weeks of the year. That's how it is if you work with somebody like that, they take you to their hearts. I do enjoy being in the bosom of a family. I love the de Freitas family, and the Walstons likewise. I do enjoy having a family around me.

I think sometimes, when I look back on it, maybe I have missed out in not marrying and creating a family of my own. I think there's a tide in the affairs of men – and women – as Shakespeare said, 'which, taken at the flood, leads on to fortune.' It wasn't that I didn't have a lot of men friends, I did, but if you've spent your life going off to Vietnam, going off to America, going off to France, being very independent, there's no man going to wait until you come back. I mean, he wants to see you, he wants to take you out, he might want to propose to you. You can't say, 'Can you hold on until I get back?' And then you get back, and you're packing, you're off again! Nobody's going to wait around for you like that. It wasn't part of my planning. There was nothing planned about it. If it had come my way, wonderful, but it didn't. I had a job to do, I had a full life which I enjoyed enormously. I very much admire my female colleagues in the House who have managed to have a husband, to have a home, to have children, and still have a very big professional life. I admire them enormously that they're able to cope. I guess there are times, I admit to you, when I feel sorry for myself that I haven't got [a family] of my own. But I'm not sure I could've done what I have done. You've got to make choices in life, and maybe unconsciously I made my choice.

In 1973 I was selected to fight West Bromwich in a by-election. Ted Castle was my press agent. He'd had a heart attack just before, and I called Barbara up, and I said, 'The only person I want as press officer is Ted, but is he able to do it?' She said, 'It'll be the making of him, you ask him.' Ted came up, stayed the whole of the time there, and Barbara came to do meetings with me, as she always did any election I fought. You're made such a fuss of in a by-election because everybody comes to help. Everybody I know came up. It was tremendous, this great flood of support from old friends from all over the country, who put themselves out, just determined that we were going to make it. It was great. And that was when I first got in [*pointing to a black-and-white photograph above the door of her office*] – that's a picture of my mother and me at two o'clock in the morning when, after all those great trials of strength and those unsuccessful campaigns, I finally made it. It was very thrilling.

It changed my life considerably, of course. From being a secretary/personal assistant, I had a full-time job to do myself. And I loved it! I was almost sick when I made my maiden speech, though I can't remember what I said. What I enjoyed most, in the early days, was the constituency work. The grass-roots is enormously important; this is where you draw your strength from, and I just don't mean political strength; it's where you get rejuvenated, because it's all there. I like looking after people; I like being in my constituency; I like meeting people; I like talking to them, helping them. I like visiting factories; I love industry, coming from an industrial area; I like meeting the voluntary organisations. I could go into a supermarket in my constituency, and everybody comes to talk to me. I felt that here was a great big family, to get to know and be with.

There were about twenty-five women MPs in 1973, out of six hundred and thirty in total.

In 1974 we had the two elections when Labour went into

Government and I remember Bob Mellish, who was then Chief Whip, Chief Government Whip, calling me up and saying, 'I'd like you to come into the Whips' Office.' I don't know why he asked me but it was a very great honour because it was a Ministerial posting. Maybe he thought it would be a good idea to have a woman; it would bring a new dimension into the Whips' Office. I was so taken aback, I said, 'Well, Bob, I've hardly said anything in the house yet, I haven't made my mark. I've hardly spoken.' And he said, 'Oh, you come into the Whip's Office, keep your trap shut, and your majority will go up at the next election.' He was right. It did!

It's a very detailed job. It's the nitty-gritty of making this place function. You look after the Members in the West Midlands, see who's going to speak and encourage people to speak on various issues; you deal with Ministers; you organise the speakers in the Chamber. You've got to get the best out of Members; you're seeing to it that your party gets the best out of what is available, that you get the best speakers. You're not using them, but you're moving people about and getting the best that you can for your own party. I enjoyed it because I like learning. All the time I was learning about procedures here, about human beings, about Members who have come here, about some of the problems they have, their families, their excuses. I remember there was a woman Member who liked to go off to the opera house, and Bob Mellish said to me, 'Tell [her] she can't go tonight, it's a three-line whip. I don't care if her mascara runs, you go and tell her she's not going.' And I had to tell her. All of those human things one has to deal with. You're learning the whole of the time. It's not always what you give, it's what you learn in these things, and being in this place it's a great learning process the whole time. I believe if you stop learning, you might as well quit the job.

I left the Whips' Office when I went to the European Parliament. It was a great experience, to mix with Europeans [all working] to create a better group in the European Community. But we had trailed behind Europe for years and years and years, and we were feeling our way. We had a lot to make up, and we couldn't be pushy. We only came in after the referendum, so it wasn't for us to move in and boss everybody else around. We had to take it gradually. But we set the pattern for what has taken place later. What makes me sad is that Britain has never taken the lead that it should in Europe. I've been very critical of my own party on this. I want to see Britain leading Europe. I don't want it going in as the old man of Europe, having to wait two years before we can sign this or sign that. There's a lot of nitty-gritty stuff about Europe that I don't like, about the size of eggs and what the colour of lipstick should be, but there's no doubt that is where Britain's future lies.

When the European Parliament became directly elected, I preferred to stay at Westminster. I was then asked by Mr Speaker to join the 'Speaker's Panel of Chairmen', which is about twenty Members drawn from both sides of the House to chair Standing Committees. All the major bills have to go through Committee and they take months, which very few of the British public are aware of, before they come back to the floor of the House and to the Lords for their final sessions. I used to sit all night, have a break for ten minutes, come back again at one o'clock and go on until five or six o'clock in the morning. I saw the dawn coming up over the Palace of Westminster many times.

My first major bill was a housing bill. I'd seen that everybody was in the room and just before a Division, as I said 'Lock the doors,' the Opposition Whip nipped out because he thought one of his Members was missing. I hadn't seen him go and I said, 'Lock the doors!' and locked him out of the Committee! He was beating on the door, 'Let me in! Let me in!' He was very upset about it. I was very unhappy about it too. It happened on a Thursday and I went home that weekend, very upset, because he reported me to the Chairman of Ways and Means, who was then Jack Weatherall. I'd had a sleepless weekend and on the Monday morning Jack called me up and he said, 'Will you come and see me as soon as you come into the House?' I came in, this very room next door, and there was Jack Weatherall and he said, 'I don't know what you've done. I don't mind very much. I'm totally on your side.' I explained what had happened, it certainly wasn't deliberate – why should I want to lock my own Whip out? But these things happen, you make mistakes and you take them to heart when you're only a baby at the job.

I did that for about eight years. You may say, 'Why were you selected for that?' and the answer is, 'I don't know, but by Jove, it stood me in good stead for when I became Deputy Speaker.' I was also on the House of Commons Commission, a very important committee here, I was the only woman member of that. Maybe *because* I was a woman I got these advantages. I mean, sometimes you can look at it like that: maybe I was advantaged being a woman.

Working in politics and working with women like Barbara Castle who had fought their way through, it just seemed that if one was determined enough, one got there. I don't think one was so aware of women's issues as one is today. (But as we see from all the statistics, women are still not breaking through into the professions as they should be.) When I was selected for West Bromwich I was the only woman on the short-list and I remember a woman saying, 'I don't think we want you; you've never been married, you don't know what it is to struggle to try and make ends meet, to stand against a kitchen sink and do the washing-up. You've never had all that to do.' Those were unfair accusations; with the type of background I had, with a mother who worked all her life, I was very much aware of it all. The only thing I could say in response was, 'Because I haven't had that to do, and because I don't do that, I can devote more of my time to looking after the interests of people like you.' If there was discrimination in that period, it tended to come from women. But then women at that time rather looked to a man. They'd think, 'It's a man's job. It's a man's world, is politics.'

I'd like to see more women in this place, and I'm always very keen to see many more women in public life in other jobs, like on the Bench, in professional life, in the law, getting on in the civil service, making progress there. I can use my influence to advance other women. One way [is] by nominating women JPs that I think are responsible and will do a good job on the Bench. I use my influence there.

This country hasn't really made any progress over the last ten years. When I see the areas that I love and represent that have made such little progress, the hard lives of the people there, the unemployment, the poverty, the low wages, that affects me tremendously. I see what changes could be brought about and I see people who want change and who have faith and confidence in that, and yet it has not been possible. It is very heart-breaking. Very discouraging. It would have been marvellous to have had my Party in government at the same time as I personally made this progress. That would have been absolutely splendid. I feel it is a tragedy that a major party like the Labour Party has been in the wilderness – because it *is* in the wilderness and it has been for too long.

I feel very strongly about democracy. I'm very concerned about a party, whichever party it is, that is in power for such a long period of time. I don't think it's healthy for a democracy. I would like to see a Government in power that had a good working majority, but that paid more attention to the quality of the legislation that it brought in, rather than to have slapdash legislation. Nevertheless, I have to say that when the Labour Party does take office, it is going to need a very long time to put things right.

It's a constant [process] of dripping away all working hours of the day. You make this commitment to bring about changes for the better [in women's] lives; by improving the housing conditions in which they live; by seeing to it that the education system is improved, that the schools that their kids go to are decent; by the factories, the foundries, the places they go to work, that they have a reasonable deal there; that both their husbands and themselves get a fair rate of pay for the job. There are far too many women today do a job that a man does and don't get the same rate of pay. I never think of Margaret Thatcher being a good role model for women, because she never advanced any women at all. I would've said that she wasn't a good role model at all. Whether I am remains to be seen; I don't think I can judge that about myself.

Never, never in a million years did I imagine [I'd become Deputy Speaker]. But things happen here, oh, it's a whirlwind here sometimes when things happen! My name was put to all the parties with perhaps two or three others, and it was finally agreed that I was a non-contentious personality and in June 1987 I was appointed. That was a great moment. That was one moment when I was really more sad than at most other times that my mother wasn't alive – she died in November 1982. I was really very, very sad that she wasn't around to throw her chest out a little bit, even though I wouldn't have been around to see because she'd never let me do that. Lots of friends said, 'Oh, if only your mother was alive, she'd be so proud.' And I think she would have been, she'd have been that.

It's changed my life very considerably. I like my constituency and I like spending time there, but I can only get there now on a Friday evening. There were many times that I would go up for a day during the week to see people working, and schools and factories and foundries and what have you; I can't do that now. I'm not allowed to speak in the House and I'm not allowed to ask Parliamentary Questions and I do not vote. I miss that. All those things that are meat to every other Member of Parliament. It was an abrupt change for me. I've been doing this now since June 1987, which is nearly four years, it's still not something I've got very accustomed to. It's a very full day. I come in at nine-thirty. I look at my post. I do my own briefing. I have a meeting with Mr Speaker at twelve o'clock every morning which I wouldn't miss for anything. We go through the procedures of the day. The clerks explain everything, how you do this, how you do that, what has gone on the day before. It's a learning process the whole of the time. I wouldn't miss that briefing for all the tea in China. I enjoy it enormously. Then I do my duties in the Chair. I have long hours, five hours in the Chair every day, and I'm here all day. I left the House at three o'clock this morning [and was back again at] half past nine. I need a lot of sleep, but I have to manage without it as best I can! I like doing the job. I like being in control of the House. I love the traditions of the House. I would defend a Cabinet Minister who was being barracked, just as much as I would defend a back-bencher who was being barracked. I really am very keen to see that everybody here has a right to be heard. They don't have to be listened to. But they have a right to be heard, however unpopular their views are. That's what they're here for.

I feel very honoured that this is what has happened to me. That makes up for a great deal of what I miss in other things. The support that has been given to me by all the political parties gives me enormous strength and encouragement. I feel very honoured by it. The fact that there was no objection in over 600 people is very good. You have the support of all these people. They have placed their trust in you and you have got to respond to that trust, and cherish it, and treat it very carefully. Again, we're coming back to this family thing.

I don't think people should go on and on and on. I've seen too many people around this House who have just stayed on, believing that they were indispensable in their constituency to their Party and to their electorate. The time comes when we've all got to go and I don't mind that at all. When I retire, I shall travel as much as I can. I shall go to the theatre, I shall see friends, I shall make new friends. I shall have people come and see me, and I shall go and see them much more. I shall be as active in the Labour Party in my local community as I've always been. And I shall dig my garden. All the things that I've neglected to do, I shall do. It sounds very humdrum, but I shall do that.

I've never been overly ambitious. When I came into this House to work for other Members, I didn't come in with the idea in mind to be a Member of Parliament myself. It's the inevitability of gradualism. I never thought I'd be a Deputy Speaker until it came about, so the Speakership is all for the future. If I'm nominated I shall be nominated willingly, but it is entirely up to the House. It's not a matter for any political party. The Speakership of the House is for the entire House to determine when the time comes after the next election.

In May 1992, a few months after this interview, Betty Boothroyd was elected Speaker, the first woman to hold the post in the history of Parliament.

I've enjoyed everything that I've done and I've always thought it a little step in the right direction, all the things I've wanted to do. But undoubtedly, when I look back, becoming a Member of Parliament was crucial because, of course, without being Member of Parliament, I couldn't become Deputy Speaker. But, undoubtedly, to have the confidence of my peers, in becoming Deputy Speaker, that is something that I cherish very much.

I don't believe that I have any regrets. If I have any, I think it's family. The fact that I have no family is a regret. Not just parents, because parents have to pass on, but that I haven't created a new generation. If I have to focus on any one regret, that is the only thing. I don't regret anything I've done in my professional life, that's all right. But I would have liked to have, to have had, a husband, a partner, and to have created, to have seen a family around me.

I'm a person who is on a very even keel. The only times I have been down are when I have fought and haven't won by-elections or elections. Thank God I don't think I've had any depressions or real sadnesses, other than my family deaths which everybody has. I don't think I've had periods of great gloom. I don't think I have suffered in that way. Maybe it's because of my make-up, my resilience. I always think that there's nobody really to look after me but me. I have got to earn a living, I have got to do my job, because nobody is going to do it for me, nobody looks after West Bromwich if I'm ill or depressed. So I just do it. I'm not introspective at all about myself. I've been brought up like that. It's a stoic thing – I think this is a lot to do with being North Country, I really do. I don't analyse myself, my feelings, I just get on with it.

CONCLUSION

Many themes recur in these ten life stories: discrimination at work; the strain of trying to combine marriage and motherhood with a demanding professional job; the impact of the Second World War; the influence of older women; the importance of education; the abiding sense of social duty; the importance of family support systems; the reliance on paid and unpaid female labour in the home; the importance of a supportive partner; the centrality of motherhood to female identity; the personal qualities of resilience, determination and self-control; the contradictory attitudes towards feminism and femininity; the tension between the individual and the collective. The significance of these themes, beyond their historical interest, is that they are very little different from those that might emerge from interviews with ten professional women today. The concerns and pressures and difficulties encountered by these women as they forged their careers in the decades after the Second World War, resonate deeply with the experiences of contemporary women.

Undoubtedly these are ten remarkable women: their achievements are remarkable, their lives are remarkable. Paradoxically it is the very fact that their achievements give cause for remark that shows how much progress remains to be made. Women's history is full of admirable women, but we will be getting somewhere when women do not need to be out of the ordinary to do these sorts of things. The ratio of remarkable women to unremarkable men in senior positions in every profession is still the clearest indication that we live in an inequitable society. As Baroness Turner said in a House of Lords debate on 'Opportunities for Women' (February 1992): 'The exceptional individual will normally make out, but there are hundreds of thousands of reasonably talented women who still find it difficult because of the social and family pressures upon them.'

These interviews tell of a generation of women growing up in a society overshadowed by two World Wars. The absence of fathers, brothers and uncles was commonplace; women were often left to bring up families single-handedly or with the help of other female relations; economic prosperity and political optimism in the 1920s and 1940s was quickly replaced by the austerity and conservatism of the 1930s and 1950s. They watched their mothers' generation and then their own wooed into the workplace, then thrust out of it again. Hardship and opportunity came hand in hand.

The parallels to be drawn between the generation of professional women who grew up in the inter-War period and the generation of women now in their twenties and thirties are, as I have already suggested, both surprising and significant. Like the former, young women today are operating in a period of political and cultural conservatism and economic austerity. They too are the beneficiaries of progress won for them by the generation before, yet take many of those gains for granted: the right to contraception, the right to education, the right to equal pay, the right to a mortgage. Like them, young women today are marrying later and having children later. The women interviewed here married relatively late for their generation. While they were unusual for their time, later marriage and later childbirth are now prevalent in professional middle-class women. The Office of Population Censuses and Surveys (Population Trends 67, HMSO) forecast in 1992 that by the year 2000 more than forty per cent of babies would be born to mothers over the age of thirty, and cites later marriage as an important factor. An increasing presence in the workplace and the desire not to relinquish the financial freedom and autonomy that accompany the pay-cheque in part explain this delay. Births to women over thirty are currently rising almost four times as fast as the general increase in birth numbers, a trend most pronounced in middle-class professionals in the South-East, while birth rates among women in their twenties are at their lowest since 1945, and continuing to decline. Research carried out at the Emma Willard School by Carol Gillingham et al (*Making Connections*, 1985) found that amongst the thirty adolescent girls interviewed, professional aspirations came a long way ahead of romantic ones on their list of priorities. Mary Wollstonecraft would have approved: education and employment have given today's women more things to do than wait for marriage.

Like the women interviewed here, young women today are juggling the conflicting demands of family and career without adequate support systems for doing so. Britain lags behind other European countries, notably France, Belgium and Sweden, in terms of maternity leave, paternity leave, tax relief incentives and child-care facilities. Only two per cent of under-fives in Britain have access to publicly-funded day care, and there are just 300 workplace nurseries nationwide. By contrast, Germany, Holland and Belgium have been guaranteeing a crèche place to all under-fives for over a decade. Only seven per cent of British workers with small children are happy with child-care facilities at work, according to a recent report by the Henley Centre for Forecasting (*Frontiers: Planning for Consumer Change in Europe*, November 1992). The report concludes that 'it remains starkly the case that in many parts of Europe the arrival of children simply removes women from the labour market.' As Valerie Grove writes in the introduction to her book, *The Compleat Woman*: 'It is motherhood which divides women; not marriage, or work, but children . . . Feminism and family life may be hard to reconcile, but reconciled they have to be.'

Increased opportunities for working flexible hours, job-sharing and career breaks have to some extent made the juggling act easier. Women now make up forty-five per cent of Britain's labour force and twenty-five per cent of the self-employed: between 1979 and 1990 the number of self-employed women rose by 122 per cent, from 348,000 to 773,000. The number of women working part-time has also gone up by over one fifth since 1984. But these figures are open to interpretation. In this case, statistics that apparently indicate progress can also be seen to support Betty Boothroyd's comment that 'women do a job and a half' (page 181). Women spend over twice as much time as men on domestic duties, according to the Henley Centre report (quoted above), and in matters relating to food and children the differential increases sharply. Women's earnings are still thirty per cent lower than men's and only six per cent of women earn over £15,000 per annum. Much apparent progress in the workplace in fact conspires to maintain rather than challenge the status quo. While such measures apply to women's work, very rarely do they apply to men's. A 1990 survey of two-parent households with dependent children showed that almost sixty per cent of women were either working part-time or not at all. Part-time workers are not entitled to sick pay, maternity pay, holiday pay or pension entitlement and have far fewer training and promotion opportunities than full-time workers. Eighty per cent of them earn less than the decency threshold set by the Council of Europe. Enacted in this way, measures ostensibly designed to help women, do just the opposite: they do little to improve the quality of women's lives and simply compel them to work harder. As Naomi Wolf claims in *The Beauty Myth*, 'the economics of industrialised countries would collapse if women didn't do the work they do for free.' The domestic realm is still women's responsibility, and women's paid work is still implicitly regarded as a dispensable indulgence; how to combine the two is still overwhelmingly seen as her problem. There will be no real progress until these so-called progressive measures in the workplace extend equally to male employees. Until then, the system forces mothers into dependency on men. Unless the system changes, the structures of employment that hamper women's professional opportunities and preclude men's domestic involvement will remain intact, holding both women *and* men in thrall to a system that allows no genuine flexibility or freedom to choose how to organise their lives.

These ten interviews reflect not only women's continuing struggle with a system that still resists genuine, far-reaching equality, but also an internal struggle to comprehend and realise what it means to be a woman in the latter half of the twentieth century. In this respect too, contemporary women share much with the generation who grew up between the Wars. After a period of intense political activity and popular appeal, feminism has somehow failed to capture the imagination of younger women, who have, like their grandmothers' generation, retreated from the clarion call of collective interest and withdrawn once more into the private world of home, marriage and motherhood. A Gallup Poll in *SHE* magazine in 1992 interviewed 1,000 women and found that eighty-eight per cent felt the term 'housewife' was derogatory and that motherhood was undervalued. These findings were confirmed when a survey by the National Council of Women published later in the same year found that an overwhelming ninety per cent of women felt their work in the home was undervalued. The 1992 Farley Report found that of 401 mothers with children under eighteen months, forty per cent had returned to work after their statutory maternity leave, but of those, two thirds would rather have stayed at home. These figures point to considerable dissatisfaction amongst women, both about how their actual time is spent, and about the restraints on how their time could be spent. Nevertheless an emphasis on the positive aspects of womanhood, as opposed to female oppression, has brought with it a reluctance to identify with the injustices that women still face. Ironically this is precisely the dilemma that eroded feminist support in the 1920s.

At the heart of adult female identity is the struggle to be a woman in one's own right, not only a continuation of one's mother; the struggle to recreate the meaning of one's femaleness for oneself, simultaneously indebted to and in revolt against the model of femaleness represented by the generation before. In doing so we often pick up where our grandmothers left off. Surveys and statistics show that women now do not wish to fight men – political lesbianism is someone else's battleground. They seem instead to want to find ways of fulfilling all aspects of their selves in both the private and public realms. Their concern is compromise, not absolutism. They watched their own mothers either shackled by domesticity or struggling to combine work and family. Their mothers were always inadequate: they 'failed' either by trying to live through their children and spouse or by neglecting their children for the sake of their careers. Today's women want more status for motherhood, more respect for the domestic route to fulfilment, but they also want greater access to top jobs, improved professional opportunities, more say in how the country is run at every level. It is sobering to realise, for example, that in the English judiciary women are still under-represented at every level. Of the ten Lords of Appeal, ten are men; of the eighty-three High Court judges, eighty are men; of more than 7,000 barristers, almost 6,000 are men. When it comes to the professions, women are working in what is still resolutely a man's world.

The 'failure' of feminism is baffling when one considers only the 'successes' of the suffragists and the sixties' Women's Movement. But history is made up of more than headlines and there was another generation of women between these two who tell another, equally valid, story of women's experience of twentieth century life. It is wrong to say that feminism has failed. Rather we should recognise that a tension exists at the very heart of female identity between the individual and the collective, the private and the public, the conservative and the radical. Women are still socialised into a fundamentally conservative position of being the ones who conserve, preserve, maintain and restrain, yet the evidence of their lives violates that restrictive definition and upholds also the impulse towards creativity, exploration and self-determination.

Conclusion

Progress for women does not follow a straight trajectory, it is more like the algebraic sine wave. A pattern emerges throughout this century of waxing and waning politicisation, and contemporary feminism must be seen in the context of this overall pattern.

Anti-feminism, or 'individualism' as it may be more appropriate to call it, does not necessarily mean 'reactionary'. While the 1920s and 1930s have been depicted as a conservative, inward-looking period, there is also an undeniable strand of modernness that comes through in these interviews. Do these women seem modern because their conservatism is familiar to a generation itself living in a period of anti-feminism? Or are they familiar because in them we catch the first glimpse of the modern women they have allowed us to become? The suffragettes are quaintly intriguing, old-fashioned, fascinating as dinosaurs. In their long skirts and parasols and hats, they are relics from a past that has little to do with our lives today. These ten women by contrast are quietly, determinedly contemporary. It is a mistake to equate individualism with conservatism, though the two may have elements in common. The concerns of these ten women are our concerns: how to use *on our own terms* a freedom earned by the generation before; how to negotiate a way between the implications of greater freedom and the appeal of more traditional roles and responsibilities. Public and private jostle for place in these women's lives as they still do in the lives of young women today. The contemporary relevance of these ten life stories is a striking and salutory reminder both of what has been achieved in the past and of all that remains to be achieved in the future.

Rebecca Abrams
Oxford 1993

SELECTED FURTHER READING

Branson, Noreen & Heinemann, Margot, *Britain in the Nineteen Thirties* (Panther, 1973)

French, Marilyn, *The War Against Women* (Hamish Hamilton, London, 1992)

ed. Gilligan, Carol, Lyons, Nona P. & Hanmer, Trudy J., *Making Connections, The Relational Worlds of Adolescent Girls at Emma Willard School* (Harvard University Press, Cambridge, Massachussets, 1990)

Grove, Valerie, *The Compleat Woman* (Chatto & Windus, London, 1987)

Harrison, Brian, *Prudent Revolutionaries: Portraits of British Feminists between the Wars* (Oxford University Press, Oxford, 1987)

Lewis, Jane, *Women and Social Action in Victorian and Edwardian England* (Edward Elgar, Publishers Ltd., Hampshire, 1991)

Liddington, Jill & Norris, Jill, *One Hand Tied Behind Us: The Rise of the Women's Suffragette Movement* (Virago, London, 1978)

Light, Alison, *Forever England: Femininity, Literature and Conservatism between the Wars* (Routledge, London, 1991)

McLoughlin, Jane, *Up and Running: Women in Business* (Virago, London, 1992)

Rowbotham, Sheila, *Hidden From History* (Pluto Press, London, 1973)

Seldon, Anthony & Pappworth, Philip, *By Word of Mouth: Elite Oral History* (Methuen, London, 1983)

Smith, Harold L., *British Feminism in the 1920s* (Edward Elgar, 1990)

Stevenson, John, *British Society 1914–1945* (Penguin, London, 1984)

Thompson, Paul, *The Voice of the Past: Oral History* (Oxford University Press, Oxford, 1978)

Wilson, Elizabeth, *Only Halfway to Paradise* (Tavistock, London, 1980)

Wimbush, Erica & Talbot, Margaret, *Relative Freedoms: women and leisure* (Oxford University Press, Oxford, 1988)

Wolf, Naomi, *The Beauty Myth* (Chatto & Windus, London, 1990)

Wollstonecraft, Mary, *A Vindication of the Rights of Woman* (Everyman edition, J. M. Dent and Sons, London, 1992)